JULIA CHILD'S KITCHEN

JULIA CHILD'S KITCHEN

The DESIGN, TOOLS, STORIES, and LEGACY of an ICONIC SPACE

Paula J. Johnson

Principal photography of the National Museum of American History's Collection by JACLYN NASH

ABRAMS, NEW YORK

To RAYNA, NANCI, STEVE,
and ALL MEMBERS *of* TEAM JULIA
at the NATIONAL MUSEUM *of*
AMERICAN HISTORY,
PAST, PRESENT, *and* FUTURE

CONTENTS

FOREWORD
A PLACE OF HAPPINESS BY JACQUES PÉPIN 15

INTRODUCTION
The Value of the Real Thing 19

CHAPTER 1
"The kitchen needed *complete* rethinking." 33

CHAPTER 2
"This is my test kitchen as well as everything else." 59

CHAPTER 3
"This is certainly the soul of our house." 85

CHAPTER 4
"Everybody should listen to the cooks." 107

CHAPTER 5
"Welcome to my house and to my kitchen." 169

CHAPTER 6
"I'm absolutely delighted that the Smithsonian is taking my kitchen." 191

CHAPTER 7
"If I can influence anyone…" 223

AFTERWORD 257

APPENDIX A:
ABOUT THE JULIA CHILD FOUNDATION FOR GASTRONOMY AND THE CULINARY ARTS 263

APPENDIX B:
ABOUT THE SMITHSONIAN INSTITUTION, THE NATIONAL MUSEUM OF AMERICAN HISTORY, AND THE SMITHSONIAN FOOD HISTORY PROJECT 265

RESOURCES 267
ACKNOWLEDGMENTS 268
NOTES 270
PHOTOGRAPH CREDITS 279
INDEX 281

FOREWORD

A Place of Happiness

Julia's kitchen on Irving Street in Cambridge, Massachusetts, where she cooked many meals for her family and friends, was a place of joy, conviviality, and entertainment. It was certainly different from the way a kitchen was generally seen in the American food culture in the 1960s—a dreary, joyless, boring part of the house. American women were trying to escape the drudgery of kitchen work. But for Julia, it was a place of happiness. I remember entering the back door that opened right into her kitchen, the true heart of her home, for the first time. It was in the mid-seventies, not long after I published *La Technique*. I walked in, saw the big table covered with a colorful tablecloth, the crumbs that were left over from breakfast. She swept them away with her hand before she turned to me and asked, "What do you want to cook?"

Clay coin banks that stood atop Julia's refrigerator, shown here in recognition of Jacques Pépin's well-known use of chickens in his artwork

We had met for the first time at Helen McCully's apartment in New York City in the 1960s and we had cooked together that first evening. Helen, the food editor of *House Beautiful* magazine, was reviewing the manuscript for *Mastering the Art of French Cooking*, and she wanted to get us together. We spoke French because Julia's French was better than my English at the time. Cooking with someone is a way of getting to know them, especially cooking in their home kitchen. A decade later, at the end of the seventies, I started teaching cooking at Boston University for a couple of weeks during each term. I always met Julia when I went to Boston, and we often cooked together in her kitchen. The pleasure we both took from cooking together cemented our friendship. In the mid-eighties we started giving classes together at BU.

Julia's passion was to educate home cooks, and that in and of itself explains why her home kitchen was so important. She was the first to say that she was not a chef. She had never worked in a restaurant kitchen but brought her talent and love to the home kitchen. She was always interested in the latest and greatest kitchen gadgets for the simple reason that she wanted to help make cooking more accessible and enjoyable for people. This is also made evident by how she made her kitchen work for her. Everything was there. Food processor, blender, mixer, large butcher block, pestle and mortar, and especially her big love—the large, six-burner gas Garland stove. A professional, powerful stove that she put to good use. The counters were made to be comfortable for her height. The pegboard wall kept a big array of copper and cast-iron pots and pans within reach at all times. Pots and pans were not to be hidden; they were decorative, handsome, and worth looking at. She was breaking free from a culture that imagined cooking was not worth people's time—on the contrary, cooking, for her, was to be shared, enjoyed, and experienced together. Julia elevated food from something that was a simple, necessary fact of life to something that should be celebrated, considered with care, and prepared with love. She also felt that cooking should be enjoyed and shared every day, not just on special occasions. That connection with food was what she wanted to share with people, and her kitchen was where that sharing happened.

In 2001, I cooked with Julia in her kitchen the day before the Smithsonian came to disassemble and move it to Washington, DC. It was a last hurrah as well as a dinner to raise money for charity. We both cooked along with the twelve students in our class. We had chairs at the dining room table, and we moved back and forth between the kitchen and the dining room throughout the meal. It was fun. At this point I had come to know Julia and her home and her kitchen very well; we were close friends and we had filmed twenty-two episodes of *Julia and Jacques Cooking at Home* there. That night was the first time I ate in the dining room, and I remember that we made corn and oyster chowder and apple galette, classic dishes that Julia liked to prepare and eat.

    I appreciate the Smithsonian's preservation of that wonderful room and am happy to be part of sharing its history with everyone. I know that the memories of these meals we cooked together and shared together in her home kitchen will stay with me the rest of my life. We had fun, we drank wine, we shared ideas, we argued, but most of all, we loved our special time at the stove and around the table.

Happy cooking!

Jacques Pépin

Jacques Pépin and Julia Child during taping of *Julia and Jacques Cooking at Home* in 1998

Jacques Pépin *is one of the world's most celebrated chefs. Through his long and distinguished career as a professional chef and instructor, host of fourteen popular public television series, and author of dozens of cookbooks, the most recent of which is* Cooking My Way, *Pépin has advanced the art and craft of culinary technique as much as any other figure of the past century. His dedication to culinary education led to the creation of the Jacques Pépin Foundation in 2016.*

INTRODUCTION

The Value of the Real Thing

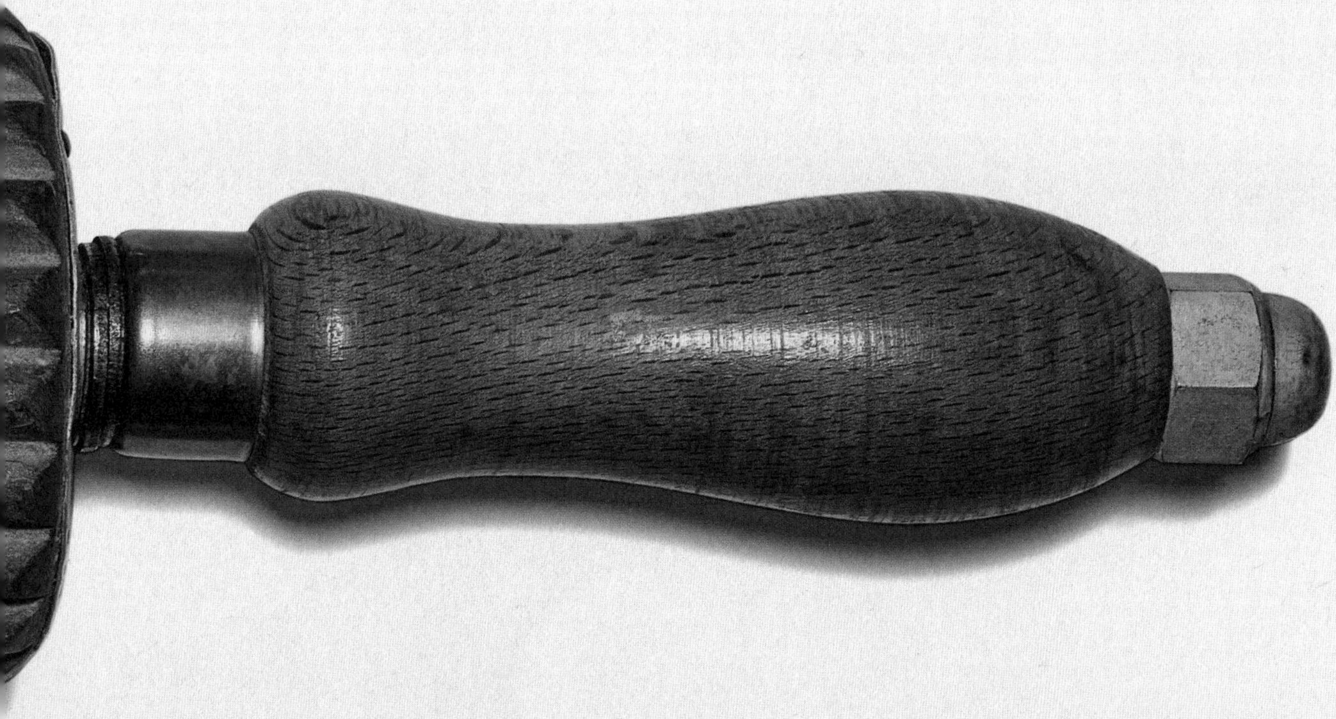

On August 18, 2002, three days after her ninetieth birthday, Julia Child stepped into her home kitchen, turned around slowly, and declared, "I feel like turning something on and starting to cook!" Under normal circumstances this wouldn't have been an unusual comment, but Julia was in Washington, DC, and inside an exhibition at the Smithsonian's National Museum of American History. The exhibition featured her home kitchen from Cambridge, Massachusetts, with every appliance, pot, pan, knife, and work of art placed precisely where it had been a year earlier, when she closed the door on her Cambridge home after forty years as America's favorite television cook, author, teacher, and gastronomic muse to return to her home state of California. A few hours later, Julia was joined at the museum by members of her family and some forty chefs from DC-area restaurants who had prepared special dishes in honor of her birthday and in celebration of her extraordinary gift to the American people—her home kitchen.

previous spread: Two of Julia's rolling pins

Julia Child surrounded by chefs marking her ninetieth birthday and the opening of her kitchen exhibition at the National Museum of American History, August 18, 2002. Among the chefs in attendance were Todd Gray (front row, third from left), Michelle Giroux and Ris Lacoste (front row, fourth and fifth from left), Jamie Stachowski (second row, center, with beard), Jamie Leeds (second row, second from right wearing black chef coat), Jeff Eng (third row, far left), and François Dionot (back row, center, silver hair).

Julia Child's Kitchen: The Design, Tools, Stories, and Legacy of an Iconic Space reveals the story of Julia Child and her famous kitchen, from the moment she and her beloved husband, Paul, began renovating it in 1961 to the whoops of delight as visitors to the museum discover anew (or yet again) the kitchen where Julia tested recipes, rehearsed cooking programs, and cooked with and for family and friends, and where three of her television series were taped in the nineties. In the numerous articles, books, feature films, documentaries, and television shows that are still broadcast and available online, Julia herself is always the star, as well she should be.[1] Julia is at the center of this book, too, but the story is told through her kitchen and the objects within, a story she began narrating herself almost as soon as the blue-green paint was dry on the kitchen cabinets. As we will see in the pages ahead, Julia spoke about her kitchen in great detail to journalists and food media, writers eager to interview this thoroughly charming and disarmingly knowledgeable woman about her popular cookbooks and television series. Julia often brought the conversation around to her home kitchen, describing the functional arrangements and aesthetic vision for her favorite room in the house. Over many years she introduced readers and television audiences to specific tools that she used in her home kitchen, which was pictured regularly in popular publications, from *House & Garden* to *Architectural Digest*, the *New York Times Magazine*, the *Boston Globe*, and many more. There was nothing mysterious or secretive about Julia Child's home kitchen; she made sure people knew that a serious cook needed a serious workspace. If Julia was the original narrator of her kitchen, this book picks up the narrative thread to reveal its—and Julia's—ongoing significance and legacy.

As one of the museum staffers who met with Julia in 2001 to discuss the future of her home kitchen, I have spent much of the past twenty-odd years immersed in American food history and delving deeply into the stories behind this marvelous room. I have had the joy and benefit of learning from and alongside my museum colleagues as we examined more than one thousand objects that we collected and together created exhibitions and programs that have placed Julia and her kitchen into the larger context of American social and cultural history. But I must confess that cooking had never been my passion—staying *out* of the kitchen was my goal as a college student in the seventies, when supporting the Equal Rights Amendment and the National Organization for Women appealed to my idea of a path to a bright future that could somehow accommodate my ambitions for a career outside of the home. But after moving from the Midwest to the East Coast and entering the museum field in 1981, I became more aware of how food and culture intersected. The worlds that opened up by experiencing a variety of cuisines, plus the allure of fine dining, and the sensory jolt from encountering truly fresh ingredients, awakened something that had lain dormant.

Then, *whomp*! Our friend Debora gave my husband and me an unexpected wedding present: a copy of Julia Child's *Mastering the Art of French Cooking*, Volume One—a serious tome if ever there was one. Curious, we started in with boeuf bourguignon, a dish we had seen Julia prepare on her television series *The French Chef* in 1963. Transformational. We gingerly moved on to other recipes, as if we were taking a course on cooking. And of course, we were, not realizing that we were part of a large cohort of Americans who were adjusting their thinking about food and cooking.

As the years have gone by and especially since meeting Julia and collecting her entire home kitchen, I have found that her message about being open to trying new recipes and cuisines—and enjoying the social and creative process of cooking—resonated even with me. As I came to know more about her and her culinary legacy, as well as how she lived her life fully and with unwavering passion, I have embraced the vast universe of food history and culture. This universe includes cookware, recipes, kitchen design, cooking techniques, food memories, and larger issues of food systems, health, and access that I would have dismissed in my youthful focus on a professional identity outside of the domestic sphere. What I didn't realize then was that Julia had flipped the script: Her home kitchen—that domestic place—was the rigorously professional space that launched, nurtured, and made possible her remarkable career.

For most of their history, museums have housed collections of artifacts, documents, artworks, and other types of what scholars call "material culture"—the objects that reflect where we came from, who we are, what we have created for various purposes, and what has mattered to us over time. While digital technology has both added to and shifted our ideas about preserving and sharing interpretations of the past, most museums continue to value the "real thing," the material evidence of life as experienced by diverse people over time.[2] With storage and exhibition space limited, and the costs of caring for artifacts ever rising, twenty-first-century museums in the United States are grappling with the realities of collecting more objects. Arguments to cut back on collecting are often bolstered by explanations that preserving the material past is no longer justified in a digital world.[3] This book takes exception to that view and aims to demonstrate that collecting the real thing—including an entire home kitchen—provides a wealth of opportunities for reflection, inspiration, and understanding, in ways that cannot be accomplished on a screen.

Julia's kitchen has been on view almost continuously since 2002, providing ample opportunity for us (known as "Team Julia") to observe how the Smithsonian's large and diverse audiences respond to seeing it and learning about it from our word-limited (but lively!) exhibition labels. The kitchen draws people closer, they speak to and ask questions of each other, and sometimes muse silently by themselves. They want more and they tell us so. This book aims to bring together the stories about the kitchen from people who actually spent time there cooking with Julia, helping her to test recipes, enjoying a meal, and taping three television series. In book form, readers can page through the sumptuously illustrated pages at their leisure and access the backstories of objects, including tales that go beyond the familiar themes such as "more butter" and "dropping a carcass on television" that true or not are firmly ensconced in the popular imagination surrounding Julia Child. This is a chance for us, after caring for (another way of saying *curating*) the kitchen for two decades, to share the stories we've learned in our research, to answer questions asked frequently by our visitors, and to offer all readers a window into Julia's formidable legacy.

Julia Child was an extraordinary individual, whose influence and legacy continue to expand, even twenty years after her death in 2004. The basic contours of her story are by now well-known to many, but always worth revisiting for new generations of fans.

Born Julia McWilliams in Pasadena, California, on August 15, 1912, she grew up in a world of wealth and privilege. Her father, John McWilliams, was a conservative businessman and her mother, Carolyn (Caro), was socially active and, like her peers, not one to spend time engaging in domestic chores. Their three children—Julia, John (born in 1914), and Dorothy (born in 1917)—were athletic, active, and friendly with other children in the neighborhood. Julia's childhood awareness of food and cooking was largely limited to the labors of hired cooks, who prepared "typical American fare—fat-roasted chicken with buttery mashed potatoes and creamed spinach; or well-marbled porterhouse steaks ... delicious but not refined food."[4] Many years later she described the kitchen in her Pasadena home as a "dismal place."[5] She attended a boarding school, the Katharine Branson School, in Marin County, and was admitted to Smith College, her mother's alma mater, in Northampton, Massachusetts.

In this image from the 1934 Smith College yearbook, Julia McWilliams (Child) (back row, second from left) poses with her fellow members of the campus charity organization, Community Chest.

Julia described herself as "an adolescent nut" in college[6] and labeled her college career as a "wild ride." The trip from the West Coast to eastern universities was an adventure, with some forty to fifty students traveling together by train. She recalled that "the trip was one long party," which lasted about five days. On campus, she continued having a good time, remembering "consuming large quantities of jelly doughnuts and driving around to speakeasies [yes, this was during Prohibition], the car packed with giggling girls."[7] At Smith reunions she admitted to campus pranks, describing how she painted a toilet seat red and how she hung a green rug across a fire rope to divide her dorm room so that her studious roommate could work in peace. Still, Julia couldn't resist tossing jelly doughnuts over the rug, a prank that led to separate but side-by-side rooms for the two friends the following year.[8]

Julia McWilliams and Paul Child (far right) with OSS colleagues in Kunming, the agency's headquarters in southern China.

When Julia graduated in 1934, she didn't have much of a plan for the future. Expected to find a husband and settle into a life of comfort, she worked briefly in New York before returning to California in 1937, where her restlessness and dissatisfaction grew. Years later she spoke about the disquietude of that time when she explained, "In my generation, except for a few people who'd gone into banking or nursing or something like that, middle-class women didn't have careers. You were to marry and have children and be a nice mother. You didn't go out and do anything. I found that I got restless a year or two after going home to Pasadena... I must have always been independent because that kind of life, I just couldn't do. It didn't fulfill anything."[9] Yearning for a larger purpose, in 1941 and with the possibility of war looming, she volunteered for the Red Cross, taking the civil service exam after the attack on Pearl Harbor. Like thousands of young women from across the country who became known as "government girls," Julia moved to Washington, DC, in 1942, to help the war effort via an office job.[10] She began working for the Office of War Information in the Department of State and was transferred to the OSS, the Office of Strategic Services (the forerunner of the Central Intelligence Agency), where she was a file clerk—a file clerk with access to sensitive documents, to be sure. Although she was not a spy, she worked for a spy agency.

To her excitement, Julia was selected to travel to remote areas of the world on behalf of the OSS, an opportunity that fed her curiosity about lives lived outside of her limited experience. It was on this assignment that she met Paul Child, her future life partner, who had been hired by the OSS for his considerable artistic skills to create maps, charts, and diagrams.[11] Child was also a photographer, writer, poet, and renaissance man who was ten years older than Julia and had already traveled the world and experienced the pleasures of good food and wine. Their work assignments took them and their colleagues to Sri Lanka (then known as Ceylon) and China, where Julia's senses were jolted awake. She found Chinese food "wonderful!" and later declared, "the War was the change in my life."[12] Indeed, not only did it give her a sense of purpose, and a chance to see the world, but it also brought her and Paul Child together into the strong and lasting partnership that shaped her life in food.

After the war, their OSS work came to an abrupt halt as the unit was summarily disbanded. The couple married in Pennsylvania in 1946 and moved to Washington, DC, where they lived in Georgetown and purchased a house on Olive Street in 1948. Soon after, they departed for Paris, where Paul served as the exhibits officer for the U.S. Information Service. Julia's palate was aroused again when they stopped in the historic city of Rouen for a meal of perfectly prepared sole meunière, salade verte with vinaigrette, her first real French baguette, a bottle of Pouilly-Fumé, a dessert of fromage blanc, and dark, strong café filtre. She recalled that "at La Couronne I experienced fish, and a dining experience, of a higher order than any I'd ever had before."[13]

This set of tea tins in Julia's kitchen prompted her to reminisce about their time in Sri Lanka. Paul suffered a bout of dysentery and switched from coffee to tea as the more soothing drink. Shortly thereafter Julia also became ill, and from that point onward, they preferred drinking tea. The turquoise tins are from the Mark T. Wendell Tea Company, a Boston firm that kept them in tea for many years.[14]

Julia kept this signaling mirror in her kitchen junk drawer as a reminder of her World War II service. Such mirrors were to be used to signal for help if needed in remote areas.

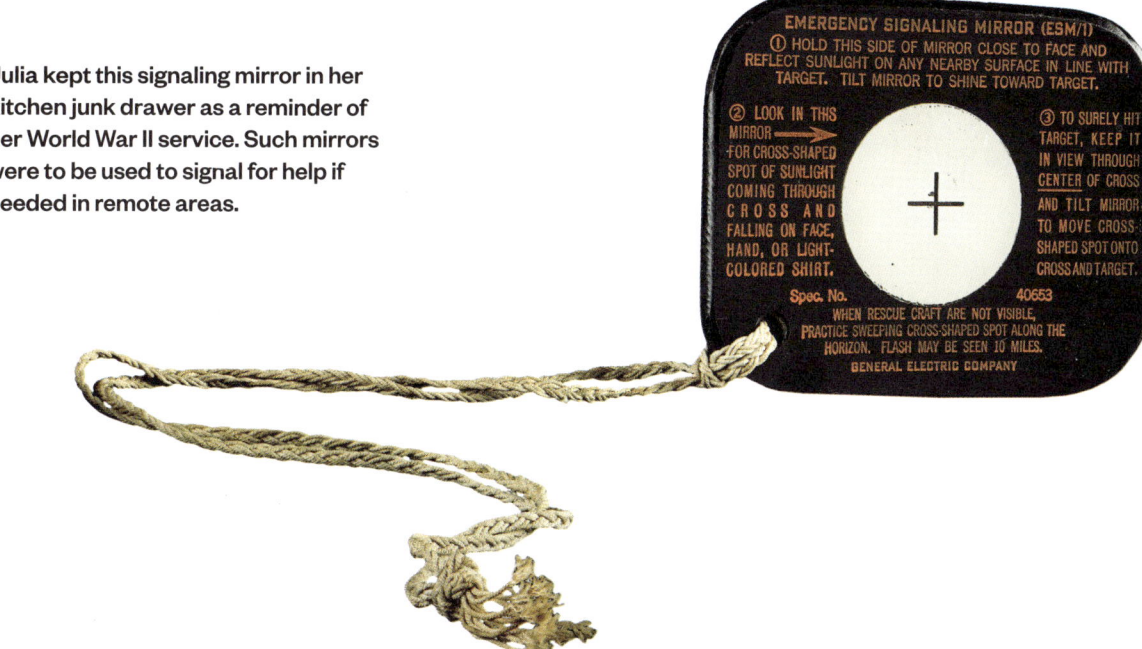

This epiphanic meal, enhanced by the excitement of embarking on a new life chapter in France with the husband she adored, clarified for Julia that her restless yen for something more was crystallizing around her passion for food and her desire to learn the fundamentals of French cooking and cuisine. Off she went to culinary school, and not just any academy, but the famous Le Cordon Bleu, where she spent two days in a course for women that Julia judged too elementary for her level of knowledge and ambitions. The school's owner, Madame Élizabeth Brassart, declared that Julia was not advanced enough for the haute cuisine course but offered her a spot in a class for professional restaurateurs. Julia accepted and met her fellow classmates—eleven former GIs who were enrolled under the auspices of the GI Bill of Rights. Looking back, she remarked, "Luckily, I had spent most of the war in male-dominated environments and wasn't fazed by them in the least."[15] Though she was the only woman in the class, at six feet, three inches, she stood taller than her French instructors as well as her fellow American students.

At age thirty-eight, Julia turned out to be a serious student after all, and with a great deal of practice and diligence, she mastered the techniques of classical cuisine at Le Cordon Bleu. As the spouse of an American diplomat in postwar Paris, she also had an active social calendar and met many people, including two French culinary experts, Simone "Simca" Beck and Louisette Bertholle, with whom she formed key relationships. The three set up an informal school in Julia and Paul's

above left: Julia with her mentor, chef Max Bugnard, and another student at Le Cordon Bleu
above right: Louisette, Julia, and Simca in Julia and Paul's Paris apartment kitchen. Julia is using the soapstone mortar and pestle, and Simca is using a tamis to make quenelles.

Julia received her diploma from Le Cordon Bleu in 1951, but not without controversy. In March she had failed the school's final test, having decided to study some of the most challenging recipes she had learned instead of focusing on the basic dishes described in the school's official booklet. The school's owner, Madame Élizabeth Brassart, refused to allow Julia to retake the exam, despite the entreaties of Chef Max Bugnard, who believed Julia was well qualified to receive the diploma. Madame Brassart finally relented, and Julia took the test, passing with flying colors. When she received her diploma in September, she noticed that Madame Brassart had backdated it to March, the date of the original exam.[16]

apartment for American women wishing to learn the basics of French cuisine. Called L'École des Trois Gourmandes (The School of Three Hearty Eaters), they used these teaching sessions also to test their ideas for a cookbook, one that would teach American home cooks the fundamental techniques and recipes of French cuisine. This experience revealed to Julia her love and affinity for teaching and learning, which never diminished throughout her long life.

Les trois gourmandes turned their attention to compiling and testing French recipes for American cooks, an endeavor that took on epic dimensions for the

JULIA CHILD'S KITCHEN

Paul Child designed the logo for L'École des Trois Gourmandes, and the three women wore patches with the logo on their aprons. Julia continued to wear the patch pinned to her blouse on her first television series, *The French Chef*.

entire decade of the fifties. As told by Julia and her great-nephew Alex Prud'homme in their 2006 book, *My Life in France*, as well as in her voluminous correspondence published in *As Always, Julia*, edited by Joan Reardon, the three friends, strong personalities all, took very different approaches to writing and testing recipes. Julia was very disciplined about operational proof—setting up experiments and meticulously tracking the results—while Simca wrote from her deep knowledge of French cuisine and cooking techniques. Louisette was less involved overall.[17]

For years, the three were wedded to the idea that the cookbook would be a compendium—a thorough guide to French cuisine's master recipes and their variations. It is important to point out that this work was carried out without computers, email, or even fax machines, but in typed pages that Julia produced on a manual typewriter, a proficiency gained during her years of office work during World War II.[18] What's more, the project extended well past Julia and Paul's residency in Paris, which ended in 1953, when they moved to Marseilles, in the South of France, for Paul's new posting, still as a cultural attaché with the U.S. Department of State. It extended through their next move to Bonn, Germany, where they resided from 1954 to 1956, then through their brief return to the United States and through Paul's last posting in Oslo, Norway (from 1959 to 1961). This meant that the cookbook collaborators had to communicate with each other and exchange drafts of recipes by mail. Unsurprisingly, the process of editing and revising each other's work became an often-exasperating exercise in cultural relations.

Throughout this time, the challenge of securing an American publisher tried Julia's patience and ordinarily cheerful disposition. Avis DeVoto, a friend in Cambridge, Massachusetts, provided guidance toward an eventual contract with Houghton Mifflin in Boston. (Avis's husband, Bernard, an eminent Harvard historian, had first caught Julia's attention with a column in *Harper's Magazine*, complaining about the sorry state of American stainless-steel knives. Julia sent him a letter on March 8, 1952, agreeing with his assessment of American cutlery, and enclosed a "nice little French model" in appreciation. This gesture inspired Avis

30 INTRODUCTION

to send a warm and lengthy reply to Julia and led to their lifelong friendship.)[19] When the publisher received the tome in 1958—more than 700 pages on sauces and poultry—they backed out of the deal, leading Julia to write to Simca, "HELL AND DAMNATION, is all I can say. WHY DID WE EVER DECIDE TO DO THIS ANYWAY? But I can't think of doing anything else, can you?"[20]

The following year, with Avis's skillful intervention, a revised and improved manuscript was sent to a New York publisher, Alfred A. Knopf, where a young editor, Judith Jones, immediately grasped the value of the work. Years later she wrote, "From the moment I started turning the pages, I was *bouleversée*, as the French say—knocked out." She tried the recipes and realized that "the genius ... lay not only in explaining all the techniques so meticulously but in the structure, which was based on master recipes and their variations. Once you had done the basic boeuf bourguignon and absorbed all the essential information, you could apply that know-how to other stews and braises in almost any cookbook."[21] She championed the manuscript to her colleagues and to Mr. Knopf himself, who famously joked he would eat his hat if anyone bought a book with the title *Mastering the Art of French Cooking*.[22]

In 1959, the Childs purchased a house at 103 Irving Street, in Cambridge, Massachusetts, with the encouragement of Avis DeVoto, who would now be a neighbor as well as a close friend. Before they moved in, however, they departed for Oslo, Norway, Paul's last posting for the State Department. In every place they lived or visited during Paul's foreign service career, Julia made it her business to frequent the local bakeries, as well as the vegetable, meat, and fish markets, to learn about local culinary customs, and to acquire kitchen tools and equipment for her ever-expanding "batterie de cuisine," the term she used often for her kitchen equipment, and Oslo was no exception. There she made some key acquisitions, including her kitchen table and chairs, which we will see in more detail in the pages to come.

By 1961, Paul Child, at age fifty-nine, had had enough of government work, and as he and Julia thought about his retirement, they imagined a life in Cambridge that would involve reading, writing, painting, cooking, entertaining, and traveling. That idyll didn't last. No one could have predicted what would come next and how their lives would revolve around food and cooking, with their home kitchen as the center of a new, creative chapter in American culinary history and with Julia as the star.

CHAPTER 1

"The kitchen needed *complete* rethinking."

JULIA CHILD'S KITCHEN

Three major life events converged for Paul and Julia Child in 1961. Paul retired from his State Department career, Julia's first cookbook, *Mastering the Art of French Cooking*, Volume One, was published, and the pair moved into their Cambridge house, which became their permanent home together and their base of operations during the as-yet-unimagined adventure that would be the rest of their lives.

Within shouting distance of Harvard University, 103 Irving Street was a solid, three-story home in a neighborhood replete with powerful intellectuals and academic discourse. Indeed, the house had been built in 1899 for Josiah Royce, an American philosopher and historian of the American West. Royce and his neighbor, William James, also a Harvard philosopher, allegedly continued their spirited academic debates on religious experiences, dubbed the Battle for the Absolute, in the neighborhood after returning home from class.[1]

previous spread: A series of photographs by Paul Child showing the newly designed kitchen, ca. 1962
above: 103 Irving Street, 2001

[FOOD PANTRY]

[ENTRANCE]

[PASTRY PANTRY]

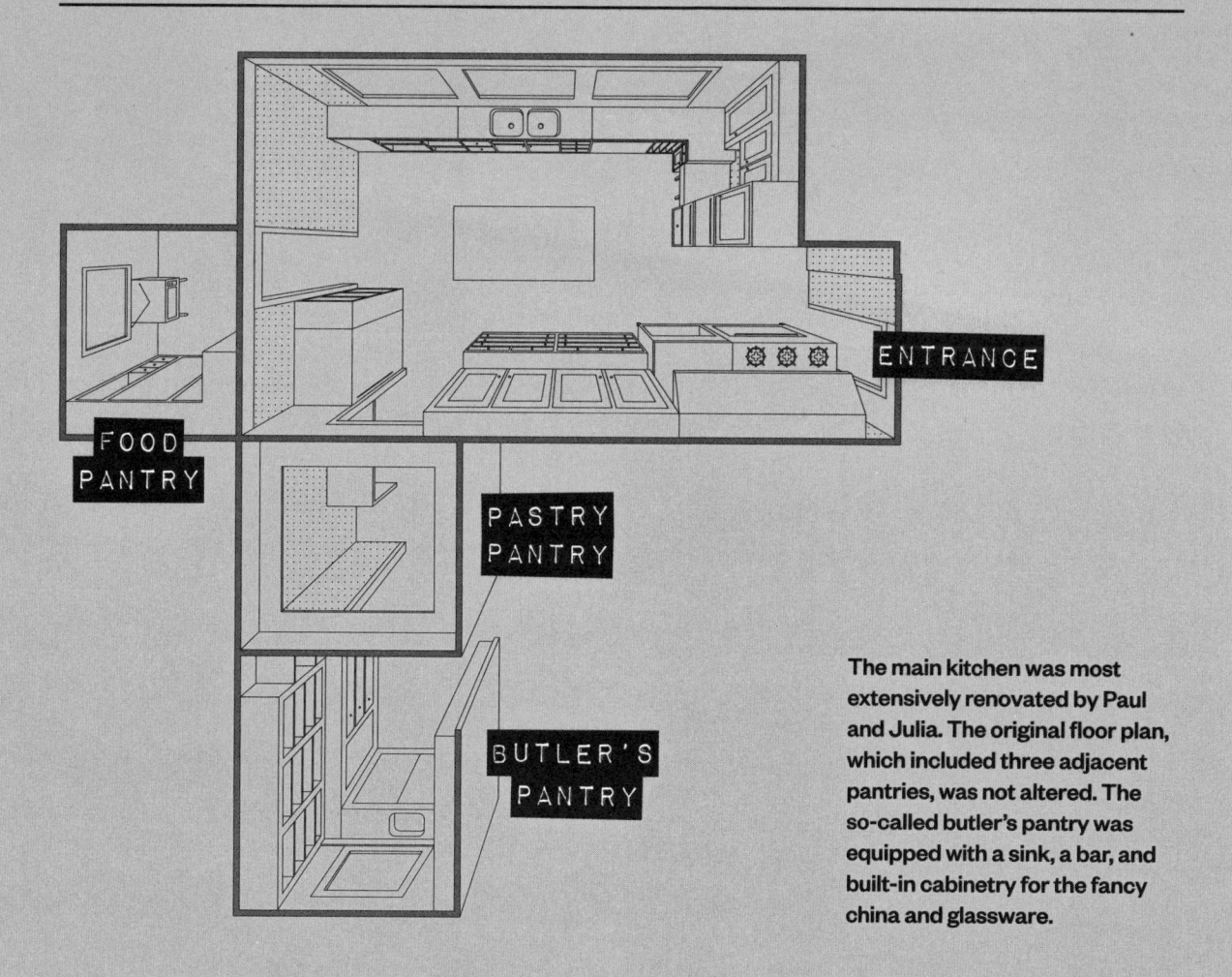

[BUTLER'S PANTRY]

The main kitchen was most extensively renovated by Paul and Julia. The original floor plan, which included three adjacent pantries, was not altered. The so-called butler's pantry was equipped with a sink, a bar, and built-in cabinetry for the fancy china and glassware.

The large house was in fair shape, for the most part, and the Childs imagined how it would accommodate their new life back in the United States. There was space for a library or two, an artist's studio for Paul, an office for Julia, as well as large rooms for entertaining, displaying artwork, and making music. Ample space to host visiting family and friends. A full basement. Gardens front and back. There was much to admire, except for the kitchen. Despite its spacious floor plan and adjacent pantries, the kitchen itself "needed complete rethinking," according to Julia.[2] Having adjusted to many European domiciles with tiny kitchens during their years abroad, the kitchen in Cambridge, the ninth of their married life, represented an exciting new beginning. This 20 × 14-foot room was their chance to create something together, a room that reflected their ideas about the importance of food, cooking, and sharing the pleasures of the table with family, friends, and, sometimes, strangers.

The kitchen renovation project took many months and was overseen by Robert Woods Kennedy, an architect Julia described as "sensitive to old Cambridge houses."[3] As an artist, photographer, and the more visually oriented of the couple, Paul generally took the lead on matters relating to the renovation, but Julia was also very much involved, even as she began doing interviews and handling correspondence relating to the long-anticipated publication of *Mastering the Art of French Cooking*, Volume One. Together, they settled on the color scheme—white walls with simple wooden cabinetry and trim painted in shades of green and blue.[4] They also chose wooden countertops made of cherry butcher block and raised them to 38 inches high, instead of the more typical 36 inches, to accommodate Julia's height. For the countertops in the adjacent pastry pantry, they added slabs of marble, a choice both smooth and cool to the touch, to facilitate working with pastry dough. In the main kitchen, a stainless-steel sink and black appliances completed the look.

"Built to Fit Your Wife," in *Popular Science*, 1953

How did Julia's kitchen compare with popular kitchen designs at the time? Were the Childs swayed at all by design trends? Were they ahead of or behind the times? Or were they on their own track, perhaps inspired by their time abroad?

SINK CENTER has storage bins behind sink for fruits, vegetables, soaps, detergents. There's a footrest and chair so the housewife can sit at the sink. Dishwasher may be added.

MIX CENTER contains built-in bins for flour and sugar and a flour sifter. There's an electric outlet for the mixer. Cake pans are racked in cabinet below the counter.

OVEN AND REFRIGERATOR are both waist-high at center for greater accessibility. Refrigerator contains freeze chest and pull-out drawers that eliminate reaching in.

- Separate work center tailored to fit your family now, and ready to be taken down any time by a handy man for rearrangement to meet new family needs.

All these things, and many other fresh ideas, were included in the kitchen because so many experts worked on it. The experts came from the campus, from manufacturers, from federal, state and private agencies. Their work was coordinated by Glenn H. Beyer, professor of Housing and Design, and director of

SEPTEMBER 1953 173

SUBURBAN DREAMS AND REALITIES

Kitchen trends in the postwar United States reflected the opportunities and aspirations of mostly middle-class, white Americans, and a smartly designed kitchen became a symbol of an idealized way of life. For people who could afford to move to the suburbs in the postwar boom, the new developments offered homes designed for family living. This typically meant homes with sizable kitchens that were more integrated with the dining and living rooms and not walled off at the back of the house. Focused on efficiency, all-electric kitchens in the fifties were equipped with labor-saving appliances and easy-to-clean materials like laminated plastics for countertops and cabinet surfaces, projecting a sense of modernity and progress. This suburban dream, however, was not available to everyone, and in places like Levittown, Pennsylvania, Black families were actively discouraged from moving in and harassed by white neighbors when they did.[5]

Popular Science magazine portrayed the modern kitchen as a serious workspace while reinforcing the traditional notion of the kitchen as a place for housewives. This article described a project at Cornell University that reengineered the kitchen, setting up efficient work zones that would "fit your wife." The partnership between Julia and Paul Child provides a counterpoint to this idea that women needed men to design a kitchen to suit them and that shiny stainless steel and uncluttered countertops were the way to go.

Just three years later, in 1956, *House Beautiful* published an article with the heading "The best kitchens are planned by exasperated women," referencing the Gilbreth time and motion studies that had been used to "improve" work methods and reduce inefficiencies in various industries.[6] Dr. Lillian Gilbreth had been writing on home management for many years and in 1940 introduced her theory of "circular routing" that became known as the kitchen "work triangle," an idea that influenced generations of kitchen designers. The triangle formed by the stove, sink, and refrigerator in a kitchen were, according to Gilbreth, ideally placed 5½ feet from each other to reduce the number of steps the cook had to take while preparing a meal. Gilbreth also recommended that ergonomics be considered in kitchen design, allowing women to stand at a countertop and not have to uncomfortably bend over or raise their arms to chop and stir.[7]

Julia Child would have agreed with Lillian Gilbreth about the need to raise her counters, but she never went in for creating the so-called efficient work triangle. Aware of the theory of saving steps for efficiency's sake, Julia quipped that she liked to traverse her kitchen while cooking because it was a form of exercise.[8]

Although they didn't subscribe to the work triangle theory, Julia and Paul thoughtfully laid out the kitchen's general work zones (sink, range, refrigerator) and distributed the tools most frequently used within each. They also rejected the popular trends for easy-to-clean Formica countertops and the modern look of vinyl or metal-covered cabinet doors, preferring butcher block wood for the counters and wood for the cabinets, painted to match trim around the doorways. Their one concession to modern materials was in the floor covering, selecting airport-grade vinyl flooring in a mid-century pattern of tiny, overlapping squares of gray, pink, green, and cream.

"Floor covering... I refuse to suffer about anymore."

"Now it seems to me I have spoken about almost everything but floor covering, and that is something I refuse to suffer about anymore, having endured the beauty of red tiles in Provence, and large squares of pure white and pure black vinyl in Cambridge. Both were handsome indeed, but every footstep showed on each of them, every grease spot glowed or glowered and I spent my life cleaning them. Now we have pebble-design airport-strength vinyl in Cambridge and fleck-design vinyl in France [at their second home in Provence, La Pitchoune] and nothing shows on them at all except the built-in design. They get a washing only when I think it's about time I did the kitchen floor, and that is psychological rather than esthetic."[9]

FOCUS: FLOOR COVERING

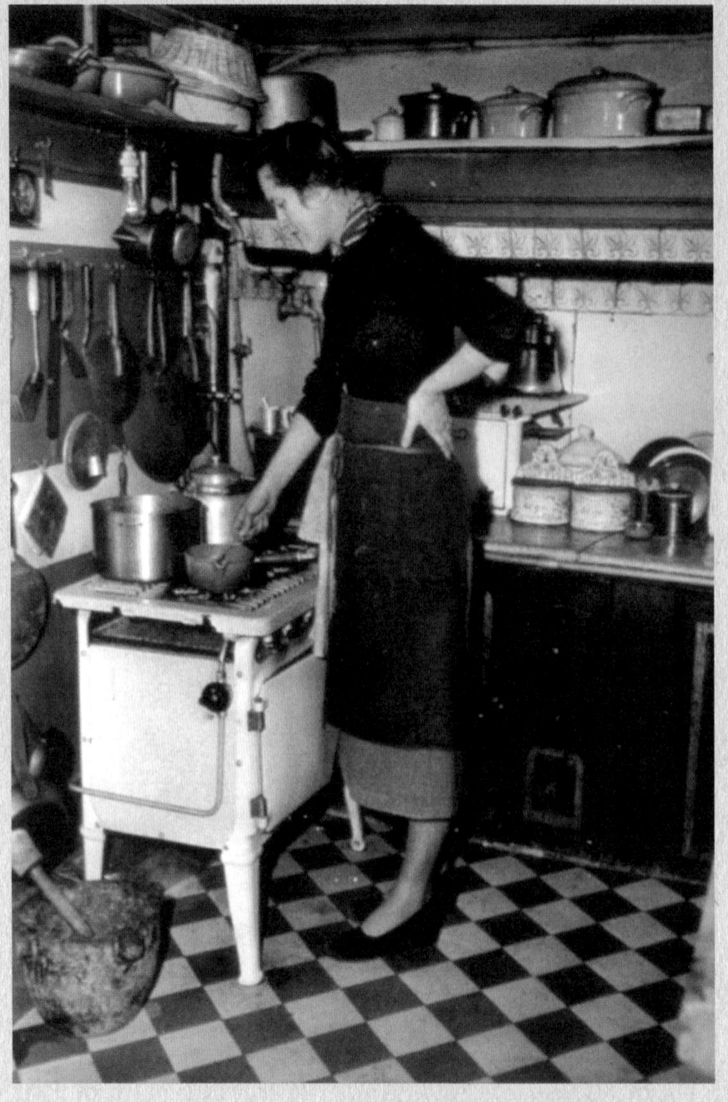

The uncluttered surfaces of trendsetting kitchens in the sixties contrasted with the philosophy that Paul and Julia had brought with them from their time abroad. As they had practiced in their tiny Paris kitchen, they wanted to hang their pots and pans on nearby walls for ease of use but also as a part of a design aesthetic. Julia remarked, "Since we rejoice in the shapes of tools, cooking utensils become decorative objects, all carefully orchestrated by Paul, from pots and pot lids to skillets, trivets and flan rings."[10] They installed the pans Julia used most frequently on pegboard within an arm's reach of the Garland range and hung utensils from the hood or grouped together in crocks that sat comfortably on the shelf above the range. She confessed, "I have always been a hanger-upper, since I like to see where everything is. But one must make a careful plan for this kind of arrangement, or the kitchen will look like a junk shop."[11]

In a 1977 essay for *Architectural Digest*, Julia described the aesthetic approach she and Paul had taken for the display of their kitchen tools, writing: "Even the knives are graduated according to shape and size on vertical magnetic holders. Glass measures and earthenware pitchers are hung just so, while scissors hang in harmony with olive pitters, bottle openers, and nutcrackers."[12]

Most notably, Paul designed a system for hanging Julia's prized copper pots and pans on a pegboard-

opposite: Julia standing over her stove in the Childs' Paris apartment, 1953. Note the pots, pan lids, and utensils hanging above the stove, and the soapstone mortar and wooden pestle resting on the floor. *above:* This image from a 1964 publication about the "World's Fair House" is a good example of the bold colors for cabinetry and the "long-lasting carefree beauty" of Formica-covered islands or peninsulas that were trending in the 1960s, as well as depictions that were also common at the time of home cooks as stylish women without a care in the world.[13] In sharp contrast, Julia and Paul's kitchen design choices were not based on easy-care glamour or made with the thought of a carefree cook standing behind a counter to serve up a meal.

covered wall. While living in Paris she turned into an enthusiastic and frequent customer of E. Dehillerin, a cookware specialty store in the Les Halles district, where she purchased copper bowls, saucepans, gratin pans, straight-sided frying pans (sautoirs), and more. She also added cast-iron pans, skillets, and special pans for sautéing fish or poéle à poissons to her growing "batterie de cuisine." So, when it came time to design their display in the Irving Street kitchen, the task was not taken lightly, but instead was a complex artistic project in and of itself. While Julia gathered the cookware together, Paul prepared the painted pegboard, resting it on the floor to facilitate moving various items around until just the right look was achieved. He arranged and rearranged individual pieces to find the most aesthetically pleasing configuration and, according to Julia, "We both looked at them and said, 'This is the way it should be.'"[14] He then outlined everything with a black or a red/copper marker so that anyone using the pans would know exactly where to return them. The entire kitchen renovation took months and, finally, Paul declared in a letter to his twin brother, Charles, "Our kitchen is now finished, as of tonight, when I put the last stroke on the last under-the-pot-diagram on the wall. Can't believe it! But she's a real wowzer and a pleasure-dome-to-be-in if'n I wuz ever in one."[15]

JULIA CHILD'S KITCHEN

opposite, left: Julia's kitchen ca. 1962. Note the television set through the doorway to the food pantry. *opposite, right:* Detail of kitchen tools in Julia's kitchen, including shears, an herb chopper, measuring spoons, an apple corer/slicer, and a fish scaler with a heart-shaped head. *above:* The original markings by Paul Child on the copper-pot-wall pegboard remain, as seen in this photograph of the wall in the museum taken in 2021, when the pots and pans had been removed temporarily for photography.

THE KITCHEN NEEDED *COMPLETE* RETHINKING

FOCUS: KITCHEN BOOKSHELF

Paul and Julia envisioned their new kitchen as a place for social interaction, involving wide-ranging conversations on myriad topics. Their plans and design included a bookcase that would hold volumes for consultation in the give-and-take of their frequent discussions over a meal or in day-to-day activities in the kitchen. On November 1, 1962, Paul celebrated the completion of this important element of the kitchen in a letter to his brother Charles: "We've had a bookcase built into the kitchen, up against the Frigidaire, for all those books of reference one always wants when conversation gets going around the Norwegian table. I've bought a 1957 edition of the *Encyclopedia Britannica* second hand, in perfect shape, which will go in first as the basic layer."[16] Paul's description of their intent for the kitchen bookshelf provides a starting point for comparing how the contents changed as they acquired new books and adopted new technologies over the following four decades. Later we will see what the shelves held when the Smithsonian collected the kitchen in 2001. Hint: Don't expect to find two shelves' worth of the 1957 *Encyclopedia Britannica*.

left: The bookshelf with encyclopedias in "The Kitchen Julia Built," *New York Times Magazine*, May 16, 1976, p. 81
opposite: Instead of sending out holiday cards, Julia and Paul adopted the tradition of sharing Valentine's Day greetings with family and friends. This Valentine from 1964 shows their strong affection for their home kitchen and its culinary tools.

Nos cœurs en casserole, farcis d'amour pour vous. P. & J. 1964.

COUNTERTOPS: "I SLIPPED UP... AND AM FOREVER FURIOUS"

Media interest in Julia's kitchen expanded with each new cookbook and television series. Julia often wrote the articles herself, but she also gave great interviews to journalists eager for insight into the kitchen that was home base for the unlikely culinary star of television. By 1975, with the publication of *From Julia's Kitchen*, Julia shared even more details about her home kitchen, including one memorable admission in a 1976 article for the *New York Times Magazine*, where she revealed a mistake they had made when first installing the butcher block countertops in 1961.[17]

"Ours, which have been in constant use for 15 years, are of restaurant-quality laminated maple 1½ inches thick, and were bought by the yard. They are easy to keep. I scrub them about once a year with a heavy brush and a barely diluted standard brand of liquid ammoniated soap. I let the wooden surfaces dry, rub them with olive oil, which I leave on overnight, and give a final rubdown in the morning with clean paper towels. Because we have room, we also have a large pastry marble, and I very much recommend one if you go in for pie doughs, feuilletes and such. If space is limited, get a portable slab ⅝ to ¾ inch thick (look under "marble" in the Yellow Pages, or find a furniture-in-parts store) and of a size that will fit on a refrigerator rack so that you can chill it during hot weather; store it up-ended in your tray cupboard when not in use. A final word on work tops: Be sure to have an overhang of 2½ to 3 inches so that you can hold a plate or bowl under the surface and scrape off into it cheese, crumbs, chopped vegetables or whatever. I slipped up on this consideration for one of my most used cutting areas, and am forever furious."

Julia's years of fury were surely vanquished with the installation of proper countertops. A 1977 article noted that "all of the counters have an overhang of 2½ to 3 inches so that a plate or bowl can be held under counter to scrape off crumbs, chopped vegetables and the like."[18]

opposite: A section of the maple countertops, which at 38 inches high are clearly higher than her Garland range

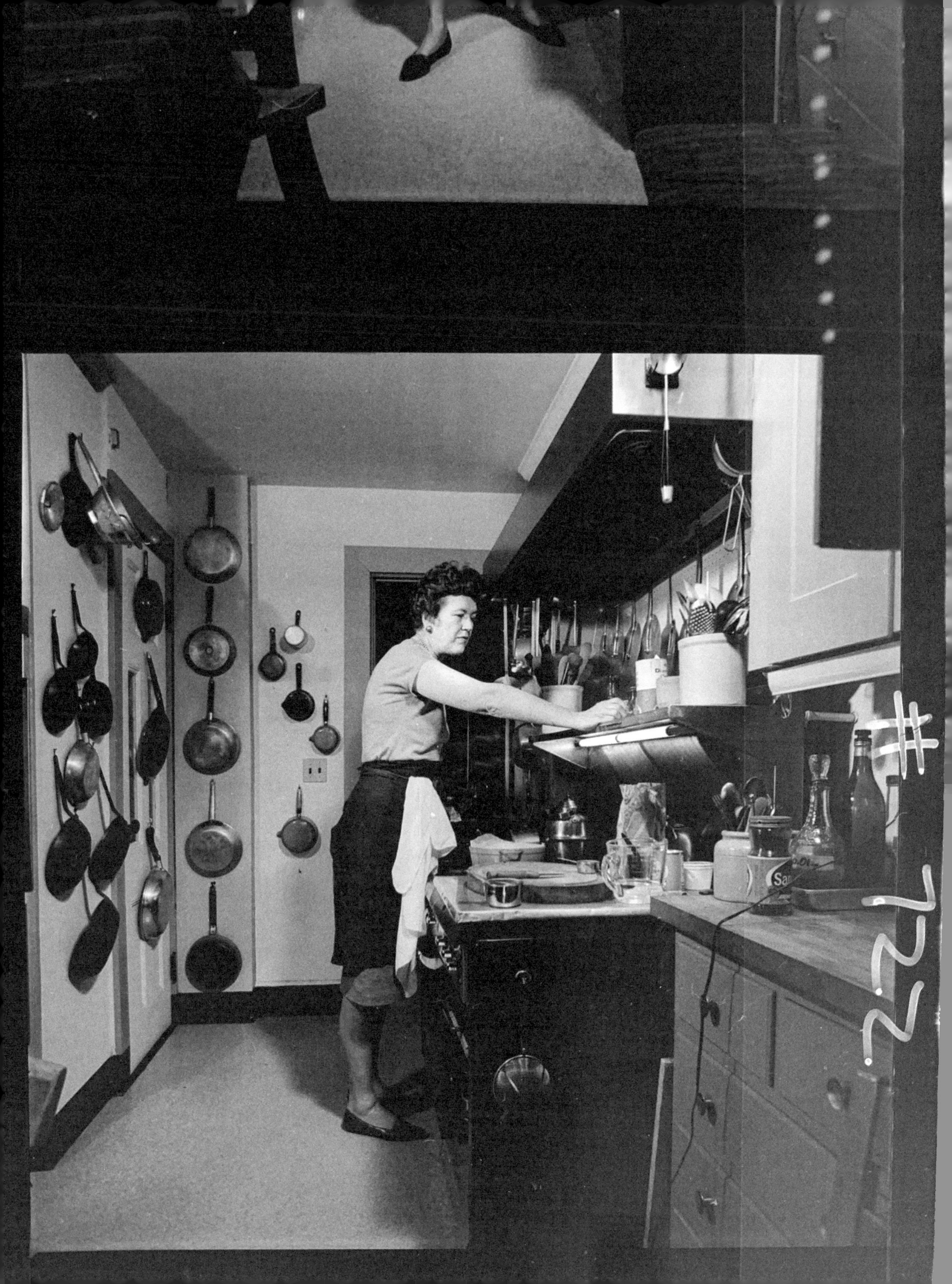

KITCHENWARE FROM EVERYWHERE

Paul Child was a tireless photographer with a keen eye for design. His photographs of their decade abroad in the fifties capture the architectural details of urban buildings, the quality of light on landscapes, and the beauty, pace, and intimacy of their lives, especially in Paris.[19] As they settled into 103 Irving Street, Paul's penchant for photography was aimed at recording the transition to their new (and ultimately permanent) home. His early photographs of the kitchen—and Julia in it—provide an intriguing point of comparison to the Cambridge kitchen we think we know. The kitchen walls and surfaces seem strangely vacant and uncluttered compared to the number and mass of things that eventually populated the kitchen after decades of use.

above: The table and chairs from Norway, and the fruit bowl and copper pots from France, were part of the kitchen's design from the beginning. *opposite:* "Julia holding pot, kitchen sink," Paris, 1952

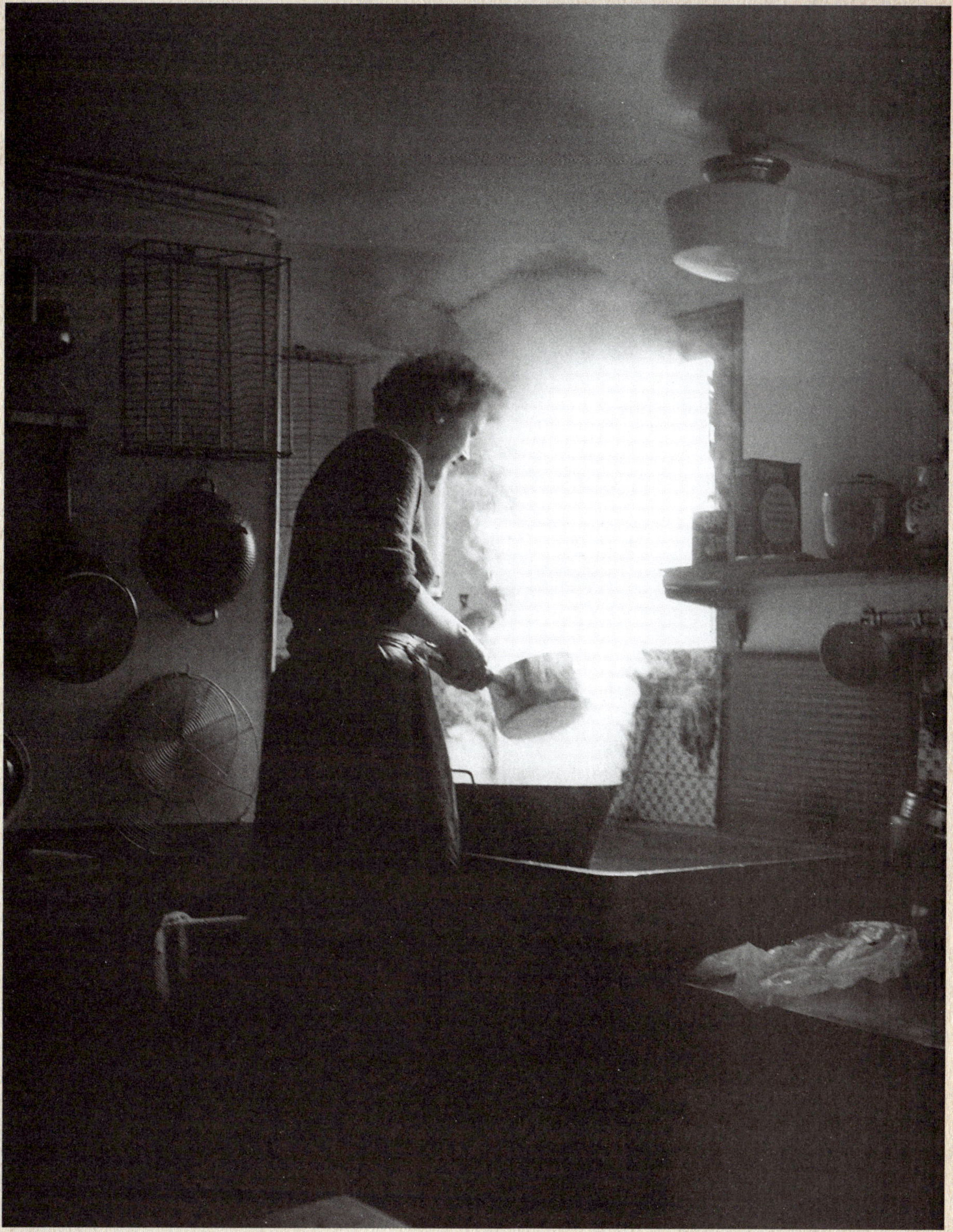

FRANCE: MORTAR AND PESTLE

Some iconic objects were part of the kitchen from the beginning, including many items the couple had collected during their years in Europe. For the most part, those objects remain in the same spot, or very close to where they were first placed by Julia and Paul in the early sixties. Julia described the large soapstone mortar and wooden pestle in a 2001 interview:

> "Now before the food processors, if you really wanted to make wonderful French sauce, say a wonderful lobster dish or wonderful shellfish mousse what you wanted was a big marble [*sic*] mortar like this and a big pestle and you would pound it like that. This is very important for French sauces, too. If you wanted to make a lobster butter for instance, you put your butter in here and lobster chunks and you pounded them all together and pounded and pounded until they were very fine, then you put them through a drum sieve, put the stuff in there and then you rubbed it through. Then you scraped it off. The terrible thing is you had to wash the sieve off afterwards. That was a big job. But it worked… When we were over there (in France) I wanted a marble mortar and we happened to go to the flea market, which was wonderful in those days, and at the very end of the flea market we found this wonderful marble [soapstone] mortar. Paul had to carry it, it weighs a ton, but Paul carried it, he was very strong, about a mile. And I've had it ever since. It's just wonderful."[20]

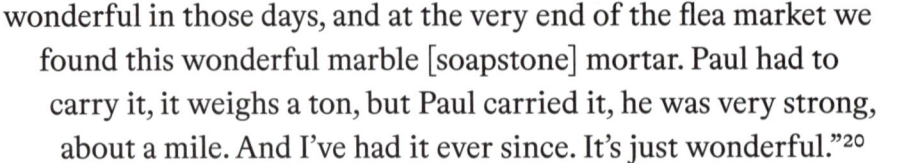

Mortar and pestle that sits on the floor beneath the butcher block table in Julia's kitchen

FRANCE: FRUIT BOWL

Set in the middle of the kitchen table is a white ceramic bowl made in Moustiers-Sainte-Marie, in Provence, France. Located in the Alpine area of southeastern France, and with sources of fresh water, clay, and plentiful wood for firing the kilns, Moustiers-Sainte-Marie became a major center for the production of *faience*, tin-glazed earthenware, in the eighteenth century. Although it was known for its delicately painted ceramics, Julia and Paul purchased this plain white, braided bowl when they were living in Marseilles in 1953–54. It remained one of Julia's favorite pieces in her kitchen, and for years it held Paul's morning fruit—bananas.[21]

FRANCE: FOOD MILLS (MOULI)

Hanging on pegboard across from the Garland range are two hand-operated food mills. Julia acquired these mills, or mouli, in France and used them for applesauce, purées, and other tasks that are now easily accomplished with an electric blender or food processor. She wrote, "the French model [food mill] with removable disks and folding rubber-padded feet is still the best… One with a top diameter of 9 inches is the standard size; if you are having more than one, the 7-inch size is handy for small jobs like sieving hard-boiled egg yolks."[22]

top: The fruit bowl from France that sits on the kitchen table. *left:* Julia's food mills hanging on a pegboard near the Garland range

GERMANY: POTATO MASHER/RICER

Between 1954 and 1956, Paul's job took the couple to Germany, where they lived in military-style housing in a suburb of Bonn that was modern, efficient, and uninspired. Ever curious, Julia made it her business to learn about local culinary tools and traditions.[23] One device that reflects her time in Germany is a potato ricer, which hangs on pegboard above her telephone, along with her lorgnette, a pair of round, black-rimmed glasses with a long black handle for holding up to one's face, and other hard-to-categorize or -store items like a box cheese grater, a magnifying glass, and heart-shaped cake molds.

Julia's potato ricer from Germany

> "Now this is a great German potato masher. It's good and solid. You see, the potato goes in and then you go WUMPH! and out she comes. I love great big things like this because it really works very well and of course it all comes apart for washing, so it's a very practical instrument."[24]

Julia added that she came to prefer her electric stand-mixer for making big batches of mashed potatoes at Thanksgiving but kept the big German ricer around, occasionally using it for comic effect in cooking demonstrations.[25]

NORWAY: COPPER KETTLE

"This kettle is for very much sentimental reasons," Julia told us in 2001. "It came from Norway from my very good friend Bjørn and Eline Egge. And it's just all copper and ... I just love it."

The kettle sits on the cooktop of the Garland range and is one of the first objects one sees upon entering the kitchen. Julia's deep connection to the object is better understood knowing of the Childs' respect for Bjørn Egge, whom they met during Paul's assignment in Oslo from 1959 to 1961. Egge had served in the Norwegian Army during World War II and spent three years in concentration camps after being captured by the Germans. After the war, he served his country in important ways; Egge was a major general of the Norwegian Army and president of the Norwegian Red Cross. He also served for four years as the deputy head of the NATO Defense College.[26]

The copper kettle from Norway sits between two enameled, cast-iron casseroles, one with origins in Belgium and the other from France. Originally known as Bruxelles Ware and imported to the United States from Belgium, the orange-flame bean pot at left is a Descoware-branded item. In the fifties, the importer D. E. Sanford Company (D.E.S.Co.) became Descoware and continued to import high-quality cookware from Belgium under the new brand. In the highly competitive market for enameled, cast-iron cookware in the seventies, the then owners of the Descoware trademark, rights, and patents sold them to its competitor in France, Le Creuset. The red Le Creuset cocotte that sits at right on Julia's stovetop is similar to a Dutch oven and was used by Julia for simmering soups and stews.

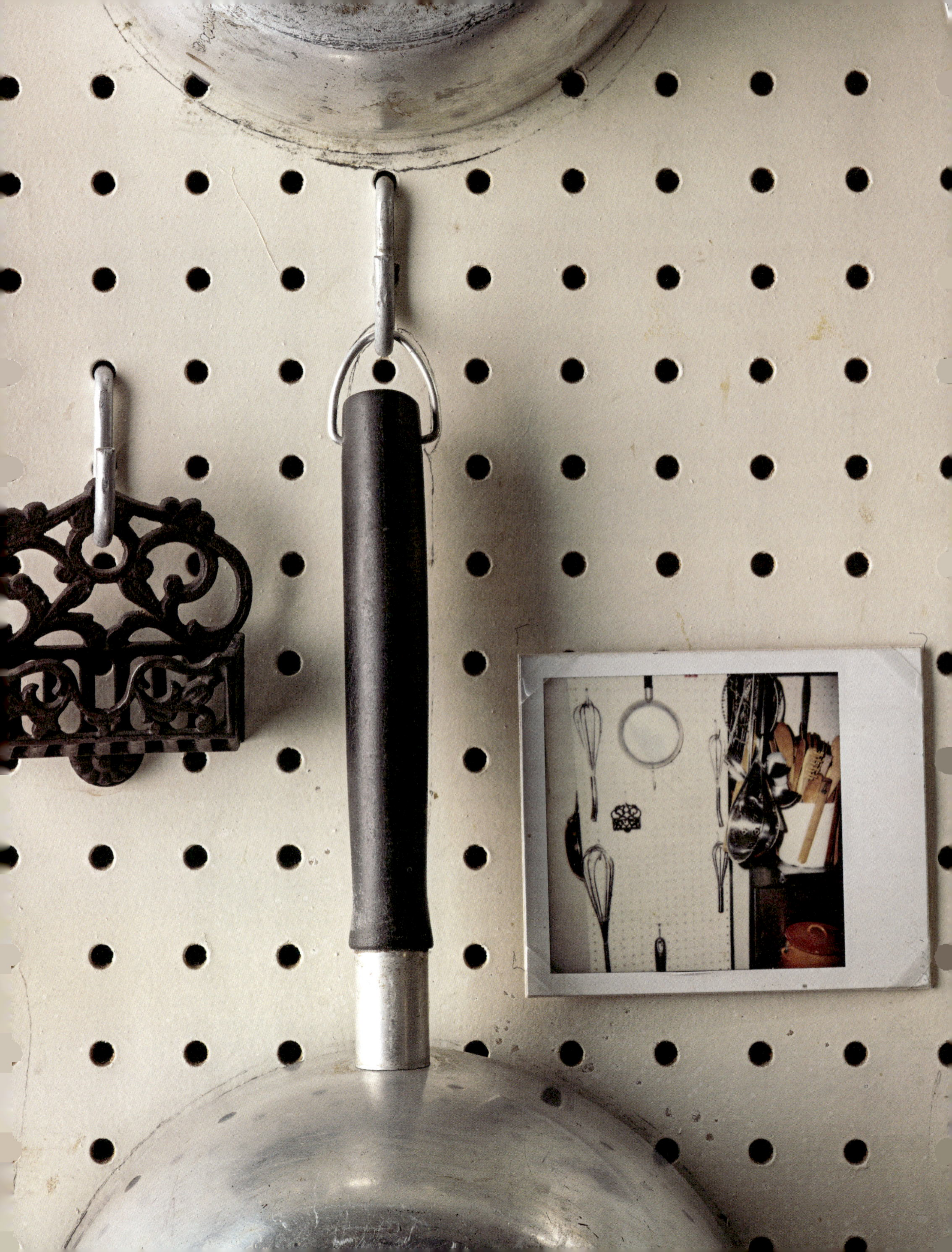

opposite: Detail from Julia's kitchen, 2023, showing a holder for matches and a photograph that helped kitchen assistants rehang cookware after use. *above:* The same general area of the kitchen ca. 1962

FOCUS: PAUL CHILD, LABEL MAKER

It is impossible to gaze into Julia Child's kitchen without eventually registering that there are a lot of labels and visual guideposts tucked among the smart and aesthetically pleasing arrangements of cookware. Hand-lettered labels on masking tape, colorful plastic labels on pegboard, and clear plastic-protected conversion tables for weights and measures can be seen among the tools and equipment. This is another example of Paul Child's influence on the design and organizational emphasis that characterizes the space. Paul's experience as a cartographer perhaps carried over into his enthusiasm for labeling utensil crocks and warning kitchen helpers about what *not* to put into the garbage disposal (also called the "pig" by Julia):

> NO GREASE... NO FAT
> NO ARTICHOKE L'S
> NO HUSKS
> BEWARE ONION SKINS

As their home kitchen was taking shape, Julia was reveling in the successful launch of the *Mastering the Art of French Cooking*. The *New York Times* food writer Craig Claiborne called the 726-page volume "a masterpiece" and "probably the most comprehensive, laudable, and monumental work" on French cuisine."[27] Julia's culinary career was taking off with an expanding schedule of book talks and cooking demonstrations, and her beautiful home kitchen was put to good use as a test kitchen, a social center, and a sanctuary. Despite the prevailing attitudes in the sixties about the wonders of convenience foods and culinary shortcuts that would free women from the drudgery of cooking, Julia was digging into a life centered in cooking, teaching, and writing, with her kitchen as another partner. She was on her way to redefining kitchens as more than mere domestic (read "women's") spaces and cooking as something transformational, fulfilling, and modern.

opposite: Dymo labels provide warnings and instructions on use of the garbage disposal.

DISPOSAL

1. REMOVE SINK STOPPER
2. RUN COLD WATER IN SINK
3. START MACHINE
4. PUSH FOOD IN GRADUALLY WITH BRUSH
5. DO NOT PACK OR JAM FOOD INTO HOLE
6. RUN 1/2 MIN. AFTER GRINDING STOPS

NO GREASE..NO FAT

NO ARTICHOKE.L'S

NO HUSKS

BEWARE ONION SKINS

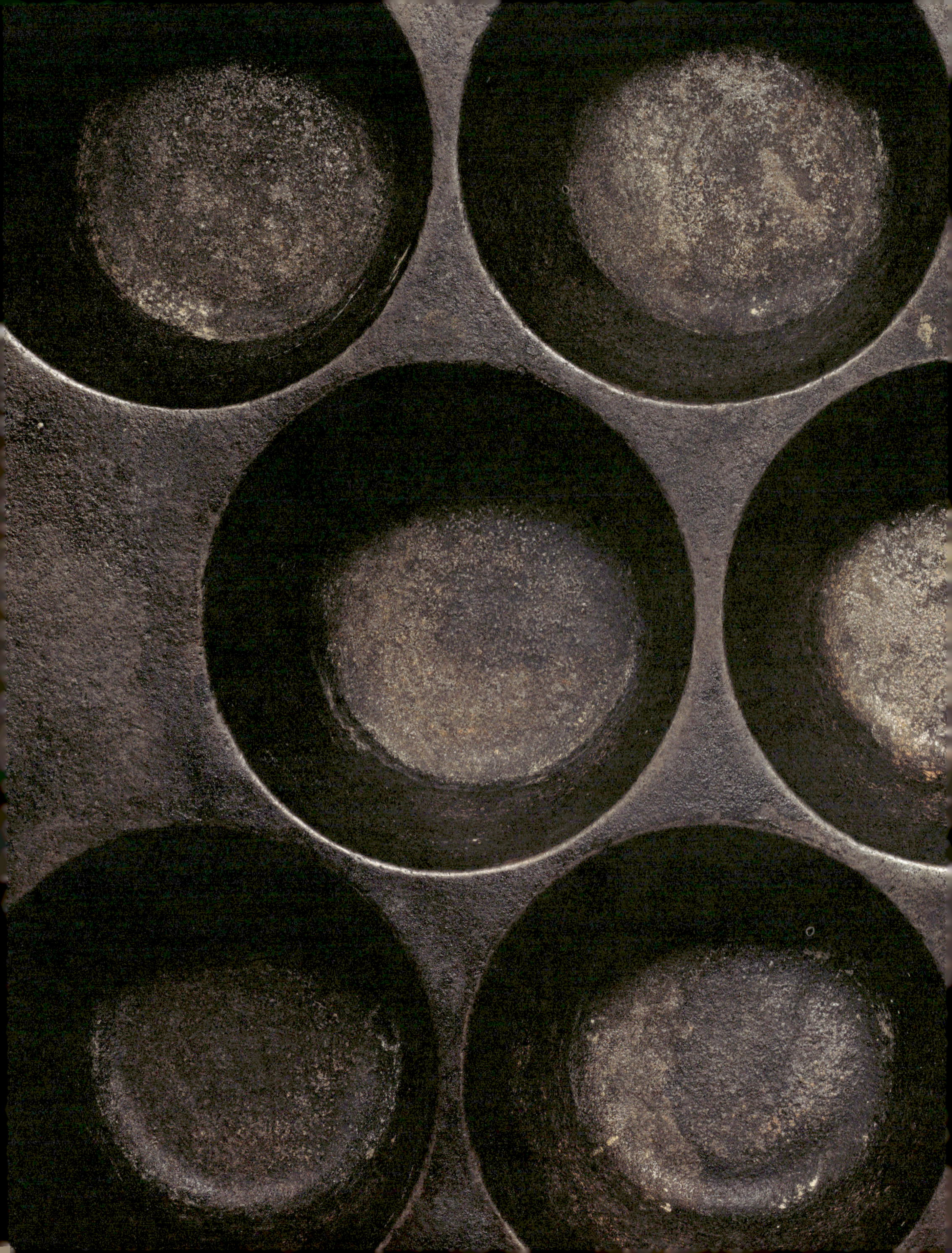

CHAPTER 2

"This is my test kitchen as well as everything else."

Less than three years after moving into 103 Irving Street, Julia and Paul Child were interviewed for the February 1964 issue of *House & Garden* magazine. By way of explaining the many roles of their smartly designed and outfitted kitchen, Julia noted, "The room is a laboratory, a sitting room, a dining room and a kitchen, and it has the forward-looking quality of a place where marvelous things at any moment may come to pass."[1]

Indeed, in the early sixties, when Julia's career was flourishing in multiple ways, the couple practically lived in the kitchen. Paul presented a picture of intellectual and domestic harmony when in February 1962 he mentioned to his brother Charles that while Julia was cooking, he would sometimes read aloud to her. On that particular day, he was reading *The Fox in the Attic*, a work of historical fiction by Richard Hughes that was to be the first in a series called "The Human Predicament." Julia had recently begun a special assignment to test recipes for "Washington Cook Book," an article by food writer and editor José Wilson that would appear in the July issue of *House & Garden*. The article focused on the role of Washington, DC, hostesses, for whom frequent entertaining at home was an important part of their husbands' work and, ultimately, the nation's business. At the time Washington was not particularly noted for its restaurants, and the home luncheons, buffets, and dinners overseen by hostess/wives (but most certainly cooked by paid staff), became Washington's way of making "the dining table a social extension of the office desk."[2] Julia and Paul would have been aware of this phenomenon, having moved to Washington after their marriage in 1946, where they lived in the tony neighborhood of Georgetown for short periods of time between Paul's work assignments in Europe.

previous spread: Muffin pan, one of two that hang on the wall of copper and cast-iron cookware in Julia's kitchen *opposite:* Some of the recipes tested by Julia for a special issue of *House & Garden* about living in Washington, DC, July 1962

Beat the eggs with ½ teaspoon salt and a big pinch of pepper until just blended. Smear a 9" enameled skillet with 3 tablespoons softened butter. Pour in eggs and stir over moderately low heat. When eggs begin to thicken, about 2 minutes, stir rapidly until they scramble into very soft curds. (The eggs must be very soft and creamy, slightly underdone. They will finish cooking under the broiler.) Immediately remove from heat and stir in 2 tablespoons softened butter. Season to taste.

Spread half the hot cream sauce in the baking dish, sprinkle with half the cheese, cover with the mushrooms and then the scrambled eggs. Coat eggs with remaining sauce, sprinkle with remaining cheese and dot with remaining tablespoon of butter, diced small. Put dish under broiler with surface 1" from heat for about 1 minute or until lightly browned. Serve immediately.

Mrs. A. S. Monroney's Winter Dinner for 8

MRS. A. S. MONRONEY, wife of Senator Monroney of Oklahoma, makes up her menus with male guests in mind—"Men," she says, "are the real eaters; women just pick." Mrs. Monroney's most successful entrée, summer or winter, is charcoal beef tenderloin. In summer, she serves it with a first course of jellied crab meat, corn soufflé and a lemon ice dessert; in winter, with oysters, soup and a rich dessert.

MENU
Blue Points
Homemade Thin Mushroom Soup
Charcoal Beef Tenderloin
*Creamed Celery and Almonds
Glazed Carrots, Peas and Artichoke Bottoms
Strawberry Bavarian Cream

Creamed Celery and Almonds

4 bunches celery hearts
2 cups clear chicken broth
Salt, white pepper
8½ tablespoons butter
1¼ cups slivered, blanched almonds
1 cup milk (approx.)
6 tablespoons flour
¼ to ½ cup heavy cream
⅓ cup dry white bread crumbs

Separate the celery into stalks. Remove leaves. Wash stalks well and cut into ⅜" dice. You should have 8 cups. Boil slowly in a covered saucepan with the broth, 1 cup water, 1½ teaspoons salt and 1½ tablespoons butter for about 10 minutes, or until celery is just cooked through but retains a suggestion of crunchiness. Drain cooking liquid into a quart measuring cup and reserve. Return celery to saucepan.

Melt 1 tablespoon butter in an 8" skillet and stir and toss the almonds for about 5 minutes over moderate heat until they are a pale golden color. Put into saucepan with celery.

Add enough milk to the celery cooking liquid to make 3 cups. Bring to a simmer. Melt 4 tablespoons butter in a heavy-bottomed, 2-quart enameled saucepan. Blend in the flour with a wooden spoon and stir slowly over low heat until butter and flour froth together for 2 minutes without coloring. Remove from heat. Pour in the simmering liquid and beat vigorously with a wire whip to blend thoroughly. Bring to the boil, stirring, for one minute. Thin out with tablespoons of cream; sauce should be thick enough to coat a spoon fairly heavily. Season to taste with salt and white pepper, then fold the sauce into the celery and almonds with a rubber spatula. Melt the remaining 2 tablespoons butter and mix with the bread crumbs.

Spread the vegetable mixture in a lightly buttered 3-quart baking dish, 1½" to 2" deep, and sprinkle with the buttered bread crumbs. If dish is to be served immediately, set under a moderately hot broiler to reheat and brown the top. If prepared ahead, set aside uncovered; reheat for about ½ hour in upper third of a preheated 375° oven until sauce is bubbling and crumbs light brown.

Mrs. Stewart Alsop's Luncheon for 6 or 8

MRS. STEWART ALSOP, whose husband is a well-known political journalist, takes cooking seriously; she and a group of friends even organized do-it-yourself private cooking sessions where they could experiment with recipes. Despite a busy family routine (she has five children, a large house), her dinner party menus always include at least one dish which she makes in the afternoon, while the cook gets other preparations under way. Soufflés, which need only the last-minute addition of egg whites, are her speciality, either as a dessert or as a luncheon entrée, baked in individual dishes.

MENU
*Eggs Clamart
Cold Roast Beef
Green Salad with French Dressing
Mocha Soufflé

Eggs Clamart

4½ cups shelled fresh peas or 3 10-ounce packages frozen peas
1 cup (pressed down) shredded Boston lettuce
4 tablespoons minced shallots or green onions
1 teaspoon salt
1 teaspoon sugar
13 tablespoons butter
1 cup heavy cream
3 tablespoons flour
Salt, pepper
6 to 8 very fresh eggs
3 tablespoons capers

Place the peas in a heavy-bottomed saucepan with the lettuce, shallots or onions, salt, sugar (for fresh peas only), 3 tablespoons of the butter, and cold water (3 cups for fresh peas, 1½ cups for frozen). Cover and cook at a slow boil (if water boils away, add 2 or 3 tablespoons more) until peas are tender. Purée in a food mill or electric blender. (Add some of the cream if you use a blender.) Blend 2 tablespoons butter and the flour to a smooth paste. Vigorously beat this paste and the cream into the peas. Stir constantly over moderately high heat for several minutes until purée has thickened enough to hold its shape in a spoon. Season carefully.

Poach the eggs. Heat the remaining 8 tablespoons butter in a saucepan until it has browned lightly. Stir in the capers and remove from heat.

Spread the hot pea purée on a lightly buttered platter, in individual dishes or tartlet shells, or on toast rounds. Make shallow wells in the purée and place a hot poached egg in each. Spoon the capers and butter over the eggs and serve.

Mrs. Hale Boggs' Dinner for 8

MRS. HALE BOGGS, wife of the House Majority Whip, finds that her husband's outdoor interests (hunting and gardening) keep her freezer well stocked with fresh fish, game, fruits and vegetables. With these, a New Orleans cook and a collection of old Louisiana recipes, Mrs. Boggs serves dinners of regional foods, ending with flaming café brûlot.

MENU
Clear Turtle Soup, Toast Slivers
*Trout Marguery à la Créole, Potato Puffs
Roast Wild Duck, Wild Rice, Giblet Gravy
Spinach Soufflé, Stuffed Tomatoes
Crab Apple Jelly
Green Salad Tossed with Anchovy Strips
Toasted Cheese Rolls
Schaum Torte
Mints, Pecans
Café Brûlot

Trout Marguery à la Créole

4 trout
½ cup thinly sliced onion
1 clove garlic
1 bay leaf
6 parsley sprigs
6 whole cloves
¼ teaspoon cayenne pepper
Salt, pepper
1 tablespoon butter, cut up
½ cup dry white wine
16 oysters, poached in their juices
½ pound fresh mushrooms, quartered and simmered in butter and lemon juice
1-ounce can truffles, diced
4 egg yolks
½ to ¾ cup melted butter
¼ teaspoon Tabasco
1 tablespoon minced parsley
24 cooked shrimps, shelled, warmed in butter

Have trout filleted and reserve heads, bones and skin. Simmer these trimmings with the onion, garlic, bay leaf, parsley, cloves, cayenne pepper, 1 teaspoon salt and 1 quart water in an enameled saucepan until liquid has reduced by half. Strain.

Sprinkle the 8 trout fillets with salt and pepper, lay them in one layer in a lightly buttered shallow fireproof baking dish, and dot with the cut-up butter. Pour on the fish stock, the wine and enough water barely to cover the fish. Bring almost to simmer on top of the stove, cover with buttered waxed paper, and set in lower third of preheated 350° oven. Bake for 8 to 10 minutes, or until a fork will pierce fish easily. Drain stock into a saucepan. Cover fish with waxed paper and set aside.

Pour the juices from the oysters, mushrooms and canned truffles into the fish-poaching stock and boil down rapidly until liquid has reduced to 1 cup. Cool slightly. Beat the egg yolks in a bowl until thick and sticky and gradually beat in the liquid. Return to saucepan and stir over low heat until lightly thickened; do not overheat or egg yolks will scramble. Remove from heat and beat in the melted butter by driblets; sauce will thicken to a cream. Beat in Tabasco sauce and parsley; season to taste.

Shortly before serving, preheat broiler to red hot. Garnish the fish fillets with the oysters, shrimp, mushrooms and truffles. Cover baking dish and heat for a few minutes over a pan of boiling water. Then spoon the sauce over the fish and garniture. Set dish so surface is 1" from hot broiler element for 30 to 40 seconds, until sauce begins to brown lightly.

The article featured nineteen women—the First Lady, and wives of senators, congressmen, and other government officials as well as journalists and business executives—and their recipes. In her home kitchen, Julia tested them all, including Mrs. Lyndon B. Johnson's Pedernales River Chili (outdoor party for sixteen); the French ambassador's wife Madame Alphand's recipe for Ouefs Interallies (luncheon for eight); the House majority whip's spouse Mrs. Hale Boggs's Trout Marguery á la Creole (dinner for eight); the wife of the former Cuban ambassador Mrs. Nicolas Arroyo's Gazpacho (summer dinner for eight); and the wife of the Washington correspondent for Ridder Newspapers Mrs. Walter Ridder's Pheasants Braised in Red Wine (Sunday luncheon for eight). Julia, known for her first cookbook and still becoming a television star, is credited at the very end of the article with the simple sentence, "The recipes in the Washington Cook Book were tested for *House & Garden* by Julia Child." That she was not referred to as "Mrs. Paul Child," in the style used for the women whose recipes are featured in the article, speaks to Julia's emerging status and identity as a professional woman.[3]

One can't help but wonder how Julia tackled testing such a range of recipes. In a March 6, 1962, letter to Charles, Paul shared his insights:

> JULIE'S BEEN HAMMERING AWAY AT THOSE WASHINGTON HOSTESSES' RECIPES. WE TWO GUINEA-PIGS NIBBLE AT THE END-RESULTS, COMPARE NOTES, DECIDE THE THING NEEDS MORE TEXTURE, OR THAT A TOUCH OF CURRY WOULD HELP, OR THAT IT SHOULD HAVE BEEN TAKEN OUT OF THE OVEN 20 MINUTES SOONER. THEN IT'S DONE AGAIN. SOMETIMES 3 OR 4 TIMES, W/ A VAST WASTE OF EGGS, BUTTER, PASTRY FLOUR, SUGAR & GOD KNOWS WHAT—BECAUSE WE FEED IT TO THE DISPOSALL [sic]. WASTE, IN THE SENSE THAT THERE ARE SO MANY STARVING PEOPLE IN THE WORLD, BUT NOT FROM THE STANDPOINT OF JULIE'S EARNING MONEY, OR FIRMING-UP HER RELATIONSHIP WITH JOSÉ WILSON OF HOUSE & GARDEN.[4]

Despite the significant amount of time, labor, and food waste, this job that kept them in the kitchen together that winter was understood by the couple as a stepping stone to more paid work in food.

Julia prepared for her first television appearance on WGBH's *I've Been Reading* by packing up tools from her kitchen to make an omelet: a bowl, whisk, butter, fork, pan, and apron.

PRACTICE AND PREP FOR TV

Julia and Paul's kitchen life took another major turn in early 1962, when Julia was invited to discuss *Mastering the Art of French Cooking* on what she later called "an egghead television show," on WGBH, Boston's educational television station. Hosted by Professor Albert Duhamel, *I've Been Reading* was formatted as a talk show, with Duhamel interviewing the featured author. Imagining that a televised chat about cooking would not be the most engaging way to introduce the public to the epic culinary accomplishment that was *Mastering*, Julia decided to bring equipment from her home kitchen—a copper bowl, balloon whisk, apron, knife, sauté pan, and hot plate, as well as eggs and mushrooms—to the TV studio. A fan of food and cooking, Duhamel had actually read the book and went along with Julia's idea to show viewers how to make proper omelets. For her part, Julia enjoyed doing the program so much she forgot to mention the title of the book, a mistake handily mitigated by an enlarged photo of the book's cover that was visible throughout the program.[5] Viewers responded to Julia's demo, sending the station some twenty-seven letters—a significant number within the context of educational TV at the time—urging the producers to bring Julia back for more cooking demonstrations. And they did, with a three-episode pilot for *The French Chef*.[6]

It is important to note that the early years of food television bore little resemblance to the food programming that is available 24/7 on television and streaming services in the 2020s. Yet shows involving food and basic cooking were among the first to be broadcast on local stations, along with game shows like *Cash and Carry* on WABD (a station operated by the Allen B. Du Mont Laboratories, Inc. in New York) and wrestling matches from various arenas in New York on WNBT (NBC Television in New York). In 1947–48, WNBT broadcast *In the Kelvinator Kitchen*, with Alma Kitchell, which featured basic (and not always well-informed) cooking instructions delivered by Kitchell in a kitchen outfitted with Kelvinator appliances.[7]

Most cooking shows of the late forties and early fifties that were produced for local television stations featured women home economists demonstrating recipes for quick and healthy family meals. Shows with names like *Hot Points in the Kitchen* (KGMB-TV in Honolulu), *Sugar and Spice* (WJAR-TV in Providence, Rhode Island), *Connie's Kitchen* (WOW-TV in Omaha, Nebraska), and *Home and Kitchen* (KOA-TV in Denver, Colorado) delivered cooking tips and nutritional advice to homemakers in regional markets across the country.[8] Professional chefs demonstrating recipes and cooking techniques were another story, and James Beard's *I Love to Eat* in August 1946, and Dione Lucas's *To the Queen's Taste* airing on CBS in 1947–49, represented early forays into that genre. Neither chef, however, was particularly comfortable or effective with the new medium and the shows were not continued. Meanwhile, in New Orleans on WDSU-TV, the city's first television station, Chef Lena Richard, a Black caterer, restaurateur, culinary teacher, cookbook author, and food entrepreneur, starred in her own cooking show beginning in 1949. That Richard forged such a culinary path in the Jim Crow South speaks to her extraordinary skills and tenacity. Her untimely death in 1950 cut short what might have been a much longer presence as the first Black female chef demonstrating her own recipes on her own eponymous television show.[9]

By the time Julia Child appeared in 1963 on WGBH in *The French Chef*, television technology had changed dramatically. Indeed, the tiny, 8 × 10–inch screens of the forties had been replaced by larger screens in furniture-like housings. The number of local stations across the country had also increased and the three national networks—ABC, CBS, and NBC—were gaining viewers with a combination of entertainment, news, and educational programming.[10] Local television stations still focused largely on instructive offerings, including "how to" shows (upholstery!), book talks, and educational lectures. It was within this context that Julia Child appeared on public television—just at the moment when more people could afford television sets and when excitement over the popular new medium for education, entertainment, and educational entertainment virtually guaranteed new viewers. What's more, her notion about what a cooking show should deliver was very different from the earlier emphasis on home economics and nutritional advice. She wanted to engage viewers in the excitement of learning new culinary techniques and recipes, and the fun of cooking with and for family and friends. With her French culinary training and her love of the cuisines of France, she wanted to demonstrate that if she, a self-proclaimed home cook, could master the techniques, tools, and recipes, so could viewers. She seemed to be speaking directly to viewers in a friendly way, encouraging them to try her recipes using tools and ingredients available to them. She was both relatable and an expert—a combination that drew people in. That, plus her big personality and engaging sense of humor, combined to make her an almost instant success on television.

Because there was no easy-to-use template for this particular type of step-by-step cooking show that managed to demonstrate complex recipes in less than thirty minutes, the Childs created one. In their home kitchen, Julia and Paul worked out recipe details as well as the timing and sequencing of the steps involved in preparing them for Julia's first television series, *The French Chef*, which followed her mesmerizing appearance on the "I've Been Reading" and pilot programs on WGBH in 1962. Julia's marvelous knack for making viewers believe that they, too, could accomplish culinary wonders in the kitchen was key to her television success, but credit is also due to the meticulous prep work and practice sessions that she and Paul carried out in advance in their home kitchen.

Each episode of *The French Chef* series was filmed in virtually one take—the substantial editing that underlies food television in the twenty-first century was not an option for the cash-strapped WGBH of 1963. To achieve the level of professionalism Julia and Paul envisioned, it was incumbent upon them to develop a system for practicing the distinct steps in each recipe, and to determine which steps would have to be shown through "TV magic" (extra dishes prepared in advance to illustrate different steps in the process and to end the program with a completed dish). And, of utmost importance, they had to make sure that Julia would finish the program within the requisite time frame.

Russell Morash, Julia's producer at WGBH, recalled:

> She was very well prepared, which was one of her secret weapons, she and Paul would really labor over these things ... We had no idea how long things took. A crippling requirement: Once you start making a program in those days, you were to go until somebody said, "Time's up," and the program is now technically over. There was no possibility of any editing.[11]

Marian Morash, Russell's wife and an accomplished chef and television personality who eventually worked closely with Julia on various cooking programs and events, explained:

> The thing here is that she really had no time to come on the set and decide what she was going to do, so she really had to do it all at home, in her kitchen, and plot it out. Paul was meticulous about getting everything organized and right, and she went along with anything he said. She really did. And so, they basically had to work at home because they didn't have time once they got to the studio.[12]

Russell also recalled: "And she would organize it so everything was on a tray, mise-en-place was fully prepared with every tool and weapon and every bit of ingredient all pre-measured out so that when they arrived at the rehearsal, she was way ahead..."[13]

Eventually they all became more familiar with the routine for a twenty-eight-minute program, and the preparations became less arduous. Still, during those early years, Julia and Paul's disciplined and systematic preparations took over their social lives.

Paul's letters to his brother Charles, who he sometimes abbreviated as Cha, in early 1963 provide a glimpse into the extent of their prep work in their home kitchen and its impact:

This General Electric Interval Timer hangs on pegboard above the butcher block table in Julia's kitchen. It was manufactured around 1953 for use in photo darkrooms, and its presence in the kitchen suggests its adaptation for timing Julia's practice sessions for television.

JANUARY 19, 1963

WE HAVE AN ELECTRIC STOVE SET UP IN THE MIDDLE OF OUR KITCHEN NOW AND ALL OUR OWN HOUSEHOLD COOKERY (PLUS PRACTICE-SESSIONS FOR THE PROGRAM) IS BEING DONE ON THE DAMN THING SO MISTRESS J. CAN GET USED TO THE DIFFERENT TIMING REQUIRED.[14]

JAN 26, 1963

DEAR CHA:

JULIE HAS NOW WORKED-OUT A SCHEDULED PROGRAM FOR HERSELF BASED ON THE RIGID NECESSITIES OF TELEVISION. IT HAS TO INCLUDE PRACTICE-SESSIONS AT HOME, WITH EITHER RUTH LOCKWOOD (PRODUCTION ASSISTANT FOR THE FRENCH CHEF) OR ME, HOLDING THE STOP-WATCH. THE 28 MINUTES OF EACH TELECAST ARE PRELIMINARILY WORKED OUT BY JULIE & RUTH INTO SECTIONS:

THERE ARE 4 SHOWS BEING TAPED EVERY WEEK: IT'S A BLITZ-TYPE OPERATION, AND WE'VE GOT THE SCHEDULED WEEKLY PROGRAMS I MENTIONED IN THE FIRST LINES OF THIS LETTER WORKED OUT TO PRESERVE OUR SANITY & HEALTH. IT IS FORTUNATE THAT WE HAVE HAD TO LEAD SCHEDULED & DISCIPLINED LIVES FOR A LONG TIME IN MY FOREIGN SERVICE LIFE, SO THIS IS NEW ONLY IN RESPECT TO JULIE'S PROFESSION DOMINATING IT RATHER THAN MINE.

WE HAVE HAD TO ELIMINATE ENTERTAINING AT HOME FROM OUR LIFE-PATTERN UNTIL THIS INTENSIVE SCHEDULE IS COMPLETED, BECAUSE THERE'S HARDLY TIME TO DO THE USUAL HOUSEHOLD SHOPPING, LAUNDRY, LETTER-WRITING, BUDGETING, CLEANING, ETC.

SATURDAY 9 FEB 63

JULIE DOES 60 STROKES ON THE ROWING MACHINE EVERY MORNING, & FEELS WONDROUSLY BRACED-UP THEREBY. SHE DISCOVERS, FOR EXAMPLE, THAT IN THE MATTER OF BEATING EGG WHITES W A LARGE WHISK IN A COPPER BOWL, SHE NOW DOESN'T GET OUT OF BREATH & HAVE ACHING ARMS. THIS MAKES A HELL OF A DIFFERENCE IF YOU'RE DEMONSTRATING EGG-BEATING ON TELEVISION, AND HAVING NOT ONLY TO LECTURE WHILE DOING SO, BUT NOT NOW HAVING TO STOP & REST. ("WHY, DAMN IT," SHE SAYS, "I THINK I COULD NOW BEAT 2,000 EGG-WHITES!") THESE EVENINGS, WHEN OTHER FOLK ARE AT THE MOVIES, OR THE SYMPHONY, OR LECTURES, FIND JULIE & ME IN OUR KITCHEN—ME W STOP-WATCH IN HAND, AND JULIE AT THE STOVE—TIMING THE VARIOUS SECTIONS OF THE NEXT TWO SHOWS. OVER AND OVER AND OVER, WITH CRITICAL COMMENTS, AND WITH SUGGESTIONS FOR NEW LANGUAGE, OR NEW DEMONSTRATION METHODS. THIS ALL COUNTS STRONGLY IN THE FINAL FILMING. THE ENGINEERS & CAMERAMEN SAY THEY HAVE NEVER SEEN A SHOW SO THOROUGHLY PREPARED BEFORE.

18 MAY 63

... WE HAD BEEN UP TIL NEARLY TWO THE NIGHT BEFORE—I WAS MAKING A 30"-SQUARE CHART OF A STEER-CARCASS, COMPLETE W BONE-STRUCTURE AND 8 OR 9 OF THE CLASSIC CUTS, AND JULIA PRE-COOKING & GETTING PACKED-UP—AND WERE OUT OF BED AGAIN AT 6 AM. THEN TWO SHOWS TAPED: THE ONE ON MEAT, AND A SECOND COMPLICATED ONE CONCERNED W 4 DIFFERENT WAYS TO PREPARE POTATO-DISHES. AND THE VERY NEXT DAY WE WERE UP AT 6 AGAIN, AFTER A FAIRLY LATE NIGHT OF PREPARATION, IN ORDER TO BE AT NEWBURYPORT BY 10, WHERE JULIE & RUTH PUT ON A DEMONSTRATION BEFORE A MOB OF WOMEN IN A CHURCH PARISH-HOUSE: A SHOW BASED ON A FISH-SOUFFLE.[15]

ANOTHER COOKBOOK IN THE WORKS

Testing recipes for *House & Garden* and prepping for television were but two of the major culinary tasks undertaken by the Childs in the first decade of their lives in their Irving Street kitchen. With the success of *Mastering the Art of French Cooking*, which sold more than 600,000 copies by 1969, Julia's fans and, importantly, Judith Jones, her editor at Knopf, were anxious for Volume Two to appear.[16] Julia and Simca (Louisette was no longer a collaborator for Volume Two) envisioned the second volume as a continuation, one that focused on extending seven areas: soups, baking, meats, chickens, charcuterie, vegetables, and desserts. At the same time, with work coming in and their love for France undiminished, the Childs looked for a way to spend more time there on a regular basis. Simca and her husband Jean Fischbacher encouraged them to build a small house on the corner of their property in Provence. The house, called La Pitchoune, or "The Little Thing," was completed in 1965 and quickly became a place of retreat from the routines and demands of Julia's burgeoning career. La Pitchoune was also a place of complete immersion in the aspects of food, cooking, and friendship that had first inspired Julia. Over nearly thirty years, the Childs would spend several weeks and months each year at La Pitchoune.[17] By 1966, Julia and Simca had begun working on Volume Two while they were together in Provence, and Julia recalled telling Simca, "Every recipe in this book must be foolproof," a principle that guided the painstaking path toward eventual publication in 1970.[18]

Back in Cambridge, Julia and Paul began testing recipes for Volume Two, deliberately and systematically using ingredients and equipment generally available to Americans. In some cases, Julia insisted on testing a dish ten or fifteen times "to make sure they withstood the operational proof."[19] The recipe that proved most elusive to Volume Two and that required exponentially more trials than anything else was their quest to create an infallible recipe for French bread. Julia's correspondence with her friend James Beard sheds light on the experience. Beard's cookbooks, articles, and cooking school in New York had, by the sixties, propelled him to widespread recognition and acclaim in the American culinary world. The two had met in New York in 1961, shortly after the publication of *Mastering*, Volume One, and he offered to introduce Julia around to his friends to help promote the book, an offer that led to people such as Helen McCully,

Julia and Simca in the kitchen at La Pitchoune during a photo shoot for *McCall's* magazine on June 29, 1970

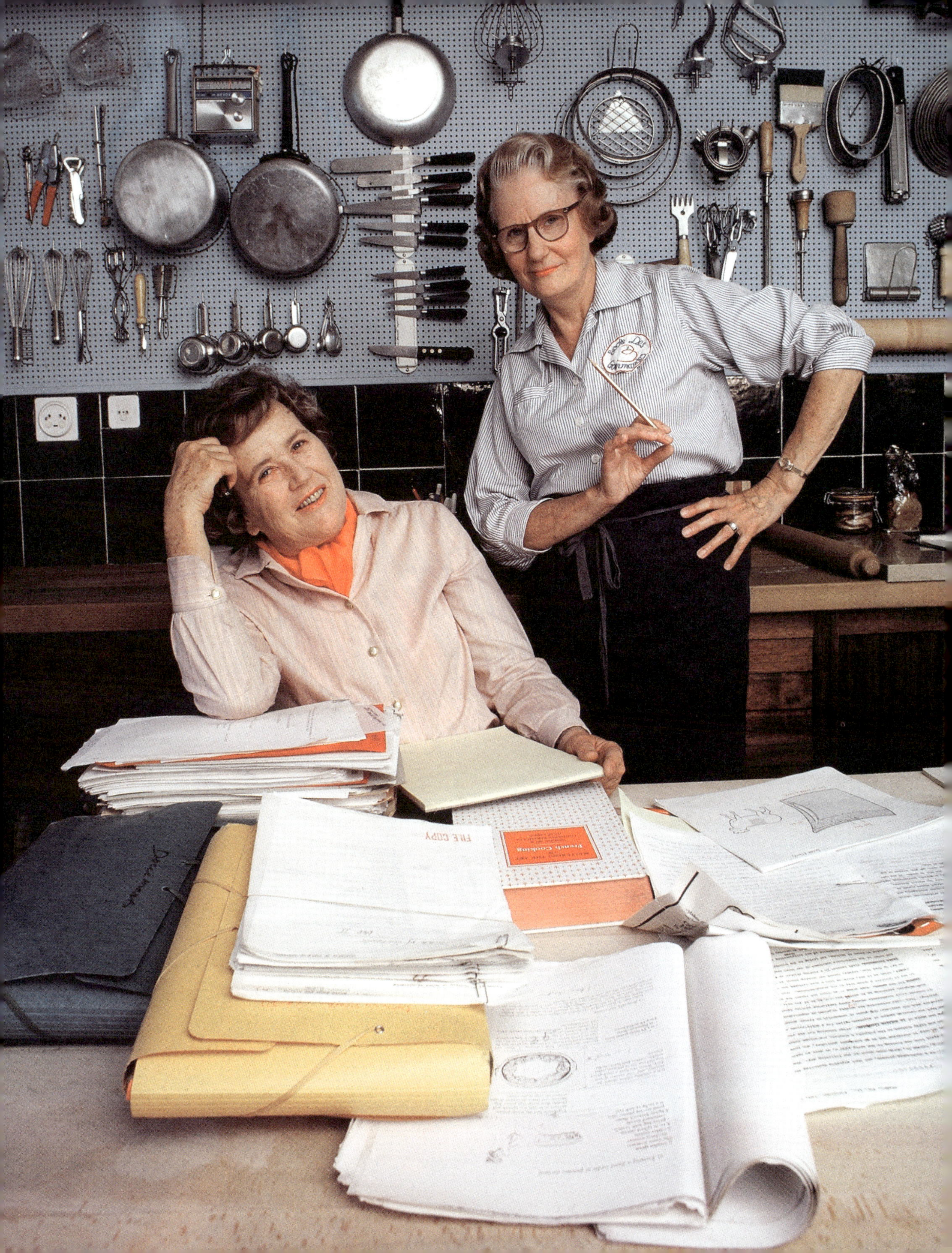
FILE COPY

editor of the magazine *House Beautiful,* and to Jacques Pépin, who was cooking at the famous Le Pavillon restaurant in New York at the time.

In a letter to James Beard on June 25, 1967, from Cambridge, Julia wrote:

"We are running The Irving Street Bakery here, with endless experiments on trying to make a really bang-up loaf of French bread which will approach that of San Peyre [the bread might reach the heights of a mountain near Cannes on the Cote d'Azur]. It is fun, and we give it all away. Getting better, but no cigar yet—so many variables, theories, and things to try. Perhaps, when next you come, we shall have succeeded, and you will give us your opinion."[20]

And a week later, on July 2, 1967, she wrote in haste about other recipes she was testing:

"I'm whacking away on recipes [for Volume Two], as usual, both in kitchen and at typewriter... This is not much of a letter, but a loving one. I have to dash down to the kitchen and do a chicken, some shrimp bisque, and a machine-made brioche. Am feeling somewhat like a steam engine lately!"[21]

"I REALIZED EVERYTHING I DID HAD BEEN WRONG."

When Julia's editor, Judith Jones, suggested that she and Simca include a recipe for real, crusty French bread in Volume Two, Julia noted that there were no French recipes for homemade bread, only recipes used by professional bakers. Undaunted, Julia set out to adapt those recipes "for the home baker, using standard ingredients and household equipment." It sounded so simple, but for Julia and Paul the road to the recipe for Pain Français (widely known as a "baguette") was two years long and dusted with 284 pounds of flour. Julia carefully measured ingredients and followed instructions for making the dough, slipping loaf after loaf into the big Garland range, only to have their hopes dashed when the crusts never met the standard achieved by every professional baker in Paris. Meanwhile, Julia's Cambridge neighbors benefited from the bread trials, as fresh but imperfect loaves were shared over the back fence among friends.

Frustrated, Julia contacted her mentor at Le Cordon Bleu in Paris, Professor Raymond Calvel. Spending a day with him on her next trip abroad, she later revealed, "As soon as we started working, I realized everything I did had been wrong... The most important thing about French bread—it is rolled and formed in such a way that it has a gluten cloak that holds it in shape. [You] bake it naked on a hot surface [like the quarry tiles]. [You] can't use a pan [like a baking sheet] because it will burn. And it is very important to have steam in the oven because that forms the crust."[22]

She went on to explain that the gluten cloak has to be slashed during baking and for that important step she uses a straight razor because it works and is easy.

Introducing steam into the oven at just the right time turned out to be the key technique Julia needed to achieve the desired baguette-like crust. Back in Cambridge, Paul experimented with quarry tiles from the local hardware store—an example of his "usual Yankee ingenuity," according to Julia—lining the oven rack with them for bread baking. The tiles held the heat like a baking stone does today. Julia and Paul experimented with introducing water at just the right moments in the baking process by spritzing water inside the oven.[23] Bakers can achieve the effect by putting a pan of water inside the hot oven on the rack below the baking stone. Some put a rolled kitchen towel into the water pan, which helps release the steam in a controlled and consistent manner.

A stack of quarry tiles Julia used for perfect French bread still sits on the shelf above the cooktop. This story speaks to Julia's persistence and creative problem-solving, two aspects that played out time and again while recipe testing for her cookbooks and preparing for cooking on television in the kitchen.

The quarry tiles, without which there would have been no perfect homemade French bread in Julia Child's home kitchen

FOCUS: GARLAND

"This wonderful oven that I have."

The big Garland range was the epicenter of recipe testing throughout the Childs' years in Cambridge. They had bought the stove in 1956 in Washington, DC, as they were renovating their house at 2706 Olive Street in Georgetown. Although they had purchased that house in 1948, they didn't actually live there then but rented it out as they moved to Paris for Paul's first posting for the U.S. Department of State. In 1956, they returned from Paul's assignment in Germany and set about refurbishing the Olive Street house. By this time, of course, Julia had completed her training at Le Cordon Bleu and was deep into testing recipes and cowriting the manuscript that would become *Mastering the Art of French Cooking*, Volume One. Their kitchen updates included adding a dishwasher and garbage disposal, and Julia was thinking about a new stove. During a visit to an old friend in Washington, Julia laid eyes on his professional six-burner Garland range, and she knew she had to have it or one like it. The friend, Sherman Kent, had also served in the OSS during World War II and had continued his intelligence career in the CIA. Kent, whom they called "Old Buffalo," offered to sell them his stove for $412.[24]

Between their extensive travels and Paul's next posting in Norway (in 1959), they must have enjoyed learning the fine points of what Julia called the "big Garland." When they were returning to the United States after Paul's retirement in 1961, they had the stove shipped to their new home in Cambridge. There it remained as Julia's favorite stove and cooktop. In an interview with the Smithsonian in 2001, she explained, "This wonderful oven that I have ... It's very solid. That's why the professional stoves are so good. This will last for generations more ... And I just love it. I would take it to my grave if it would fit."[25]

The kitchen was also equipped with an electric oven set in a wall housing within a step or two of the Garland. Julia used it for various dishes, especially when cooking for a crowd. It did not include a cooktop, so its use was limited. Julia practiced the timing for her early television shows on an electric stove brought into the kitchen temporarily for that purpose.

The Garland range in Julia's kitchen at the National Museum of American History, 2023

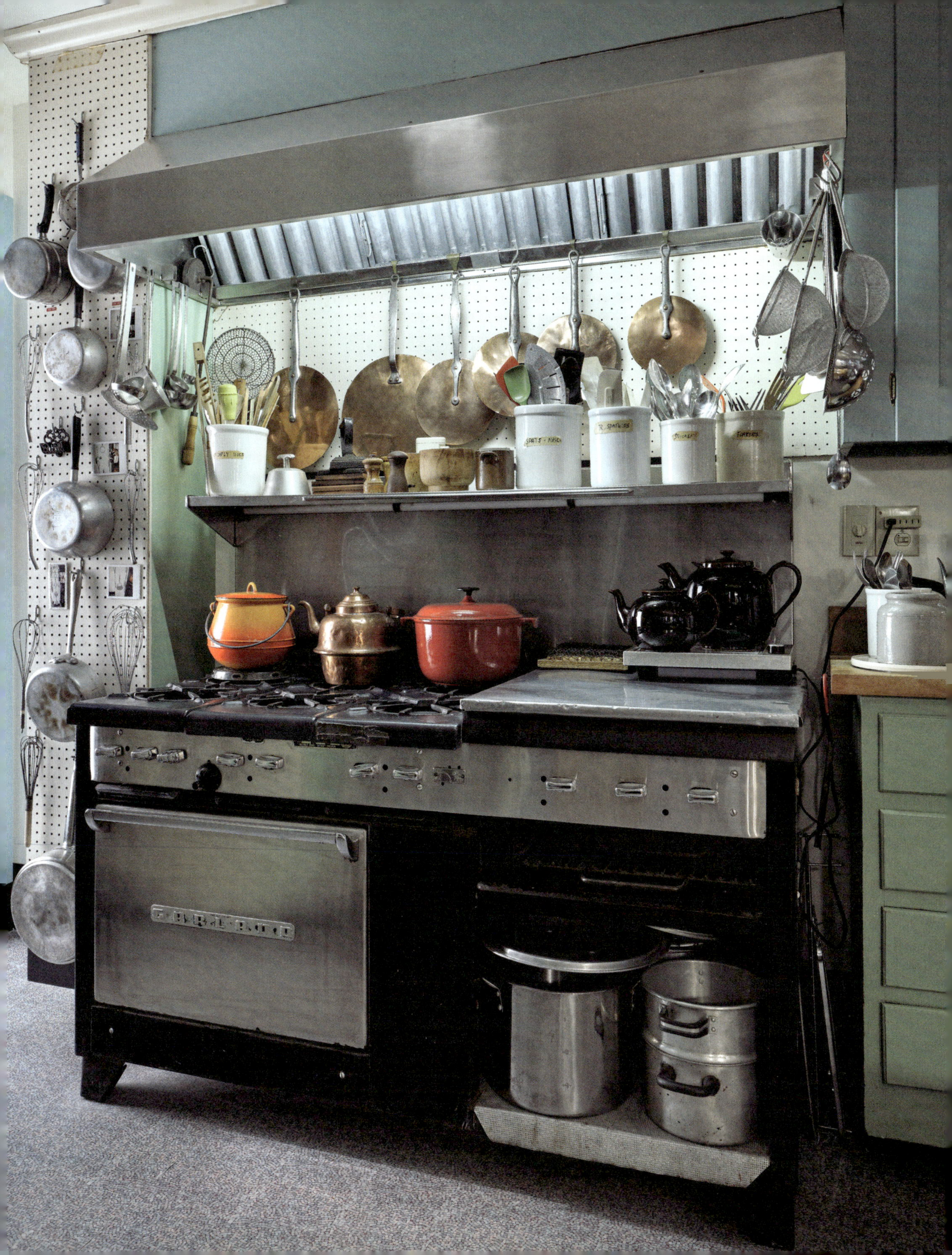
SPATS - MISC

above: "We work together," Paul says, pointing out that he is responsible for all of the how-to photographs, taken while perched above Julia's shoulders. "We wanted to show how things should look while you're doing them—not how it looks from across the table."[26] *opposite:* Julia and editor Judith Jones working at the kitchen table on *Mastering*, Volume Two

KITCHEN PHOTO STUDIO

Recipe testing was only one aspect of Julia and Paul's collaboration on Volume Two of *Mastering the Art of French Cooking*. The volume is replete with line drawings that show exactly how a recipe should look at various stages and how tools should fit in the cook's hand while a particular technique is employed. Paul brought his sense of exactitude and his skills as a photographer to the task of matching Julia's precise instructions with clear views of key steps in a recipe. In the Cambridge kitchen, he would hover over her shoulder to take photographs of her hands, tools, and ingredients that would leave no doubt about the best way to accomplish a task. His photographs were then shared with the artist Sidonie Coryn, who rendered them in line drawings. For many home cooks, the drawings appear just as a question is forming, such as, "What is that dough supposed to look like?"

Paul suffered a heart attack and underwent heart bypass surgery in 1974. The procedure was still relatively new, and he never fully recovered, with additional health ailments altering the type of assistance he was able to provide to Julia. As professional demands increased for her, Paul continued to accompany her to events and filming, but the days of their intense creative collaborations were on the wane.[27]

Julia's editor, Judith Jones, who had recognized the value of *Mastering the Art of French Cooking* and guided it through its publication in 1961, recalled the intense work sessions that took place around the table in Julia's kitchen for *Mastering,* Volume Two. Judith's hesitation about the instructions for puff pastry led Julia, ever the teacher, to suggest she try following the recipe for puff pastry, right then and there, to fully understand how to roll and fold the butter and dough. The long workdays often resulted in very late lunches that were assembled from the pantry—tuna fish (in oil) sandwiches being a favorite. By 10:00 or 11:00 P.M., Julia would declare it was time for dinner and the three—Julia, Paul, and Judith—would clear the table of work papers. Judith recalled, "Paul would set the table and make the cocktails, I'd be asked to make a nice little potato dish or a salad, Julia would whip up a delicious main course, and in no time we would be sitting at the kitchen table enjoying a soigné (to use one of her favorite words) dinner with a good bottle of wine from Paul's cellar."[28] Many years later, and after Paul's decline and death in 1994,[29] the food writer David Nussbaum similarly worked with Julia at the kitchen table on *Julia and Jacques Cooking at Home*, the cookbook based on the 1998 television series. He noted how hard Julia still worked at age eighty-six, and how her deep engagement with the process of testing and writing recipes reflected her ongoing commitment to professional standards and her understanding of what readers using the book would need in terms of instructions.[30]

"AREN'T WE HAVING SO MUCH FUN?"

Over many years, Julia worked with a cadre of women chefs and cooks who helped her prepare for dinner parties and live cooking demonstrations, and to test recipes for television shows and various publications. The teams included volunteers and paid assistants who spent considerable time in the Irving Street kitchen with Julia and each other. These assistants came to the job with various levels of food-related expertise, but they all learned something on the job as well. They shared the desire to be part of Julia's culinary world and became experts in working together in the close quarters of the kitchen. Ruth Lockwood, Marian Morash, Pat Pratt, Rosemary Manell, Sara Moulton, Susy Davidson, Liz Bishop, and Nancy Verde Barr were among the members of Julia's culinary team from the sixties through the nineties. Many of them went on to culinary careers of their own, as cookbook authors, educators, leaders of culinary organizations, and television cooks on PBS and Food Network.[31]

In 1979, Sara Moulton, a graduate of the Culinary Institute of America, had been working in Cambridge, first at a restaurant and then in catering.[32] She learned from one of her colleagues that there were volunteers who worked with Julia on her public appearances and television shows behind the scenes, and Sara wondered if Julia would perhaps need another volunteer. Berit Pratt, the daughter of one of Julia's closest friends, Pat Pratt, offered to introduce Sara to Julia, and when the two finally spoke, Julia's first question was, "Oh, dearie, do you food style?" Sara answered in the affirmative, although her CIA training had not included an actual course in the highly specialized art of styling food for media and event purposes. Still, she was hired to join the team to prep for the television show, *Julia Child & More Company*, which taped thirteen episodes at a television studio.[33]

Julia on the set with *Julia Child and More Company* cooks, including Sara Moulton (resting chin on hand), Marian Morash, and Temi Hyde (far right)

The idea of "company" here refers to guests coming to dinner, and the shows—*Julia Child & Company* (in 1978) and *Julia Child & More Company* (in 1979)—were organized as menus for dinner parties. For example, "Country Dinner" includes a menu for six people and features Mediterranean Hors d'Oeuvre Platter—Sliced Green and Red Peppers in Oil and Garlic, Anchovies, HB [hard boiled] Eggs, Olives, Syrian Strong Cheese; French Bread, or a Braided Loaf; Leek and Rabbit Pie with Buttermilk-Herb Biscuit Topping, and Snow Peas Tossed in Butter; and Petits Vacherins—Individual Meringue Cases Filled with Ice Cream and Topped with Sauced Fruits. Suggested wines were a strong dry white with the hors d'oeuvre, such as a Mâcon, white Châteauneuf, or pinot blanc; a rather mellow red with the rabbit—

Julia taking a photograph of Susy Davidson (on the butcher block) in 1984; Rosemary Manell is at the table.

Beaujolais, red Châteauneuf, Bordeaux, or cabernet; Champagne, a sparkling wine, or a Sauternes with the dessert.[34] The format provides recipes and special technical details such as how to broil red peppers to loosen and remove the skins and how to untwist the strands of string cheese and store them before adding them to the hors d'oeuvre platter.

Such a production required many assistants, and at first the experience was a bit chaotic, as no one had an official title and there was no clear hierarchy for getting the work done. About halfway through the taping, Julia recognized that people needed distinctive roles for operational clarity and created an organizational structure for the team, bestowing titles from the restaurant world that were instantly understood: Marian Morash was the executive chef and Sara Moulton became the associate chef. Julia's longtime friend Rosemary Manell became the food designer. Pat Pratt was charged with procuring and arranging flowers, and Elizabeth Bishop was Julia's executive associate, sommelier, and handler of problems.[35] While the prep work for the show was done mainly at the studio where the program was taped, Julia brought the team together in the Cambridge kitchen for meetings and to prepare food for large dinner parties, such as fundraisers, that Julia held in the formal dining room.[36]

Sara recalled her first visit to the Cambridge kitchen: "I remember trembling in my shoes and going up to that side door . . . and seeing the Garland stove right away, the fancy gas stove, professional. And walking into the kitchen, I didn't notice what became obvious to me later on [was] that everything was very high up. I was five feet tall and, according to [her niece] Phila Cousins, Julia was not six foot two [which has been widely published] but six foot three. And Julia with her husband, Paul, had designed the whole kitchen to be her size so, besides the famous pots and pans on the wall, most of which I couldn't reach, the counters were much higher and the knives were also positioned on the wall and everything was way up there. For me, it's a good thing we didn't record the show there, but we did lots of dinner parties."[37]

"The good thing for me is we didn't work there [in her kitchen on the television show *Julia Child & More Company*] because I would have needed a stool to stand on the whole time. As I tell new cooks, when you're using a chef's knife or when you're whisking, you should never have your elbow up in the air, and if the counter is too high for you, you just can't help it but do that. And if you do that you are wasting energy. Your arm is exhausted."[38]

Susy Davidson, another of Julia's assistants, who worked with her on ABC's *Good Morning America* in the eighties and went on to become the executive director of The Julia Child Foundation for Gastronomy and the Culinary Arts, was similarly challenged by the kitchen built to suit someone a full foot taller than she. While working on recipes for *Parade* magazine in 1984, she demonstrated the height issue by standing on the butcher block table to reach something on a top shelf while Julia snapped a photo.

At the very heart of these intense working sessions with women like Sara Moulton, Susy Davidson, Marian Morash, and Rosemary Manell in the Irving Street kitchen was Julia and her exceptional and infectious good cheer. They gathered to prepare meals for fundraisers and dinner parties, and while the details of the menus and the names of guests have dimmed for members of Julia's team, the one thing they do recall is what it felt like to do that work in that kitchen with Julia in their midst. Sara Moulton recalled:

> I don't remember how many [dinner parties] we did, but it was really fun. She would just get together a bunch of friends, and we would all cook together and then maybe some more illustrious person would arrive. Carl Sontheimer [inventor of the original Cuisinart food processor, based on the French Robot-Coupe], or Simone Beck [Julia's friend and coauthor of both *Mastering* volumes]. But we'd all get together and we would divide up whatever it was. It really never was that fancy, and I kick myself for not taking more notes. I didn't take any notes. What were the menus? It was French. Other than that, what do I remember?... We would be getting ready, doing things, setting the table, and in the middle of it all Julia would be looking at us all and say, "Aren't we having so much fun?" It was just contagious.[39]

FOCUS: PRIMORDIAL SOUP

Julia taped a short piece in her home kitchen for "Life in the Universe," an exhibition that would be among the inaugural displays at the Smithsonian's National Air and Space Museum (NASM), when it opened in 1976. She began the segment by announcing that she had turned her kitchen into a biochemical laboratory "to show what some scientists think could have been Nature's recipe for life on this Earth and perhaps life in the rest of the universe." Julia explained that she was re-creating scientist Stanley Miller's 1952 experiment that would transform simple ingredients into four amino acids essential to life. She set up a container of water (representing the ocean) that was connected by glass tubes to a flask of ammonia, hydrogen, and methane (the atmosphere). By heating the water, vapors rose into the flask and when she added an electrical spark (energy/lightning) the chemical transformation began.[40]

Julia's role in this program demonstrates her immense popularity at the time as well as her ability to explain even a complex scientific experiment in a comprehensible way. Her participation was surely supported (and perhaps initiated) by her friend, the secretary of the Smithsonian, S. Dillon Ripley, who served in the top job from 1964 to 1984. Ripley oversaw a period of tremendous growth for the institution, and he was a strong advocate for creative programming and interaction with the public. Like Julia and Paul, Ripley and his wife, Mary Livingston, had served in Southeast Asia for the OSS during World War II.[41]

Julia explaining how to make primordial soup in her home kitchen, 1973

"THERE WAS NOTHING TO GUESS ABOUT."

The labeling system that Julia and Paul adopted in the kitchen was reinforced with Polaroid photos that hung next to tools on the pegboard-covered walls near the Garland range. This clear and tidy arrangement was a lifesaver for all the culinary teams that ever worked in the Cambridge kitchen. And one can see why when looking at the photographs of people in the midst of food preparation on behalf of Julia's professional culinary life. The room is abuzz with people at the stove, washing dishes, cutting vegetables, reaching for tools. Sara Moulton appreciated the organization, saying, "Absolutely everything was labeled. There was nothing to guess about. How to make things function, where to find things ... that was brilliant. Everything had a place. It was pretty astonishing. There was nothing wasteful about it, there [were] no extras or frills, it was all necessary and that was very impressive."[42]

Years later, the professional baker and cookbook author Dorie Greenspan was working on the *Baking with Julia* series, which was filmed inside Julia's home kitchen in 1996, and recalled, "When I was there—everything was labeled, and it struck me as such a generous and welcoming thing to do. The labels said to me, 'There are always people in this kitchen. I want them to be comfortable, to move around,' so the coffee machine—I knew I could make coffee and not have to ask anyone."[43] The stories people tell about working in the kitchen with Julia settle around a few themes, with hard work, comfort, camaraderie, and fun being the consistent strands.

Section of pegboard near the Garland range with whisks, saucepans, and photographs reminding cooks of what went where

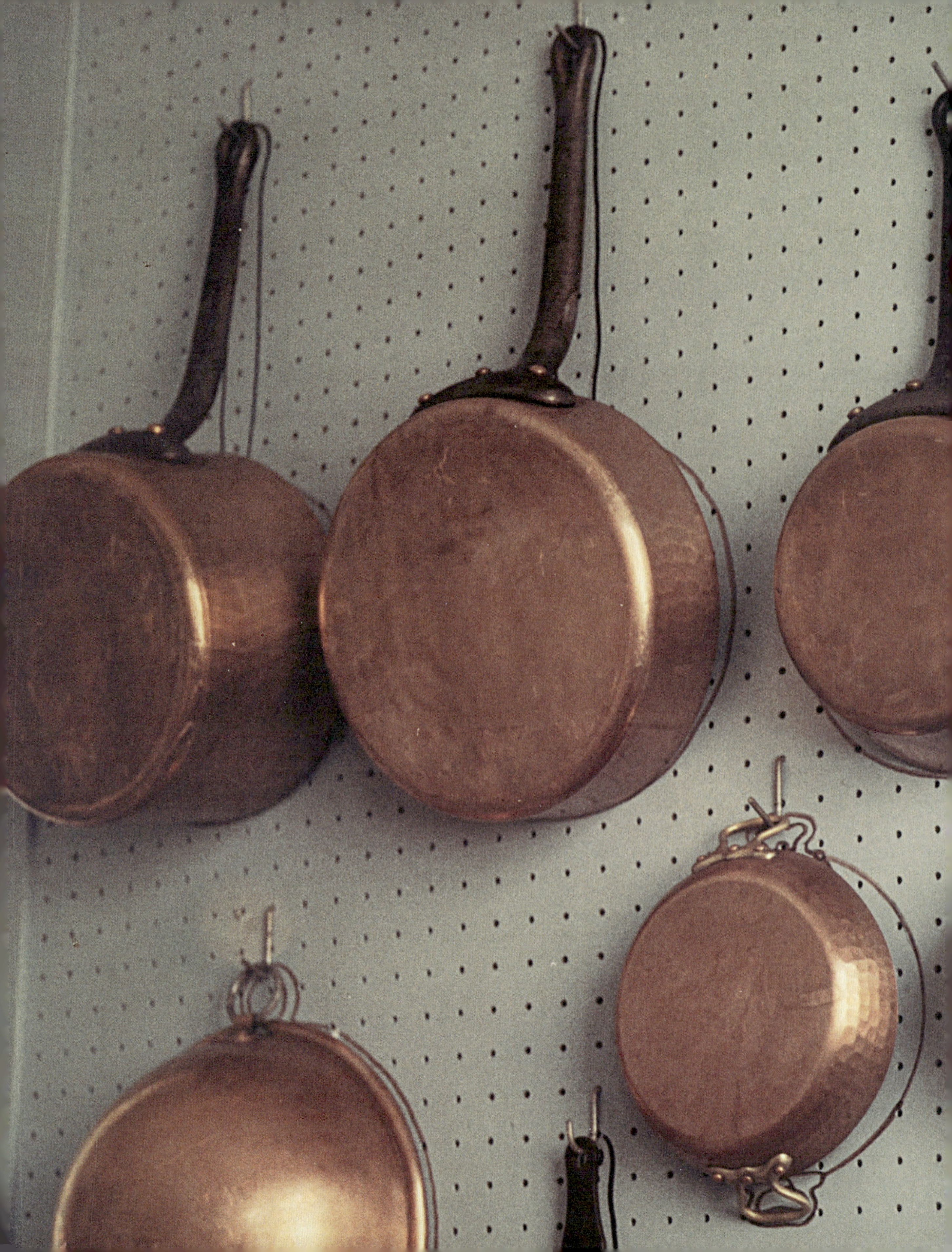

CHAPTER 3

"This is certainly the soul of our house."

V irtually everyone who visited Julia and Paul at home in Cambridge knew to arrive at the back door, an unassuming entrance adjacent to the parking area. Any doubts a visitor may have had about being in the right place would have been quelled by a glance at Julia's bottle green Volkswagen beetle (or later, a red VW Rabbit), recognizable by its slotted spoon wired to the antenna.[1] Many a visitor recalled the excitement of stepping through the back door, ascending a few steps, and finding themselves in a wide hallway with an open door to the right, where their host was likely cooking something but never too busy to greet them warmly. Whether family member, new acquaintance, or old chum, each guest was welcomed with genuine enthusiasm into Julia's home kitchen. And what happened next typically involved food: cooking, eating, discussing, and enjoying it—together.

previous spread: Section of Julia's copper wall *above:* Julia's green car at the back entrance to her home, 1974

VISITING AUNT JU-JU

Julia and Paul did not have children, but they had strong relationships with their extended families, which included invitations to their homes in Cambridge and Provence.[2] Likewise, the couple enjoyed spending several weeks each year with Paul's twin brother, Charles, and his family at their summer home in Maine. Food and cooking were always high on the list of activities during such visits, and, while Julia did not formally instruct her nieces and nephews about how to cook, they absorbed many lessons on food preparation, hospitality, and the robust conviviality that was created by cooking and eating together.

Phila Cousins, whose mother was Julia's sister, Dorothy, recalled visiting her Aunt Ju-Ju:

> It wasn't until I came to Cambridge as a freshman at Radcliffe College in 1969 that I really came to know Julia and Paul and spend time in their spacious kitchen... My gastronomic and culinary education then began in Ju-Ju's kitchen. Several times a semester I was invited over for dinner, which was a ritual. I knocked and entered from the back door. Julia came down the stairs: 'Hello, dearie! Come in!' Kisses and hugs. Sometimes I came alone, sometimes with my family members, college roommate, friends, or boyfriend.
>
> Once in the kitchen, Julia went straight to the stove, as she was always in the midst of preparing dinner. The table was set on the Marimekko tablecloth with bright ceramic dishes from Provence. I greeted Paul with a hug and kiss and he then took aperitif orders and

Julia's table set for a typical day, with a bright Marimekko tablecloth and red plates from Provence

disappeared into the pantry, a narrow room with mahogany cabinets and shelves, to prepare the drinks. We gathered around the table and discussed the events of the day, political goings on.

The dinner guests were varied and always fascinating: many relatives, Harvard professors like Dorothy Zinberg, old friends from the OSS days, WGBH folk, wonderful friends like Avis DeVoto, Pat and Herbert Pratt, and many more. Conversation was lively and above all everyone had FUN.

Julia was chatting to all there and cooking and would then say, "À table. It's time for dinner." We had a first course, often something she was working on for a cookbook or show. I particularly loved it when she was testing out puff pastry, with aromatic cheeses, sometimes some ham. And Paul always supplied the perfect white wine. Then on to the main course with a delicious salad, veggies, and red wine. Dessert was often simple, sometimes fruit and cheese, sometimes a cake or tart being tested out. Then we retired to the living room for a digestif and coffee. At 10:15 precisely, the lights clicked off on a timer, which signaled that it was time to leave, which was done with hugs and kisses all around. As I spent more time in the kitchen, Julia slowly began to give me tasks to do: making the vinaigrette, chopping the onions, washing out this or that pan [saying] "Clean up as you go along!!"[3]

above: Phila Cousins at the National Museum of American History, August 2009
left: Phila with her Aunt Ju-Ju, shortly before Julia's death in August 2004
opposite: One of a set of octagonal plates from a pottery in the Provencal town of Moustiers. Julia and Paul used the red plates in the Cambridge kitchen almost daily.

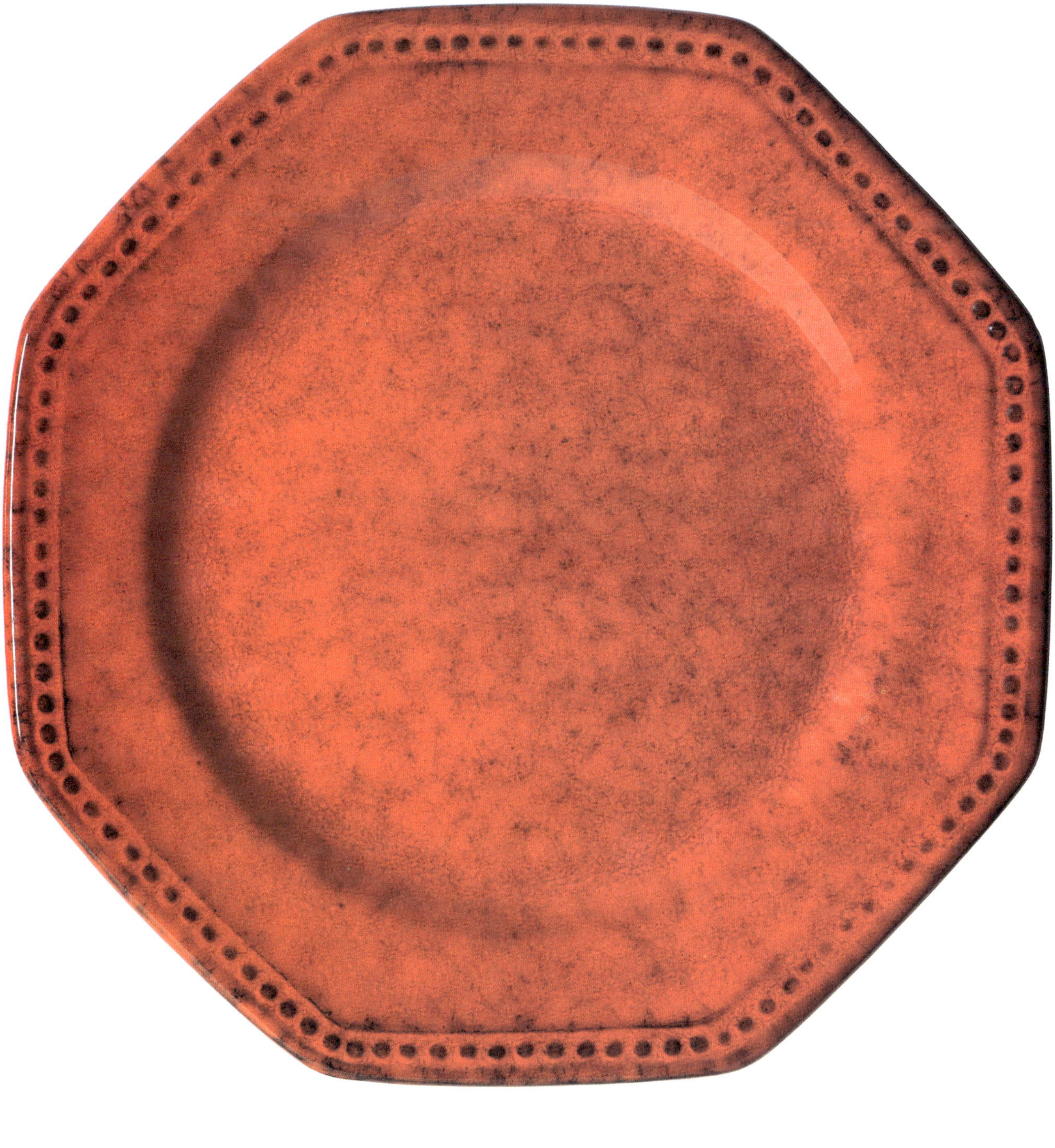

Reverse of Julia's red plates from Provence

"SHE ALWAYS MADE IT FUN."

Alex Prud'homme, Julia and Paul's grandnephew (and Charles's grandson), remembered visits to 103 Irving Street that included a lot of time in the kitchen, where he absorbed both culinary and life lessons.

> Growing up as a kid there, it was always exciting to go to Paul and Julia's house. They would often have a cocktail party where she would serve goldfish crackers and when you were a kid that was a big deal. You got away with it [enjoying a snack] at Paul and Julia's. As a young adult she introduced me to the reverse martini—the proportions are reversed. More vermouth, less gin. And as Julia always said, 'The great thing about the reverse martini is that you can have two of them.'
>
> There was always something happening in the kitchen. Julia was a workhorse. She essentially lived between the kitchen and her office on the second floor, which was funny because Paul had his office, which was very neatly organized, everything had labels and was boxed, and neat, and clean. Julia's was a whirlwind of papers and stacks of books and leaning towers of bric-a-brac.
>
> She was very inclusive and she would never give us cooking lessons, per se, she would just include us, and so she would say, "You wash the salad, you go down to the cellar and help Paul bring up some wine, you dice the butter, you over there take the garbage out." And it was fun, she made it fun. It was a whirlwind of activity, and we knew that the reward was a fabulous meal or sometimes a bizarre meal. But you never knew what you were going to eat, and she always made it fun. We kind of learned to cook and entertain by osmosis.

Alex Prud'homme, at right, with Julia and Paul Child, 1984

So, this was in the late eighties, early nineties when I was courting my now-wife Sarah and we went and spent a weekend with Julia, and she said, "Oh, we'll have a few people over for dinner."

We asked, "Who?"

"You'll see."

"What are we having?"

"Oh, I'll whip something up."

[At the dinner that evening] there was David [Liederman] from David's Cookies, a couple of famous chefs from restaurants, then random people including a woman she had met at the gas station that day. Some other guy. So, I went to a number of these parties, and you never knew who you would sit next to. Sometimes the chemistry didn't work. She didn't care, she carried on.

[Sometimes there was a] bizarre menu. People would often send her foods. She had a Virginia ham, smoky, quite delicious, [but] an acquired taste. Underdone green beans she insisted you eat with your fingers because it tastes better that way. And a potato dish that she was experimenting with... We had a friend there, a college friend [and he wondered] "This is Julia Child? What are we eating?" This is just how she operated—she didn't mind throwing different flavors together to see what would happen and different kinds of people together—and that was the experience of Julia.

And Thanksgivings, which were always epic. She kept her phone number in the phone book so all day the phone would be ringing. "Julia, the top of my turkey is frozen and the bottom burned." She generally got people to cut the bird apart. She would often calm them down. "It's going to be delicious, lovey." So, we witnessed that, and [for our own meal] Julia did the turkey but we would often do the side dishes—[what] became a competitive sport within the family. Fun! I did a chestnut puree, and I roasted the chestnuts but [then] had to peel them [an unpleasant chore].

That's the thing about that home and that kitchen, it was an aesthetic experience—sensory, visual, olfactory, taste, even physically [like] walking up and down the stairs. It was a cabinet of wonders, that kitchen.[4]

DINNER INVITATIONS

For nonfamily members and new acquaintances, an invitation to Julia's home inspired speculation and anxiety. What will she prepare? What if it's a French dish and I don't know what the food is? Will I be exposed as a rube? Turns out such worries were way off base. Julia was just happy you were there, and she swept you up in whatever was happening. For many new guests, being served in the kitchen came as a surprise, but also took the edge off anxieties about anticipated formalities. They learned quickly that Julia much preferred dining with guests in the kitchen. She believed that the room could accommodate eight, with six being more comfortable, and four guests the ideal.[5]

Marian Morash, whose husband, Russ, was Julia's first producer on *The French Chef*, and who later worked with Julia, recalled her first visit to the kitchen in the early sixties:

> I remember very well, she said, "Come over for dinner." I got a babysitter and we went over for dinner. I was expecting some kind of lavish thing and she had made an asparagus quiche. She was working on it to see how it would be best put together . . . So, she put down this asparagus quiche, and she cut a nice wedge for each of us and I thought it was probably the best thing I had ever eaten in my life. But all through the dinner she was saying, "Well, I think, what do you think, I think it could use a little more salt, a little bit more cream . . ." She was actually working on the recipe as we had dinner. And they [Julia and Paul] were so welcoming, you just felt totally at home, you felt like you were with your mother or father, or your friends.[6]

Marian Morash went on to become an indispensable assistant to Julia, earning the title "Executive Chef" for various culinary projects that involved teams of people working in the kitchen on dinner parties or preparing for cooking demonstrations and television shows. A culinary expert, restaurateur, and television star in her own right (as Chef Marian on PBS's *The Victory Garden* for twenty-five years), during Morash's first experience in Julia's kitchen her observations of how Julia's work included a lively social dimension (e.g., testing recipes with dinner guests) that came together around the kitchen table later influenced her own approach to cooking.

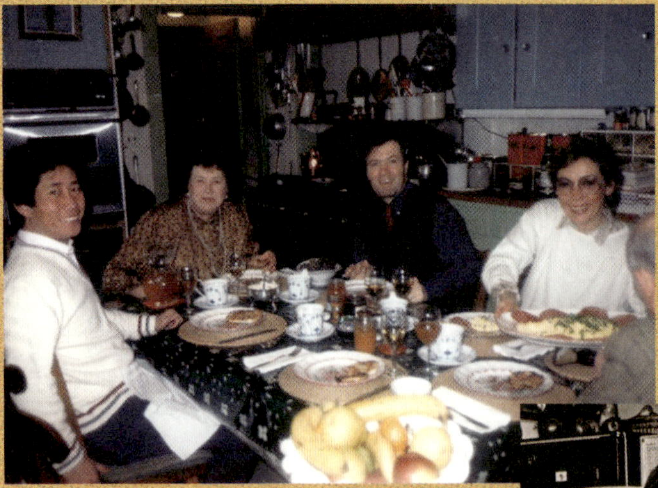

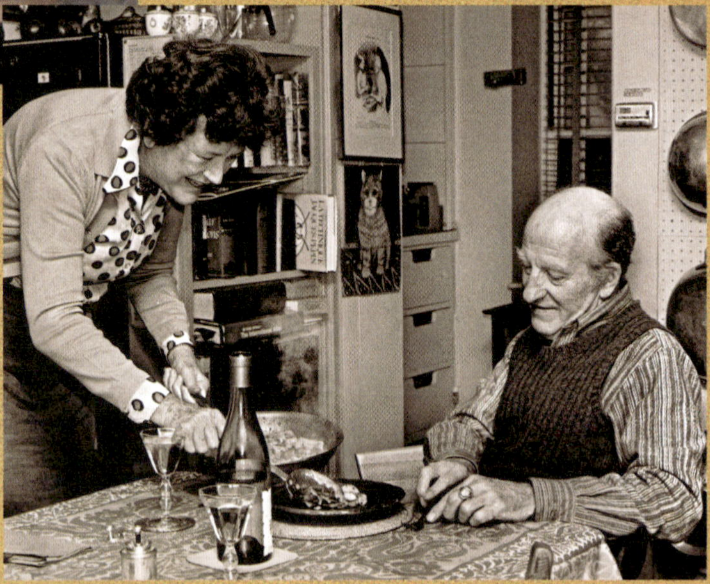

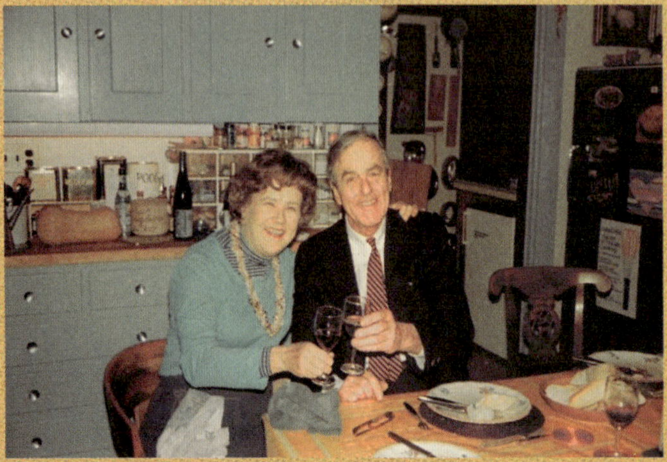

FOCUS: MEETING JACQUES PÉPIN

"What do you want to cook?"

Chef Jacques Pépin met Julia Child in 1960, shortly after his arrival in the United States from France. As we learned in his foreword to this volume, the two bonded over their mutual interests in French cuisine and the opportunity to speak French together. They became professional colleagues and friends as *Mastering*, Volume One, was published in 1961. Several years later, Julia invited Jacques and his wife, Gloria, to have dinner at 103 Irving Street. He recalled that when they arrived, Julia asked him, "What do you want to cook?" to which he replied, "What do you have?" Julia opened the fridge to reveal pork chops and string beans, which Jacques proceeded to prepare, while Gloria and Paul made drinks. Many years later, as recounted in his foreword, Jacques remembered that when the meal was served at the kitchen table, the oilcloth covering still had crumbs from breakfast. This felt consistent with Julia's casual approach. There was nothing snobbish about her or the kitchen, a dynamic that seemed very welcoming to the Pépins, who became frequent guests. Reflecting back on the kitchen, Jacques mused, "But the kitchen carried, you know, it was a love nest for her and Paul ... Paul always gave her credit but she always gave him credit, too. You can see that they had a very strong love affair between them."[7]

top: Breakfast at Julia's: Martin Yan (chef, cookbook author, and star of the long-running television show *Yan Can Cook*), Julia, Jacques Pépin, Gloria Pépin, and Paul Child enjoying breakfast around the kitchen table, sometime in the eighties. *center:* The photographer Anthony Gawrys and writer Mary Lou Kelly visited Julia and Paul at their home on assignment for *Boston Today* magazine, in September 1978. Gawrys remembered that lunch was Chicken Diane cooked in white wine with mushrooms, chicken stock, and heavy cream, and paired with a perfectly chilled Pouilly-Fuissé. *bottom:* Julia with her brother, John McWilliams, at dinner in the kitchen, 1975. McWilliams was two years younger than Julia and had been severely wounded in France during World War II. He and his family lived in Pittsfield, Massachusetts, where he worked for the Weston Paper Company.

Julia's conviction that guests were an essential and integral part of the kitchen scene played out time and again over the forty years she lived at 103 Irving Street. She wrote in 1976:

> When guests arrive for a meal, they are ushered right into the kitchen. They walk about, then sit at the table, and we have aperitifs and talk while I am finishing the dinner. It is easy and pleasant, and I am one of the party the way I like to be. Food is better, too, infinitely better, because the cook is in the kitchen, the way a chef is in his restaurant. No fresh green beans sit to warm up, losing their texture and color while I am in the dining room; no sauce will boil away nor custard curdle. Furthermore, nobody minds a bit of public stirring, tossing, and tasting; in fact, most seem to enjoy being witness to the action, although in time, I've noticed to my pleasure, nobody pays the cook much mind—unless the cook demands attention. To change courses, I pile the plates in my double sink and hide them under big stainless trays, while all finished pots are covered discreetly, and the stove light doused. Everything looks shipshape, in other words, and that is a most important consideration in kitchen dining. Then when we're through, out we go, shutting the door, to have coffee in the clean and well-ordered living room.[8]

below: A few of Julia's baking sheets and trays that were stored near the sink and put into service to cover dishes in the sink while entertaining. *opposite:* One of the Norwegian chairs at the kitchen table

"THE CENTER OF THE UNIVERSE."

If Julia called her kitchen the soul of the house,[9] the kitchen table was, in Alex Prud'homme's memory, "the center of the universe." Contrary to kitchen designs that valued sleek efficiencies over dining among the work surfaces and equipment spaces, Julia held firm to her preference for the dining table to be placed in the center of the most important room in the home. She quipped, with memorable self-awareness and candor, "I want the dining table in the middle of the room just because, like a sheepdog, I need to be right there in the midst of everyone."[10]

Alex Prud'homme recalled: "When they weren't having a dinner party per se, when they were just having friends over or family, we'd sit at the kitchen table. The kitchen table was utilitarian but also center of universe… Everything there—newspapers, tea, cookies. It was magnetic in a sense."[11]

The kitchen table itself was sturdy and utilitarian. It and the four chairs (two round-backed side chairs, and two straight-backed chairs) came from Oslo, Norway, Julia having ordered the furniture prior to their departure in October 1960. She protected the table's surface with a series of coverings, favoring designs by the Finnish firm Marimekko, which she purchased in Cambridge.

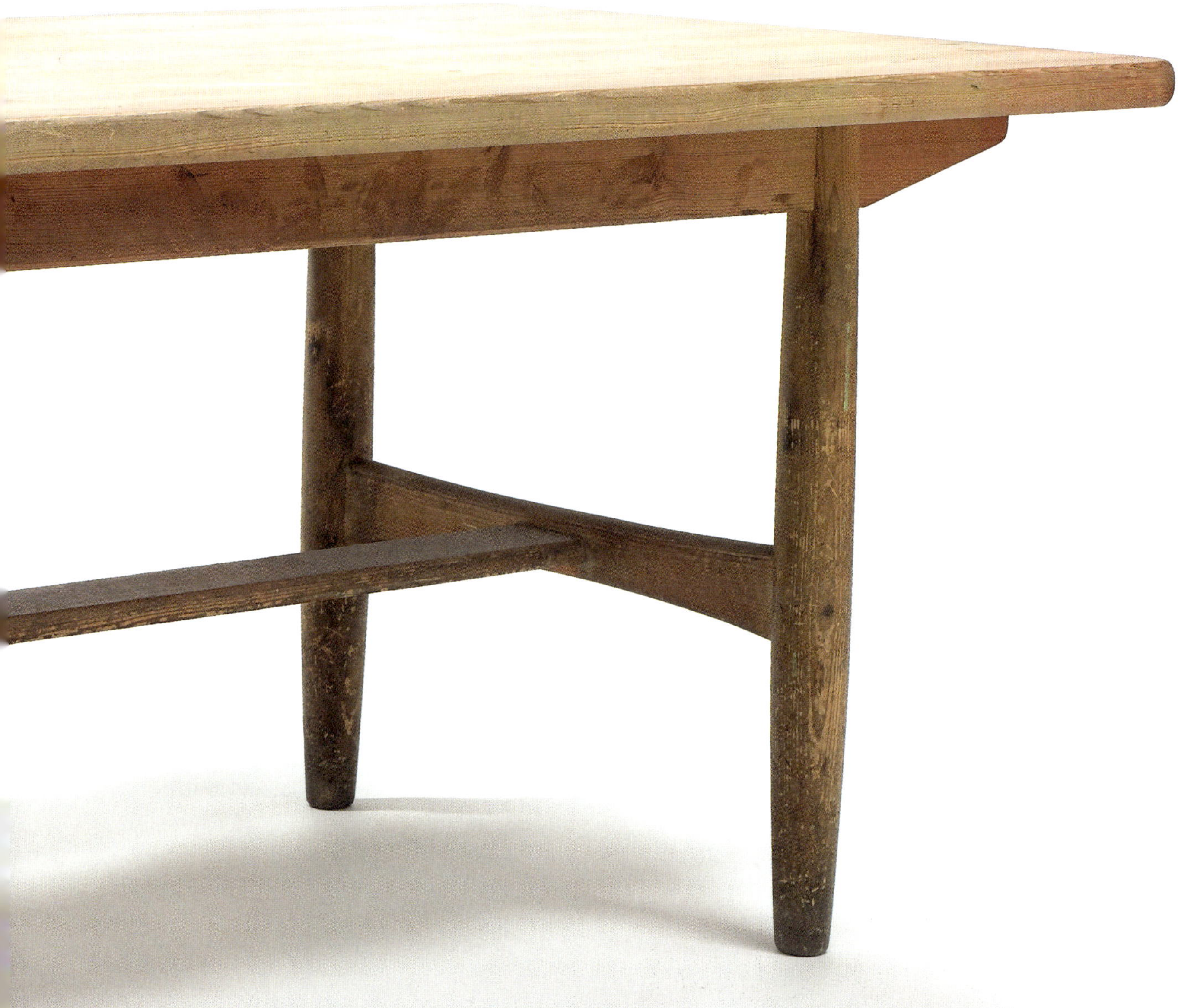

JULIA CHILD'S KITCHEN

FOCUS: CHRISTOPHER KIMBALL

"Julia liked to test you."

Julia invited people to dinner and frequently gave them assignments to help prepare the meal. For Julia, cooking was fundamentally a social act.

Christopher Kimball, the author, editor, and founder of *America's Test Kitchen* and *Milk Street* on public television, worked for many years in Brookline, very near to Cambridge. When he visited Julia's kitchen at the Smithsonian in 2012, he recollected how Julia would occasionally give him a call:

> She always called you personally, she always sent you a note—one of those little postcards. [One evening,] I walked in and... within two minutes she handed me this huge plastic tub of oysters and said, "Do you mind shucking oysters?"... So I spent, like, ten minutes, cutting my finger, opening two oysters. She asked if I wanted a church key and everything else. So finally, I was completely humiliated, and I said, "I tell you what. I'll drink the wine, you give me a big glass of wine, and you open the oysters."
>
> Julia liked to test you. She was competitive. She wasn't just the kindly professor. She liked to stick it to you. One of the times I came over, there'd be a leg of lamb and she'd just ask you to carve it to see if you knew where the H bone was. With the oysters, it was a test I failed miserably. But I think she liked people to stand up to her. I said, "You do it," and we got along fine after that.[12]

left: Christopher Kimball speaking with curators Paula Johnson (left) and Rayna Green (right) *right:* Some of Julia's knives for opening oysters

FOCUS: PAUL CHILD'S WINE TRACKER

In addition to being a devoted husband, artist, correspondent, and designer of orderly kitchens, Paul Child was a meticulous keeper of his wine cellar. He created a cardboard tracking grid that showed how many bottles of each vintage were stored. When a bottle was consumed, he would erase the proper numeral, leaving that vintage with one fewer bottle. The *New York Times* wine writer Frank Prial visited the Childs in 1975 and mentioned Paul's hand-drawn system in his article. Prial agreed that it was a good idea to track the wines on hand but added that the system would have been better if notes had been made on when the wine was consumed and by whom.[13] Opinions aside, Paul's tracker provides a wonderful record of the couple's taste in wine. The vast majority of wines listed are French, with only a handful of bottles produced in the United States, specifically California, and one Italian vintage.

Although French wines were clearly prevalent in the Irving Street cellar, by the eighties Julia's interest in California wines had grown. The 1976 Paris tasting, which pitted the best of Bordeaux and Burgundy against the best new wines from California, had vaulted California to the international stage. In both red and white categories, California wines

above: Paul Child's silver tastevin, or wine-tasting cup, hangs from a nail by the kitchen sink. The handle bears his initials "PCC." *left:* Renowned Napa Valley vintner Robert Mondavi and Julia Child sharing the microphone (and possibly a song) at an AIWF-sponsored event at the National Museum of American History in 1993. The museum's director, Dr. Spencer Crew, presided over the event.

had placed first, with the 1973 Chateau Montelena Chardonnay and the 1973 Stag's Leap Wine Cellars Cabernet Sauvignon preferred by the blind panel of tasters—all French. In the years following the "Judgment of Paris," winemakers in California and in other regions of the United States and around were emboldened to make wines that could meet and perhaps exceed the standard of good French wine. Working closely with the vintners Dick Graff and Robert Mondavi to establish the American Institute of Wine & Food (AIWF) in 1981, Julia tasted and learned about the distinctive qualities of some of the new California wines, mentioning Chalone, Schramsberg, and Mondavi in a 1986 interview in *Wine Spectator*.[14]

Adopting Prial's suggestion that Paul's wine tracker should include more details about when and by whom wine was consumed would have been a complex undertaking given the nonstop informal entertaining that characterized life in Cambridge. *above:* Russ Morash, Gloria Pépin, Jacques Pépin, and Paul Child after a memorable meal, with wine, in the kitchen, 1975. *opposite:* Paul Child kept this wine tracker in the butler's pantry, where the wine tools and glasses were stored.[15]

Region	Wine	Year	Bottles
BORD	CH. FOURCAS HOSTEN	1970	1 2 3 4 5 6 7 8
BORD	CH. GRUAUD-LAROSE	'67	1 2 3 4
BURG	BONNES MARES	'62	1 2 3 4
RHONE	CHAT. NEUF DU PAPE	'66	1 2 3 4 5 6 7 8
BURG	BEAUNE Champimonts (Drouhin)	'64	1 2
BURG	CLOS DE LA ROCHE	'61	1 2
BURG	BONNES MARES (de Vogüé)	'52	1 2 3 4 5 6
BURG	CHAMBOLLE-MUSIGNY	64>71	1 2 3 4 5 6 7 8
BURG	CH. LA CONSEILLANTE	'62	1 2 3 4 5 6 7
BORD	COS. DESTOURNEL	'64	1 2 3 4 5
BORD	CH. BATAILLEY	'73	1 2 3 4 5 6 7 8
BORD	CH. HAUT BATAILLY	'64	1 2 3 4 5 6 7 8 9 10 11
CALIF	CLOS DU VAL (NAPA)	'72	1 2 3 4 5 6
BORD	CH. BECHEVELLE	'71	1 2 3 4 5 6 7 8 9
RHONE	CLOS DES PAPES	'71	1 2 3 4
BURG	CHABERTIN	'62	1 2 3
BEAU	SAINT-AMOUR	'76	1 2 3 4 5 6
BURG	GRIOTTE CHAMBERTIN	'66	1 2 3 4 5 BEAU: BROUILLY 1 8
BURG	GEVREY-CHAMBERTIN	'62	1 2 3 4
RHONE	2org bottles - BAUMES DE VENISE	'73	16 (little bottles) '75 ST. EMILION (figeliera) 12
BURG	POMMARD-RUGIENS	'52	1 2 3
BEAU	LA VIEILLE FERME	'74	1 2 3 4
BURG	CLOS de VOUGEOT	'64	1 2 3 4 5
BURG	CLOS-VOUGEOT	'66	1 2 3 4 ∞ '62
BORD	LYNCH-PAGES	'62	1 2 3 '64 1 2 3 4 5
BURG	GRANDS-ECHEZEAUX (GRU)	'64	1 2 3 4 5
BURG	CÔTES DU RHONE-VILLAGES	'74	1 2 3 4 5 6 7 8 9
BORD	CH. LAFITTE-ROTHSCHILD	'66	1 2 3
BORD	CH. LÉOVILLE-BARTON	'66	1 2 3
BEAU	LA FEUILLE D'AUTUMNE	'76	1 2 3
BORD	LA COUR PAVILLON	1972 RIOJO: 1 2 3 4 5 6 7 8 9 10 11 (NO YEAR)
BURG	CLOS DE LA CLOCHE	1921 Dn Boroulet
MOSEL	GRAACHER HIMMELREICH (spät.)	'67	1 2 3
BORD	CHEVALIER MONTRACHET	'68	1 2 3 4 5 6 7 (de Sylou)
BURG	CORTON CHARLEMAGNE	'70	1 2 3 4 5 6 7
ALSACE	GEWÜRZTRAM. FRIBERG	'69	(GR. RES.) · 8 Bottles · × 9 Botts of '71
BURG	CHASSAGNE MONTRACHET	'68	1 2 3 4 5 6 7 Le Chateau
ALSACE	PINOT BLANC '74×	'69	1 2 3 4 5 6
BURG	POUILLY-FUISSÉ	'72	1 2 3 4
BURG	POUILLY-FUISSÉ	'73 · 21
BORD	CH. LAVILLE HAUT BRION '69>	'71	1 2 3 4 5 6 7 8
LOIRE	MUSCADET DE SEVRE × MAINE	'73	1 2 3 4 5 6
ALSACE	BRANDLUFT-RIESLING	'74	1 2 3 4 5
BURG	VOUGEOT CLOS BLANC D.V.	'72	1 2 3 4 5 6 7 8
BORD	CH. GRAVILLE-LACOSTE	'67	1 2 3
BORD	CH. SIGALAS RABAUD (Sauternes)	'55	1 2
BORD	LAVILLE HAUT BRION	'71	1 2 3 4 5 6 7 8 9 10 11
ARBOIS	CH. CHALON	'69	1 2 3 4
RHONE	HERMITAGE	'0	1 2 3 4 5 6 7
RHINE	SCHLOSS VOLRADS	'70	1 2
BURG	MEURSAULT-PERRIÈRES	'66	1 2 3 4
BURG	MEURSAULT-CHARMES	'71	1 2 3 4 5 6 7 8
RHINE	JOHANNISBERG RIESLING	'72	1 2 3 4 5
RHINE	SCHLOSS JOHANNESBURG	'67	1 2
BURG	(SP) MONTRACHET	'69	1 2 3 4 5 6 7 8
ALSACE	RIESLING SCHOENENBERG	'75	1 2 3 4 5 6 7 8 9 10 11
RHONE	CH. NEUF DU PAPE (BLANC)	'76	7
LOIRE	SANCERRE	'70	1 · '72(?) 1 2 3
LOIRE	POUILLY BLANC FUMÉ	'75	14
BORD	(Sauternes) CH. D'YQUEM 2 '62 ∞'66 · CH. LIOT BARSAC 1 '61 · CH RAYNE-VIGNEAU 1 '62 CH. CLIMENS 1 '62 (SAUTERNES)
RHINE	BORNHEIMER KIRCHENSTÜCK	'75	1 2 (Spätlese)
ANJ	ROSES D'ANJOU	'75	1 2 3 4 5 6 7 8 9 10

Region	Wine	Year	Bottles
BURG	POMMARD "CLOS DES EPENAUX"	'64	7
NUITS	CLOS DES GRANDES VIGNES	'64	(BOURG) 1 2
NUITS-ST. G.	'67 Thomas Freres (des Richemones) 1 2
NUITS-ST. G.	'71	1 2 Desaylou
BEAU	FLEURIE LA FIERTÉ	'76	1 2 3 4 5 6 7 8
BURG	CHAMBOLLE-MUSIGNY · LES CHARMES ·		5
CH	BEYCHEVELLE	'64	1 2 3 4 5 6
CH	HAUT-BEYCHEVELLE	'64	1 2 3 4
CH	GISCOURS	1 2 3 4 5 · '66
CH	PAVIE	1 2 3 4 · '66
CH	COS DESTOURNEL	'64 (ST. ESTEPHE) 1 2 3 4 5
RHONE	CHATEAU NEUF-DU-PADE	'66	9
SP	LA RIOJA ALTA	'59	1 2 3
CH	MARGAUX	'66	1 2 3 4
	BRANE CONTENAC	'64	1 2
BURG	BEAUNE GUIGONE DE SALINS	'64	1 2 3
BURG	BEAUNE BRESSANDES	'71	1 2 3 4 5 6 7
BORD	DOMAINE DE CHEVALIER		1 2 3 4 5 6 7 8
BORD	CALON SEGUR	'64 1 2 ∞ '71 1 ∞ '6: '78
BURG	MUSIGNY	'62	1 2 3 4 5
BEAU	JULIENAS · BRISE DE MER ·		1 2 3 4 5 6
	CÔTES DU RHONE (½ Bottles)		13
	CORTON-BRESSANDES · '64 · 1 2 · BURG ·
CH	HAUT BAILLY	'64	1 2 3 4
RHONE	HERMITAGE		1 2 3 4 5
BEAU	MOULIN-A-VENT LE RÈVE ·	'76	1 2
CH	DUCRU BEAUCAILLOU	'71	1 2 3 4 5 6 7 8
RHONE	CH. NERTE	'78	1 2 3 4 5 6 7 8 9 (CH. N. DU PAPE)
RHONE	CÔTES DU RHONE - VILLAGES ·		1 2 3 4 5 6 7
RHONE	CH. NEUF DU PAPE	'73 ·	1 2 3 4 5 6 7 8 9
BURG	BEAUNE CLOS DES URSULES		1 2 3 4 5 6 7 8 9
BORD	CH. GRILLET	'69 · 1 2 (Sim Adron × Sim)
BURG	CHEVALIER MONTRACHET (DE SYLOU) · 6 · '68
BURG	VOUGEOT CLOS BLANC DE VOUGEOT	'72 · 10 ·
RHINE	JOHANNISBERG RIESLING	'72 · 1 2 3 4 5
VOUV	MONMOUSSEAU	'69 · 1 2 3 4 5 ·
BORD	CH. LAVILLE HAUT BRION ·	'69 5 · × '71 · 10
	VARIOUS CHAMPAGNES · 13 · · · ·
RHINE	SCHLOSS ELTZ (Spätlese) · '71 · 7
SPAIN	AMOTILLADO SHERRY · 10
	PORTUGUESE ROSÉ · FONSECA · 0 · 1 ·
	CHABLIS · 0 · 1 2 3 4 5 6
	MADEIRA BUAL · 1860 · 2 · (Baum Bland)
ITALY	VERNACCIA (Sardinia) · 1955 · 1 ·
ITALY	MALVASIA (Naples) · 1950 · 1 ·
USA	CHARDONNAY · 1973 · 18 · (Napa Valley - Mondavi)
USA	GEWÜRZ TRAM. 1974 · 6 · (Napa Valley - Louis Martini)
ALSACE	RIESLING	1972	1 2 3 4 5 6
SAUT	CH. LIOT (HAUT BARSAC) · 1961 · 1
SAUT	CH. CLIMENS · '62 · 1
SAUT	CH. D'YQUEM · '66 · 1 2
SAUT	CH. SUDUIRAUT · '67 · 1 2
	VOUVREY · 1 2 3 4 5 6 7 8 9 10 11 12 '76
	CHARLES KRUG · '72 · (NAPA) · 1 2 3 4 5 6

Cooking at Julia's
An Elizabeth Bishop Wine Event

Reception

Beluga caviar • blinis • Fresh cured Salmon on black bread
Gougères • Rillettes of rabbit

Veuve Clicquot La Grande Dame 1990

Dinner

Oyster - Corn Chowder with Small Cornbreads
Puligny Montrachet Les Pucelles Bouchard 94

Poached Ray Valérie with black butter
Smith Haut Lafitte 95

Truffled Pâté of Pheasant in aspic
Ducru-Beaucaillou 82 and Cheval Blanc 82

Shell Roast Napa with Onion Custard • tomato coulis
Haut Brion 86 and Côte Rôtie La Mouline Guigal 83

Granité of Grapefruit
Veuve Clicquot Rosé 95

Salad Tulipe, cheeses • Pear Walnut Dressing
Vintage Port Barros Colheita 77

Coffee - Rum Caramel Custard • Lime Tuile Cookies
Chocolate Truffettes
Château d'Yquem 90
Vintage Port Fonseca 77

Jacques 01

Menu prepared by Jean-Claude Szurdak • Jacques Pépin
with the B.U. Culinary Students

COOKING AT JULIA'S ONE LAST TIME

Jacques Pépin recalled a memorable evening of cooking in Julia's kitchen with Chef Jean-Claude Szurdak and about a dozen students from the Boston University culinary program. The occasion was a fundraiser and a way of saying farewell to Julia just before she left her Irving Street home in 2001. Jacques remembered that it was "pretty tight" in the kitchen with so many cooks and that the guests ate in the dining room, one of the only times Jacques recalls eating there himself and not in the kitchen. In his typical style, he painted the menu for "Cooking at Julia's," and donated the original to the Smithsonian. It memorializes one of the last meals cooked in her home kitchen by Julia's friends and students.[16]

The menu also reveals that this was "An Elizabeth Bishop Wine Event," referring to Liz Bishop, who in 1968 started working on Julia's television show *The French Chef*. Bishop continued in her role as an associate for Julia on *Julia Child & Company* and *Julia Child & More Company*. As a trusted friend, Liz helped make Julia's many public appearances—cooking demonstrations, interviews, book tours—more professional.[17] She was also a sommelier and worked with Julia and the prominent California winemakers Robert Mondavi and Richard Graff on creating the American Institute of Wine & Food in 1981. Established as a nonprofit organization devoted to the study and enjoyment of gastronomy, the AIWF and its members—professionals and enthusiasts alike—remained important to Julia throughout her life. After Liz's death, her family donated funds to Boston University's wine program, and in 1996 the Elizabeth Bishop Wine Resource Center was established as part of the BU program in gastronomy.

The food and wine pairings on the menu for this memorable evening would have been a dream for the lucky guests, combining Julia's love for France and her American roots: Beluga caviar, oyster and corn chowder, truffled paté of pheasant in aspic, granité of grapefruit, rum caramel custard … what's not to love? The cuisine and fine wines may have taken the sad edge off the evening's purpose—to cook and dine with Julia one more time before she pulled up stakes in Boston.

The menu that Jacques Pépin painted for the special dinner at Julia's home in 2001. He donated the artwork to the National Museum of American History in 2015.

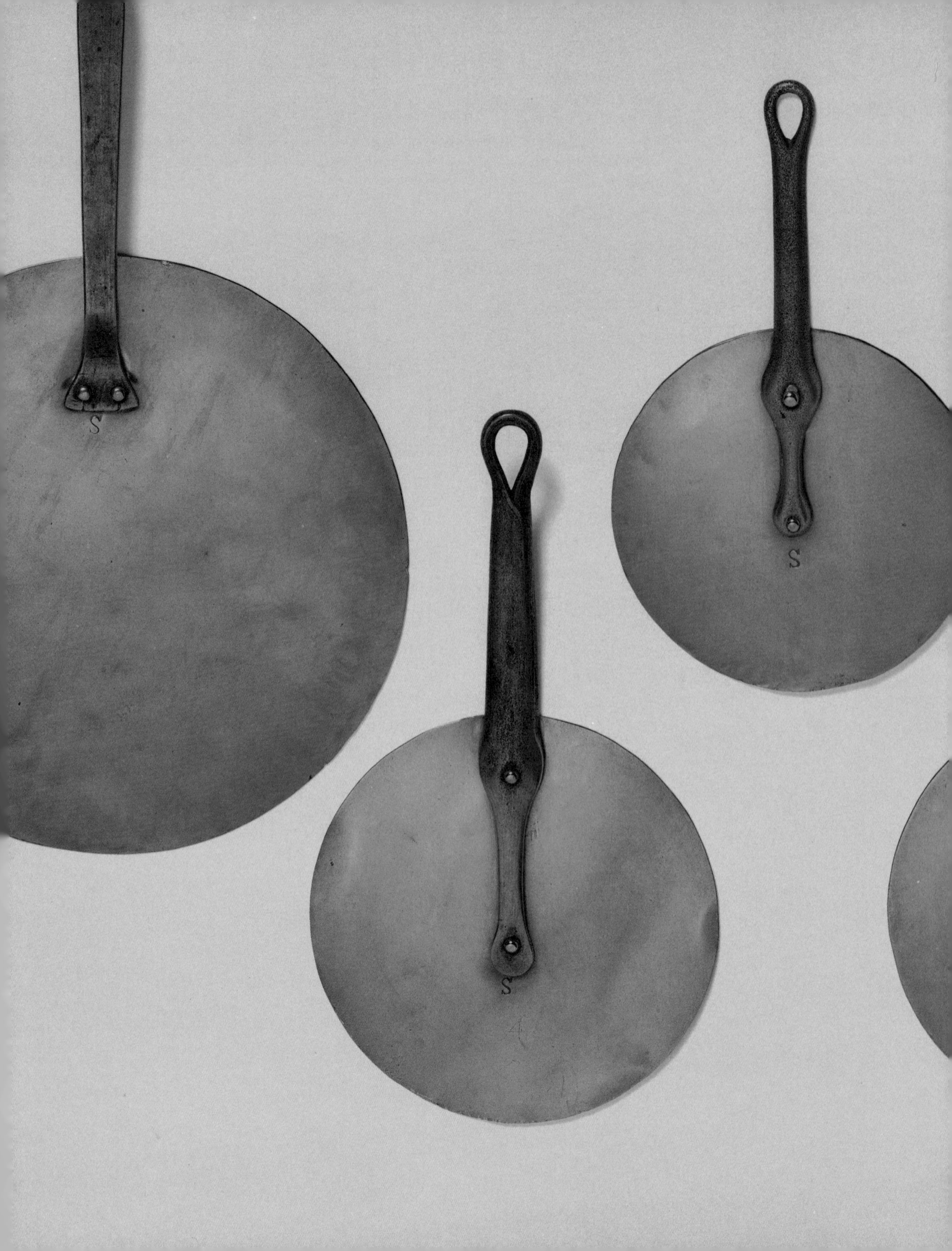

CHAPTER 4

"Everybody should listen to the cooks."

JULIA CHILD'S KITCHEN

Julia Child was justifiably proud of her gleaming "batterie de cuisine." In Volume One of *Mastering the Art of French Cooking*, she devoted seven pages to descriptions and illustrations of her essential kitchen tools and equipment. By the time Volume Two was published nearly a decade later in 1970, her dedication to helping readers understand the importance of cooking with the right tools was reflected in an expansive "illustrated roundup" of useful kitchen equipment that covered nearly forty pages. That guidance, in Julia's own voice, provides a marvelous window into her opinions and preferences regarding tools of the culinary arts. It also reveals that her role as cooking teacher extended to helping students select and care for their own equipment. Many of the tools described in Volume Two of *Mastering* are now in the museum's care, with Julia herself having provided their essential and often very personal histories.[1] An opinion she expressed often, including to the museum team, was that "Everybody should listen to the cooks" when developing kitchen tools, as cooks know what they need, what works, and what doesn't. Julia's kitchen, in essence, contains tools that passed the test.[2]

previous spread: Julia's copper pan lids *opposite:* The wall of copper and iron cookware in Julia's home kitchen, 2001

108 CHAPTER 4

JULIA CHILD'S KITCHEN

TOP ROW 1. TIN BUTTERFLY **2.** TIN FISH MOUSSE MOLD **3.** TIN IMAGE OF SAN PASQUAL **4.** TIN FISH MOUSSE MOLD **5.** COPPER SAUCEPAN **6.** RICE BALL COOKER **7.** ALUMINUM DOUGHNUT CUTTER/PINEAPPLE CORER **SECOND ROW 8.** COPPER SAUTÉ PAN **9.** COPPER SAUTÉ PAN **10.** COPPER SAUTÉ PAN **11.** COPPER SAUTÉ PAN **12.** COPPER SAUCEPAN **13.** COPPER SAUCEPAN **14.** COPPER SAUCEPAN **15.** COPPER BUTTER WARMER **16. & 17.** CAST-IRON MUFFIN PANS **18.** COPPER GRATIN PAN **THIRD ROW FROM TOP 19.** COPPER BOWL **20.** BRANDING IRON **21. & 22.** BLACK-STEEL CRÊPE PANS **23. & 24.** COPPER CRÊPE PANS **25.** COPPER GRATIN PAN **26.** COPPER GRATIN PAN **27.** COPPER GRATIN PAN **28 & 29.** CAST-IRON CORNSTICK PANS **SECOND ROW FROM BOTTOM 30.** COPPER GRATIN PAN **31.** COPPER SAUCEPAN **32–36.** GRATIN PANS **37.** COPPER SAUTÉ PAN **38. & 39.** WEIGHTS **40.** BRASS TRIVET **41.** COPPER CARAMEL PAN **BOTTOM ROW 42.** COPPER SABAYON BOWL **43.** BLACK-STEEL FISH PAN **44. & 45.** COPPER GRATIN PANS **46.** SPRING SCALE **47.** BLACK-STEEL FISH PAN

"EVERYBODY SHOULD LISTEN TO THE COOKS."

Julia's love affair with kitchen tools continued for as long as she lived. She was keen to try new devices for her own enlightenment but also felt a responsibility to her television viewers and live cooking demo audiences to "try out everything new so that I can have a valid opinion of its worth."[3] Where to store everything new was already an issue in 1976, when she admitted, "even I have almost come to the point where any further acquisition must mean the getting rid of an existing object, and that is a terrible wrench because I love almost every piece. I therefore have no helpful advice to give those with limited space except to suggest puritan restraint, strict discipline, and super organization."[4]

On principle, Julia steadfastly refused to represent any particular brand of cookware, but she gave credit when credit was due, lauding *types* of equipment—like the sturdy stand mixer and food processor—that revolutionized kitchen work. Over four decades, the Cambridge kitchen absorbed an astonishing number of tools, equipment, gadgets, and artwork, most of which she managed to fit within the basic design created by Paul in the early sixties. Paul mused that Julia had enough equipment "to stock two medium-sized restaurants," while she graciously praised his original design by declaring how it allowed for expansion without the kitchen taking on the junk-shop look that she was determined to avoid.[5]

As we explore the arrangements and particular histories of objects inside Julia's cupboards and drawers, sitting on countertops, and hanging from pegboard-covered walls, it is possible to see their utility and beauty but also their meaning far beyond the confines of the actual room. Neither a junk shop nor a collection of restaurant ware, Julia's home kitchen speaks to and reflects some of the major transformations in food that characterize the second half of the twentieth century in the United States. This way of understanding the historical context of the kitchen can be observed in old and new technologies and by recognizing the remarkable range of materials present, from copper to cast iron, from stainless steel to plastics. What's more, the manner in which common kitchen tools share space with highly specialized, professional equipment evokes a sense of time and place as well as Julia's embrace of devices that got the job done. It is important to keep in mind that Julia's open and fearless approach to cooking, teaching, and learning came together at a time when more—certainly not all—Americans had weathered the deprivations of the Great Depression and World War II and had both the means and interest

Julia and Paul surrounded by kitchen tools in their Cambridge kitchen. Many of those same tools are now in the collections of the National Museum of American History.

JULIA CHILD'S KITCHEN

"EVERYBODY SHOULD LISTEN TO THE COOKS." 111

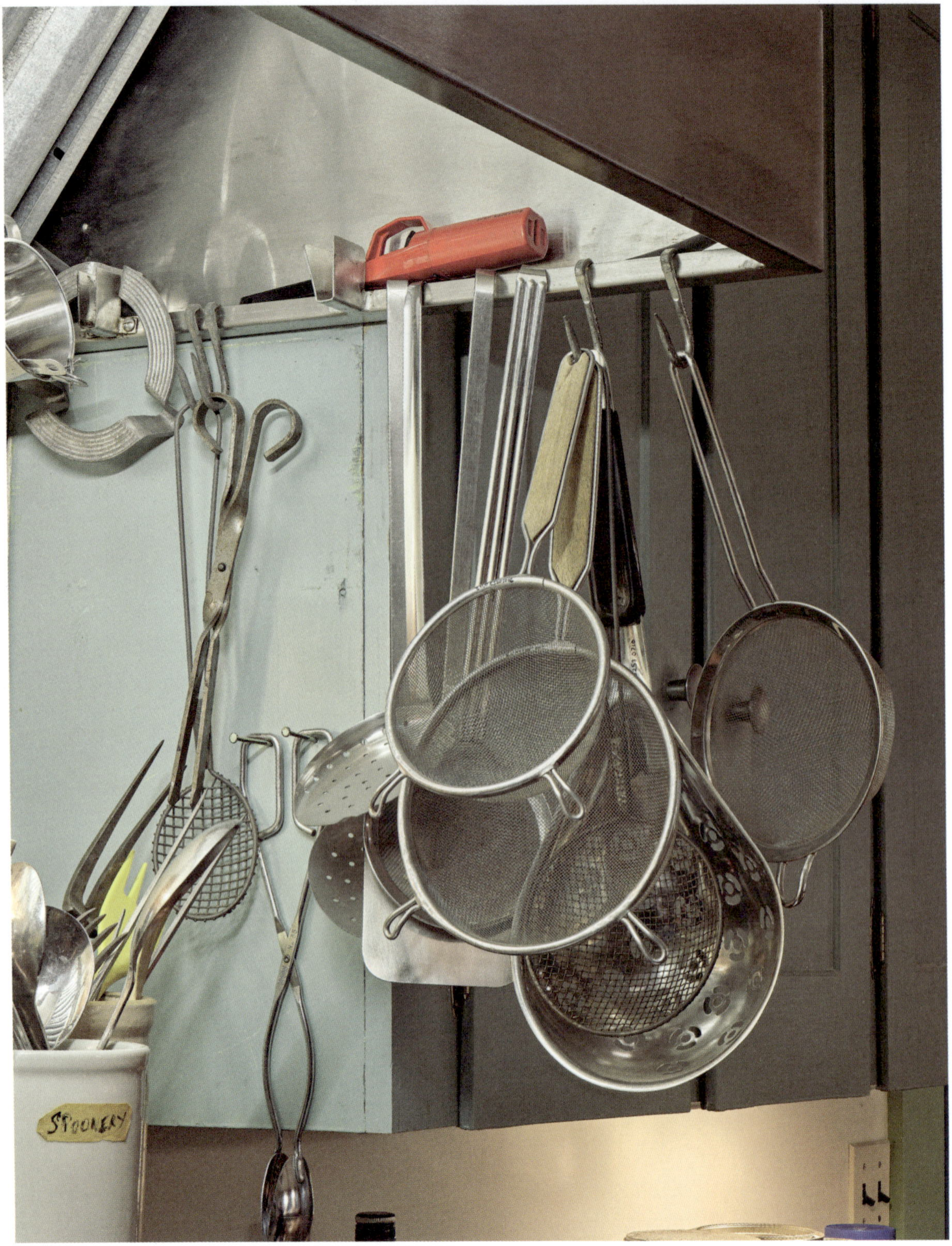
SPOONERY

to explore cuisines and cultures beyond their borders and lived experiences. This curiosity about and appetite for food beyond the products brought to Americans by the expanding food industries infused vitality to food in the United States.[6] These aspects of change, however, were often out of step with many of the prevailing views that valued convenience and minimal effort in the kitchen above all else.

In the years following World War II, food production in the United States expanded to meet the national goals of an abundant and affordable food supply, ushering in a more industrialized, centralized, highly processed, aggressively advertised, and hyperglobalized system. As food industries and popular media encouraged women to forsake cooking at home and to let processed, convenience, and fast foods relieve the drudgery of the kitchen, individuals like James Beard, Joyce Chen, Edna Lewis, Marcella Hazan, Alice Waters, and of course Julia Child represented another approach to food, cooking, and feeding oneself and others. With her enthusiasm for learning and encouraging others to experience new foods and flavors, Julia brought people toward a way of thinking about food and cooking that contradicted many of the popular and powerful voices of industry.[7]

For Julia and others, "convenient, easy, and cheap" were not the three most essential guiding principles for getting dinner on the table. Yet she understood that home cooks often desperately needed time-saving devices and culinary shortcuts. Their lives, she knew, revolved around raising children and accommodating their activities, managing a household, perhaps juggling paid work outside of the home, and typically

opposite: In Julia's kitchen, tools are grouped near where they will be needed. These strainers, sieves, scoops, and tongs hang from the hood of the Garland range. The portable lighter is nestled in the hood, where Julia could reach it easily to light a burner. *right:* Advertisement for ready-to-cook family favorites, 1960s

doing so without help. Aware that the recipes in *Mastering the Art of French Cooking*, Volume One, might strike the average homemaker as impossible to achieve, she nevertheless wanted aspiring home cooks to know that if she, Julia, could master the French classics, so could they. In addition to the more unfamiliar techniques of French cooking, she also provided basic tips that echoed lessons taught by high school home economics teachers, such as read a recipe first to be sure all ingredients and tools are at hand; learn how to substitute ingredients as needed; and, importantly, always clean as you go.

Julia was not one to get stuck in the past or to ignore the dynamic changes in social and cultural life taking place around her. She liked being around young people and exploring new ideas—habits that propelled her forward. By the eighties, she had shifted away from her early, almost exclusive embrace of France ("the French straitjacket")[8] to following James Beard's lead on celebrating American regional specialties. She continued to endorse using canned and store-bought ingredients when necessary, while also advocating for dishes featuring fresh and local ingredients, and those representing cuisines from around the globe. Julia welcomed students and guest chefs into her home with a genuine desire to teach, but also to learn from them. That spirit was conveyed through her writings, television shows, and live demonstrations in which she became the audience's kindly and trusted friend who never demanded perfection, just sincere effort.

Julia's kitchen in all its organization, equipment, and personal touches can be explored and understood in light of changes in food and Julia's role and responses to those changes over four decades. In the arena of cookware alone, the kitchen can be read in strata of time, and on a spectrum of quotidian to highly specialized. Hand-operated food mills, mortars and pestles, and an electric food processor suggest the sweep of technological change. Professional copper cookware, larding needles, chef's knives, and specialty gadgets for scaling fish and chopping parsley share space with heavily used cast-iron skillets, supermarket carrot peelers, an electric frying pan, and a homemade device for quickly and efficiently removing kernels from an ear of corn. The bookshelves hold food-stained volumes that many American cooks used (and still do), with classic French texts and wine encyclopedias lined up on an adjacent shelf. Signs of Julia's professional life in television (VHS tapes of her shows that she would critique while cooking) occupy a shelf under her own cookbooks marked "Kitchen Copy." The material culture of the kitchen connects us to Julia and her life, to be sure, but also to American history and themes of changing roles, especially for women, in both home and professional kitchens; the impacts of new technologies and culinary innovations; the tensions and contradictions in food production, marketing, and distribution; and an abiding, yet sorely tested, sense that cooking and eating with others remains central to the human experience and must not be abandoned.

The kitchen bookshelf, 2001, and a selection of material from its shelves. Julia had two copies of *The Joy of Cooking* on her kitchen bookshelf, and among her marginalia is the definition of "samp" as "coarse hominy." Like the rest of us, Julia had to look things up occasionally, and her source was Merriam-Webster's dictionary. She also took notes on details like the different sizes of Champagne bottles, from Magnum to Methuselah.

JULIA CHILD'S KITCHEN

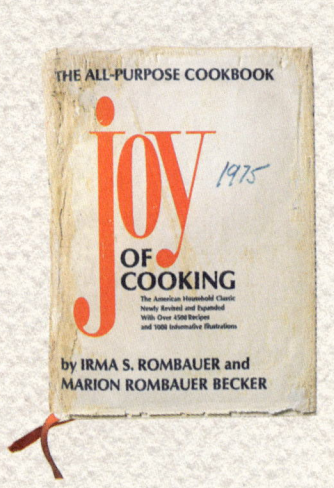

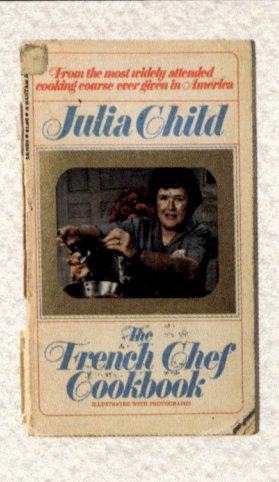

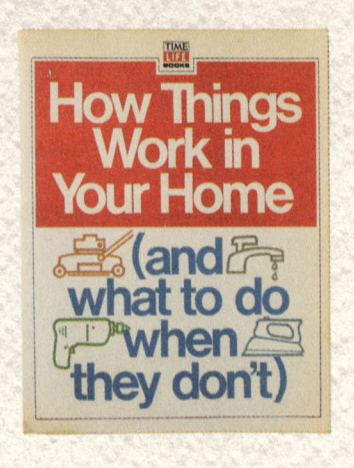

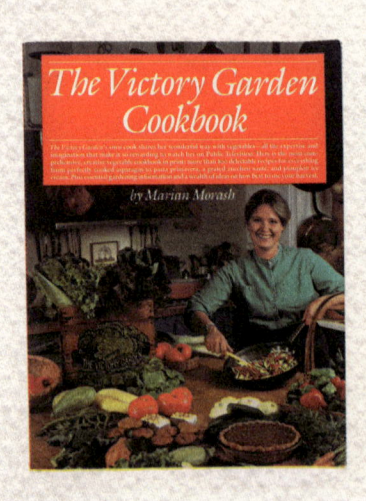

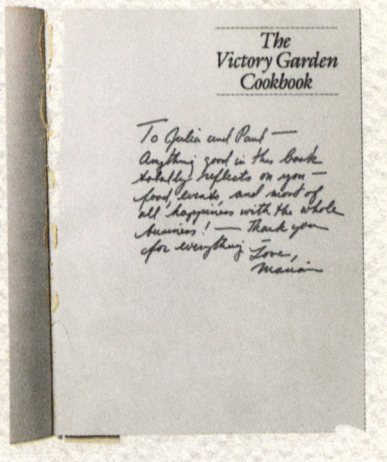

116   CHAPTER 4

JULIA CHILD'S KITCHEN

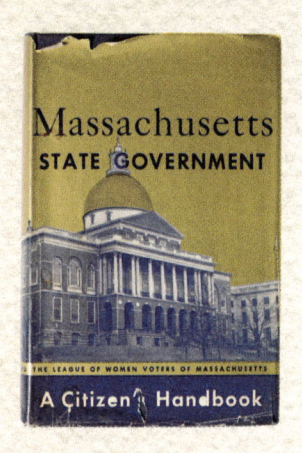

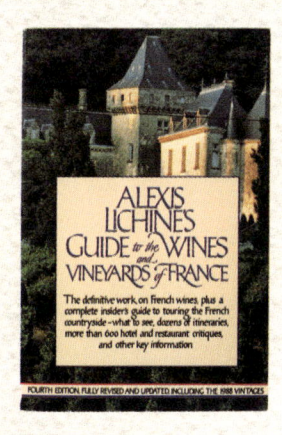

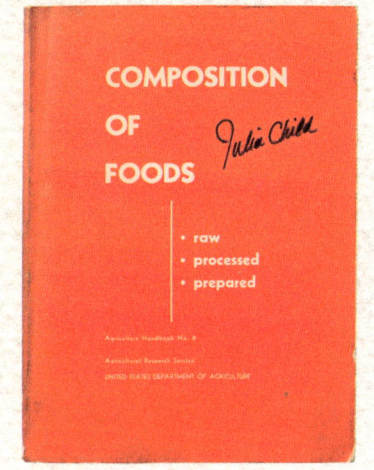

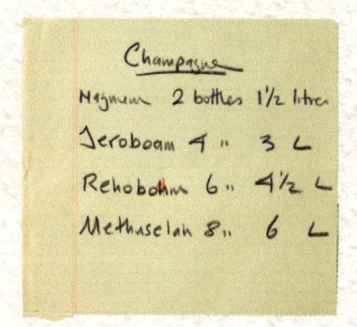

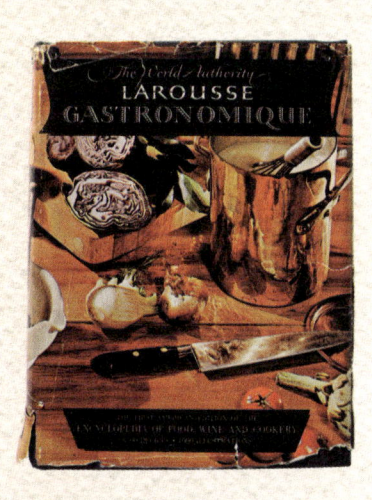

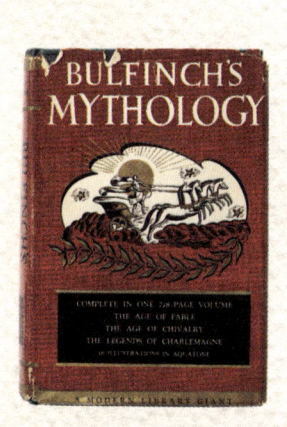

"EVERYBODY SHOULD LISTEN TO THE COOKS."   117

REVOLUTIONARY TECHNOLOGIES

Refrigeration and electrification may have been the most significant technological breakthroughs for home cooks in the early twentieth century, but culinary innovations in the post–World War II period proved revolutionary as well. Julia felt a responsibility to her fans and followers to test new technologies, and three countertop machines serve as examples that connected Julia with Americans possessing tremendously varied levels of culinary skill and interest.

FOCUS: THE MICROWAVE

"This NASA machine"

The introduction of the microwave oven for home use in 1955 wasn't exactly a rousing success. The Tappan RL-1 Electronic model microwave oven was expensive—$1,295—and large—the size of a modern mini fridge, at 10 cubic feet (27 × 24 × 27 inches). The inventors hoped it would replace regular ovens, and they designed the unit to resemble a regular stove, building a recipe drawer into the housing and publishing cookbooks with sumptuous-looking meals on the covers. The technology, developed during World War II, was not well understood or trusted by consumers, especially arriving on the scene to cook their food as the Cold War was itself heating up and fears of radiation were at a fever pitch.

By the seventies, microwave ovens were much smaller and more affordable—about $300 in 1976—and at some point, Julia and Paul invested in what she called "this NASA machine," a moniker recalled by her great-nephew Alex Prud'homme.[9] He continued:

"Julia was a fast-forward type of person and she didn't always take time to read instructions. I didn't witness this but in the early version of the microwave, [it was] an enormous machine. She put a frozen chicken, some green beans, and a piece of chocolate cake [inside], thinking that one [would] tap the buttons and it would miraculously cook everything. And, of course, the thing rattled, made all this noise, chocolate dripping out of the door. She opened it up—half frozen chicken, etc. [and said], 'Oh, I guess that didn't work!'"[10]

Famously, she also used the microwave oven to dry off a newspaper that had gotten wet in the rain, a mistake that set the unit afire.[11]

Later, Julia remarked that she had two freezers and used the microwave for defrosting and heating chicken stock, for melting butter, heating up milk or tea, and melting chocolate, but not for cooking a meal. Although many people touted the microwave for baking potatoes quickly, she preferred baking them in her oven. Like other cooks and consumers, Julia figured out how this new technology could enhance her cooking, not take it over.

The 1955 Tappan Electronic microwave oven, which included a drawer for recipe cards, in the collections of the National Museum of American History

FOCUS: SLOW COOKERS

"Cooks all day while the cook's away."

For many American home cooks, the Crock-Pot, introduced by the Rival Manufacturing Company in 1971, was a lifesaver. Electric slow cookers had been available since 1950, when the inventor Irving Naxon began manufacturing his Naxon Beanery in Chicago, ten years after receiving a patent for the device.[12] Naxon eventually sold his business to the Rival Manufacturing Company in Kansas City, and after some design alterations and fueled by a robust marketing campaign, the Rival model caught the attention of cooks looking for an easy way to prepare a home-cooked meal while they were busy elsewhere, including at paid employment outside of the home. The advertising tagline "Cooks all day while the cook's away" was an appealing idea for many women who had entered the workforce to pursue careers or to help provide financial support for their families.

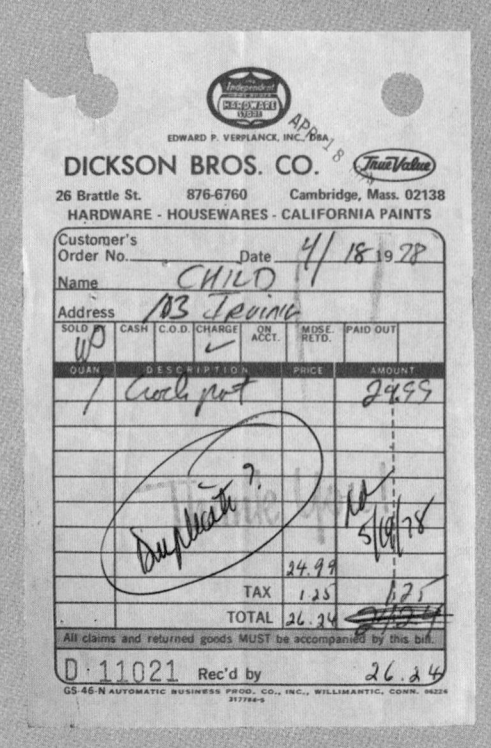

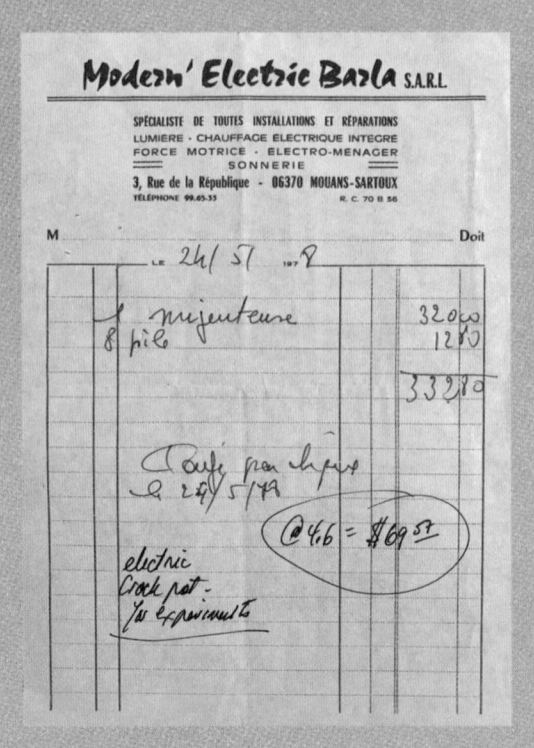

above: Two receipts for Crock-Pots that Julia purchased in 1978
opposite: A booklet of recipes and instructions accompanied the original Rival Crock-Pot.

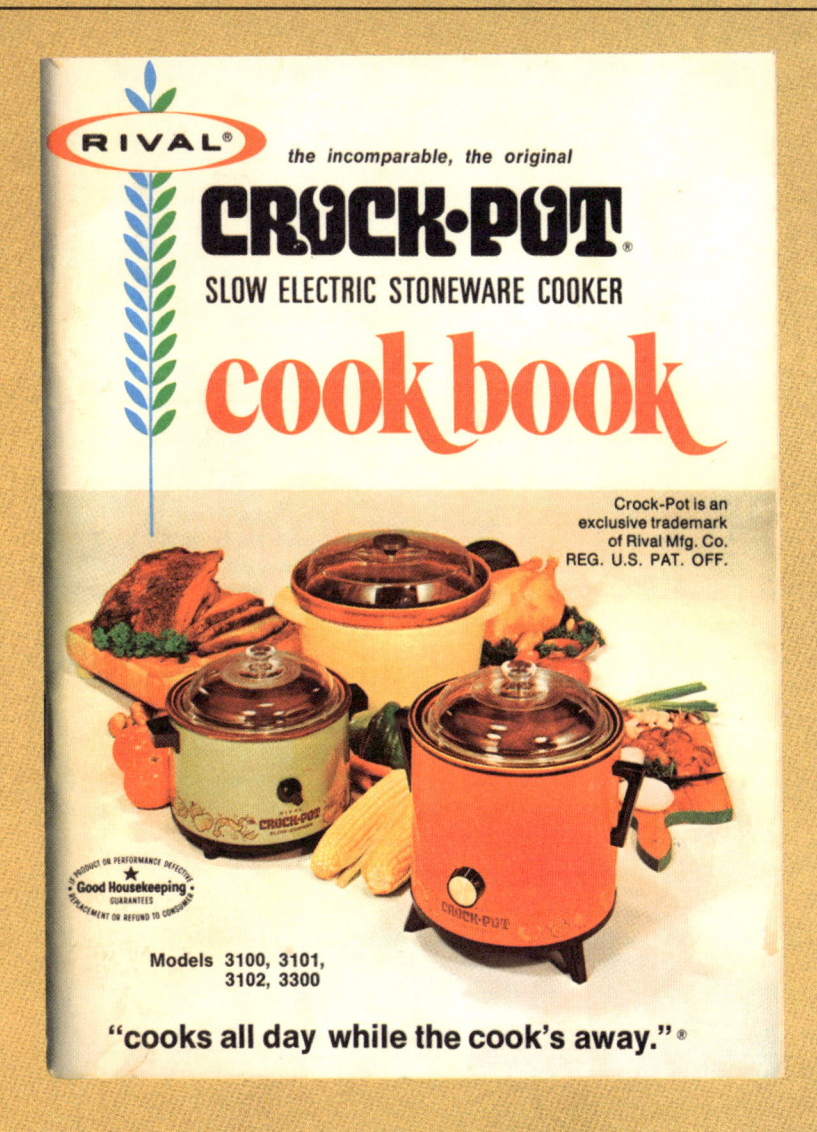

With Julia's penchant for new kitchen equipment, the question arises as to whether she was among those who tried the electric Crock-Pot in the seventies. A partial answer is found in the archives at the Schlesinger Library: In 1978, Julia purchased two slow cookers, one from Dickson Bros. Co., in Cambridge, and another from France, for her "experiments."[13]

Julia also wrote about cooking baked beans in an electric Crock-Pot in a chapter on potluck suppers in her 1979 book, *Julia Child & Company*. She noted that she had better results if she precooked the beans and sautéed the onions and pork before putting everything into the Crock-Pot to finish cooking slowly.[14]

French copper saucepans of various sizes from Julia's wall of copper and cast-iron cookware

RAISING THE BAR ON KITCHEN EQUIPMENT

The idea that home cooks could or should demand high-quality tools was not widely shared in the fifties and sixties. Manufacturers produced cookware that perhaps appealed in an aesthetic sense to homemakers but did not have the smart design, tough construction, or quality materials that professional chefs enjoyed. Julia voiced her dissatisfaction with the types of kitchen tools that were marketed to home cooks and made the case for improvements through her cookbooks and television shows, declaring that serious cooks deserved, for example, saucepans that were solid heat conductors and had handles that didn't fall off.[15] Was it too much to ask for manufacturers to design cookware that would help and not hinder the culinary efforts of cooks at home? Julia complained, "It is at times difficult to find even a decent frying pan," in department or hardware stores, "let alone a knife that will cut more than butter."[16] She was firm in her belief that cookware manufacturers should consult with cooks in designing kitchen equipment, and her kitchen reflects the increasing professionalization of the home kitchen—and, by extension, of women in the culinary field—in the second half of the twentieth century.

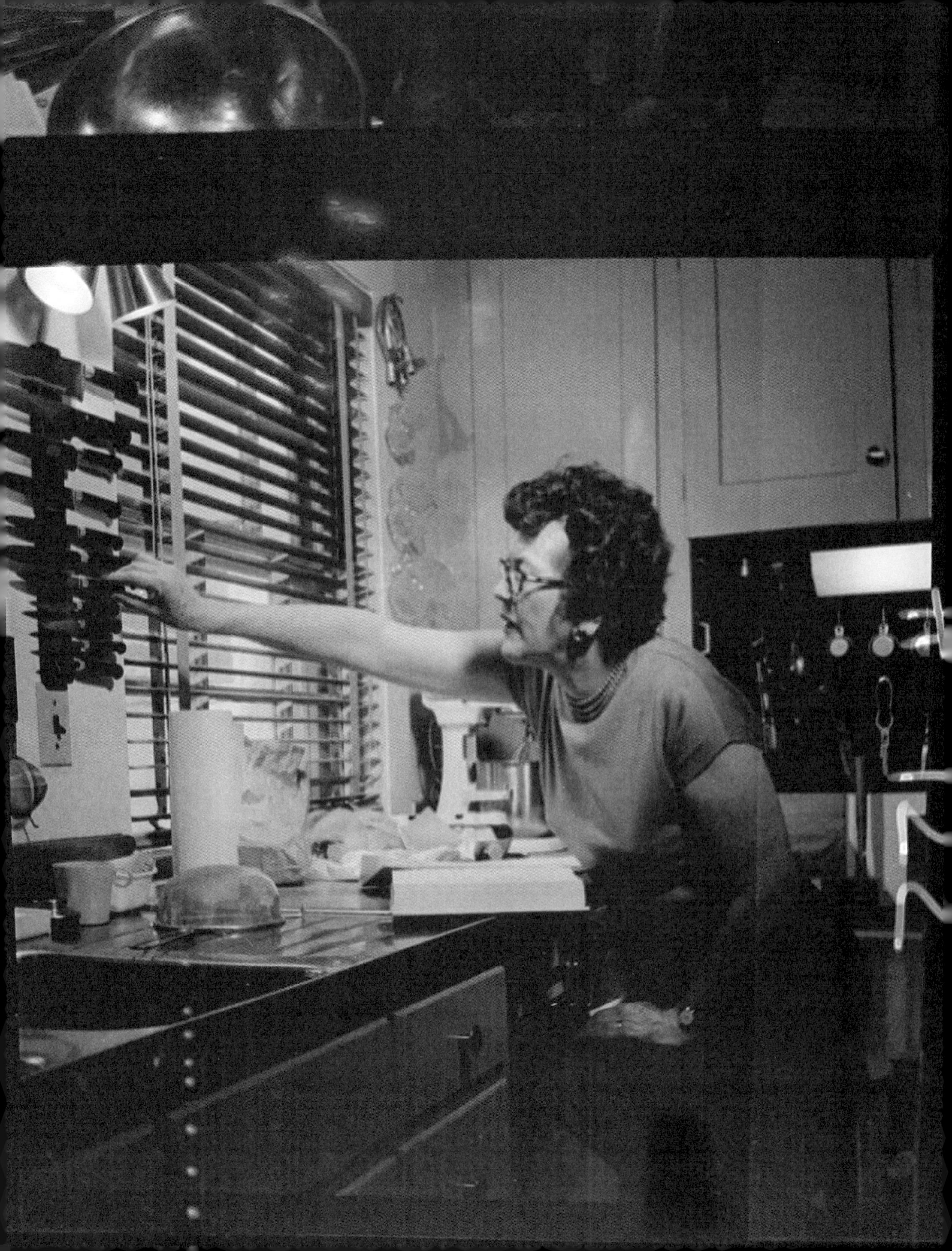

FOCUS: KNIVES

"It's essential that you get good knives."

Julia was often asked for tips about kitchen equipment, and over the years she offered basic advice through various media—print, television—and in personal appearances. She said, "It's essential that you get good knives" and consistently recommended that cooks "learn how to sharpen them and store them in a place where the blades won't be knocking together."[17] Julia's kitchen demonstrates exactly what she meant: Her good, professional knives are kept on magnetic holders mounted above the sink, where they were easy to access but out of the way of the heat and potential hubbub around the stove. Plus, they wouldn't bang around in drawers where they would get damaged and dull.

Julia called herself a "knife freak" and said she realized this about herself early on:

> As soon as I got over to France and found a really good knife and learned how to sharpen it, I realized what a different it makes in cooking to have a sharp knife. It's just very important because certainly if you're doing French cooking, which is always interesting to do because you do so much to the food, you've got to have good knives and you have to know how to use them.[18]
>
> If you're just beginning, I think these are the three essentials: a small paring knife, and a big chopping knife, and then the bread knife—you always need the serrated knife. And then this is a very good sharpener: This has diamond dust on it and it really works very well and you can feel it grip the knife.

Beyond the three essentials, she continued:

> And then I always like a "baby" [small] knife, which is very useful. And then I like this medium one, it's a little bit nicer for slicing tomatoes. But if you're a knife freak it's kind of fun to have. And then this long, serrated knife if you have beautiful pieces of roast beef to cut. And then if you have smoked salmon this one is a salmon slicing knife ... But the all-purpose shape like this is very important because you can do everything with it. And now this is rather fun, a very thin-bladed one. Every once in a while, you

Julia reaching for a knife in the series of photographs by Paul Child, "Julie in our kitchen at home," 1964

need something like that and I can't remember what, but it's kind of nice to have if you like knives. Then this one's a Japanese knife which I use for serving pie because you can cut it and then scoop it up and serve it out to people. This is kind of a serrated butcher's knife. I have that here because I like the look of it. I don't use it a great deal. And there's the grapefruit knife. You certainly always need one of those. And I guess a lot of these aren't essential, but they're fun to have.

I think it's very important with the knives once you have used it and washed it, you put it away, you don't put it with anything else because if you do somebody might cut themselves. But even worse the knives might bump against each other and it would crack, it would nick the blade. In other words, once you've used the knife, put it away.[19]

Julia used her own kitchen tools for live demonstrations and for her television programs as well, so it's no wonder that she kept purchasing knives as her work took her to various cities. Between February and July 1978, for example, she purchased knives at Sur La Table in Seattle (Henckels boning knife, tomato knife, and sharpener); Bridge Kitchenware in New York (four paring knives, a 6-inch Wüsthof cook's knife, a 5-inch Wüsthof cook's knife); Dickson Bros. in Cambridge (a butcher knife); and Jaeggi & Sons in London (a Sabatier knife and a Granton knife). As for her Ginsu knife, Julia explained, "I happened to be on a plane one day and I ran into a man who was a salesman for the Ginsu knife. And he gave me a bunch of them." It is breathtaking to think that Julia and the salesmen were handling knives on an airplane—a striking throwback to the pre-9/11-era when there were few security restrictions for carry-on items.[20]

JULIA CHILD'S KITCHEN

above: Receipt for knives and other kitchen utensils Julia purchased at Bridge Kitchenware, 1978. *right:* Receipt for knives and a sharpener Julia purchased at Sur La Table in Seattle, 1978

"EVERYBODY SHOULD LISTEN TO THE COOKS."

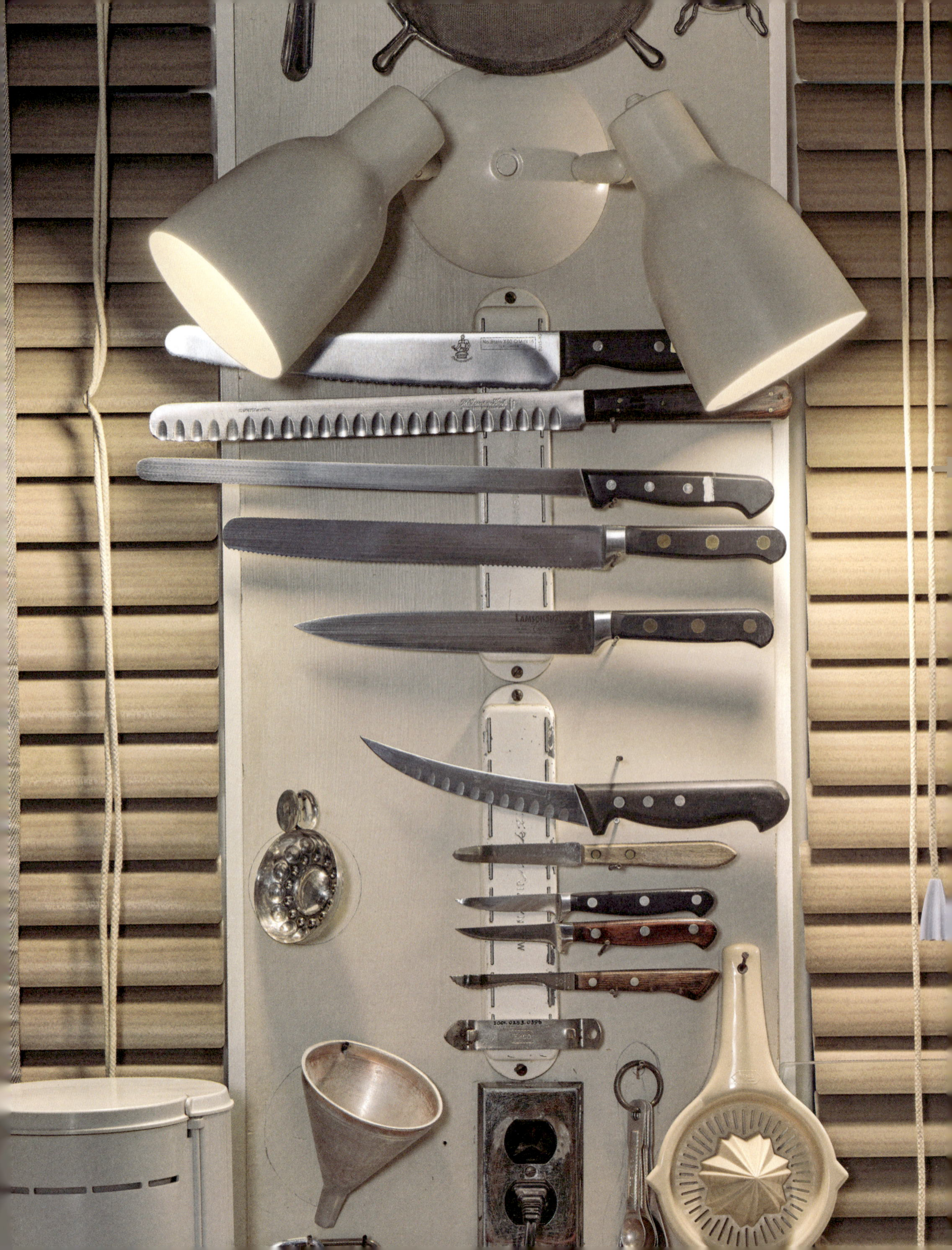

JULIA CHILD'S KITCHEN

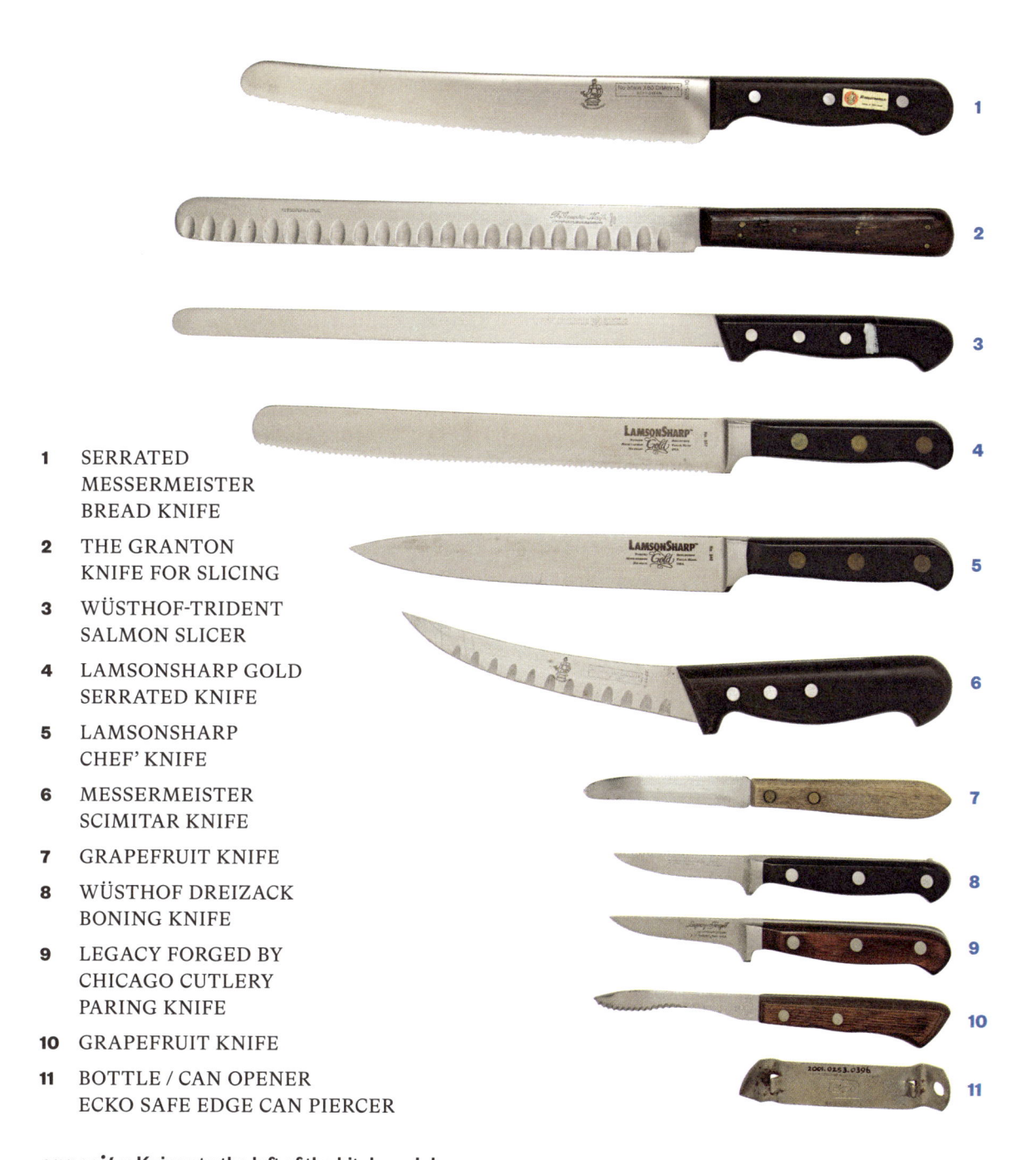

1. SERRATED MESSERMEISTER BREAD KNIFE
2. THE GRANTON KNIFE FOR SLICING
3. WÜSTHOF-TRIDENT SALMON SLICER
4. LAMSONSHARP GOLD SERRATED KNIFE
5. LAMSONSHARP CHEF' KNIFE
6. MESSERMEISTER SCIMITAR KNIFE
7. GRAPEFRUIT KNIFE
8. WÜSTHOF DREIZACK BONING KNIFE
9. LEGACY FORGED BY CHICAGO CUTLERY PARING KNIFE
10. GRAPEFRUIT KNIFE
11. BOTTLE / CAN OPENER ECKO SAFE EDGE CAN PIERCER

opposite: **Knives to the left of the kitchen sink**

"EVERYBODY SHOULD LISTEN TO THE COOKS." 129

JULIA CHILD'S KITCHEN

12 ALFRED ZANAGER COMPANY BREAD KNIFE

13 CHEF'S KNIFE, CUISINART COMMERCIAL CUTLERY **Made in France**

14 WÜSTHOF DREIZACK-WERK 8" CHEF'S KNIFE **Made in Solingen, Germany**

15 LAMSONSHARP 6-INCH CHEF'S KNIFE NO. 749 **Forged, hi carbon, no stain Made in USA**

16 CHEF'S KNIFE, WÜSTHOF DREIZACKWERK **Made in Solingern, Germany**

17 HOFFRITZ PARING KNIFE

18 LAMSONSHARP GOLD PARING KNIFE

19 LAMSONSHARP PARING KNIFE **Made in USA**

20 PETTY PARING KNIFE **Made in Japan**

21 WÜSTHOF DREIZACK-WERK PARING KNIFE

22 PARING KNIFE **Made in France**

Knives on the knife rack to the right of the kitchen sink

130 CHAPTER 4

DISPOSAL

1. REMOVE SINK STOPPER
2. RUN COLD WATER IN SINK
3. START MACHINE
4. PUSH FOOD IN GRADUALLY WITH BRUSH
5. DO NOT PACK OR JAM FOOD INTO HOLE

JULIA CHILD'S KITCHEN

23 FLAT SPATULA FOR PASTRY

24 SERRATED KNIFE

25 KNIFE WITH FORKED TIP Ginsu 2000

26 PARING KNIFE E. Dehillerin, Paris

27 CHICAGO PRO SCIMITAR KNIFE FOR CUTTING RAW MEAT

28 SABATIER SHELLFISH KNIFE Made in France

29 ERIK ANTON BERG ESKISTUNA SKINNING KNIFE Made in Sweden

30 SHARPENING STEEL

31 BREAD KNIFE

32 FILLET KNIFE Made in Sweden

33 GINSU SERRATED KNIFE

34 LARDING NEEDLE

35 F. DICKNIFE SHARPENING STEEL Made in Germany

36 MEAT POUNDER Rival Manufacturing Company

37 V...JAPANESE-STYLE KNIFE [DEBA-BOCHO] TO FILLET FISH (BRIDGE) Made in Japan

38 EZE-LAP KNIFE SHARPENING STEEL Made in Westminster, CA

132 CHAPTER 4

Julia stored more specialty knives and cutting tools in and around the butcher block table. Whether held in a slotted holder at the front or stuffed between the table and adjacent cabinetry, they were always at the ready.

FOCUS: FOOD PROCESSOR

"Ask Santa for a food processor."

Julia was tremendously interested in new technologies for the kitchen, perhaps none more so than the electric food processor. She was keen to try out the different models that were coming on the market. After a 1972 conversation with her friend James Beard, the American chef, cookbook author, and culinary expert who became a lifelong friend of Julia's at the time of *Mastering*'s publication, Julia wrote to a Mrs. Wilson at Robot-Coupe USA asking for literature on the new Robot-Coupe vertical cutter-mixer. Manufactured in France, the Robot-Coupe promised to cut raw meat, shred and slice vegetables, chop nuts, and perform various other tasks that were done by hand in home and commercial kitchens alike. Beard had already ordered a unit, and Julia was curious to know about the sizes, prices, and availability of the Robot-Coupe in the United States.[21]

She also corresponded with distributors of the Moulinex "Moulinette" electric chopper (a compact chopper and mincer) and ordered one through Fred Bridge's kitchenware store in New York.[22] By 1978, she counted some twenty-two different brands of food processor on the market and had tested about eight of them. She told a correspondent that she couldn't recommend any one model as she "wouldn't care to be stuck for the consequences!" She did, however, list the models she had used and found to be satisfactory: Cuisinart, Farberware, Norelco, Sunbeam, and Waring.[23]

Although she wouldn't declare her favorite brand, Julia did not downplay her exuberance over the technology. She advised readers of *McCall's* magazine that they should "ask Santa for a food processor." She declared:

"The food processor is the first revolutionary new kitchen dog-work machine to appear since the electric mixer and the blender, and while it does both mixing and blending, it also chops parsley and onions (which the blender does with difficulty)! It slices carrots, potatoes, cucumbers or what have you, it juliennes mushrooms and other items, grates cheese, grinds meat, purees fish, makes mayonnaise, pie crust doughs, and even cake batters. In fact, it is generally about the most useful machine a good cook—or even a semi-non-cook—can have in the kitchen since by taking so much of the time and drudgery out of many otherwise arduous operations it actually makes good cooking possible in a way it never was before."[24]

In explaining her embrace of the food processor, Julia compared the time it took to make a dish—fish mousse—using old and new technologies. In *From Julia Child's Kitchen*, her 1970 cookbook that was more personal and informal compared with her two "textbooks of classical French cuisine," *Mastering the Art of French Cooking*, she described the process of pureeing a fish fillet by pounding it in a mortar using a large wooden pestle, a process that took about thirty minutes, even with more than one cook taking turns at the task. Once sufficiently smooth, it was pounded for another twenty minutes with pâte à choux flour to form a paste, followed by more pounding as bits of egg were added. Only then, when the substance was fine and smooth, would the cooks turn out the puree into a sieve, or tamis, then forcefully rub it through the mesh with a special wooden pusher, also called a "champignon" or "sieving mushroom" because of its shape. This process took a great deal of time as the cooks had to stop to scrape the emerging mousse into the bowl. Enter the electric food processor, which managed to make in seconds what had taken hours to do by hand—a veritable miracle that delighted anyone faced with making terrines, mousses, pâtés, and quenelles, and other dishes of all sorts.[25]

Julia kept her food processor and blender on the top of the butcher block table.

"My mixing machine."

Julia's stand mixer occupies a prominent place on the counter near a window. She called it her "mixing machine" and noted that it had a heavy-duty motor and a bowl that was "just the right shape so that everything is in motion at once." She was a fan of the attachments and advised, "I think if you are going to buy a mixer, get a really good one. I think if you don't have the money, use the portable one and keep adding to your money until you have enough to buy this machine because it will last you the rest of your life."[26]

In Julia's kitchen, the big soapstone mortar and wooden pestle remain as reminders of the demanding process of making pâtés before the arrival of the electric food processor. Julia kept the mortar and pestle in her kitchen because they were so important to her early culinary work in Paris (and her beloved husband had carried them through the streets of the city from the flea market to their home on the top two floors of 81 rue de l'Université). She also referred to the mortar and pestle when teaching students about culinary techniques and technologies. Another tool essential to the process, a horsehair sieve, was stored in one of the pantries adjacent to the kitchen.[27] The food processor that Julia used at the end of her time in Cambridge was a KitchenAid model, which sits on the butcherblock table next to a blender amidst various cutting and pounding tools. The soapstone mortar and pestle sit on the floor beneath the table.

left: Julia's stand mixer on the countertop near a window.
opposite: Regal Ware ad, 1972

"Look for objects designed for real cooking."

In addition to knives, Julia recommended that home cooks invest in a variety of pots and pans, and to look for those designed for professional cooks. In a 1976 article, she recommended that cooks "look for objects designed for real cooking" and noted that "many of today's pots and pans are really useful only for defrosting frozen pouched vegetables or heating cans of soup. You want heavy frying pans with sides at least 2 inches high and long handles, so that you can stir, shake, and toss without worrying about things hopping out onto the stove. You want saucepans with sturdy handles, with heavy bottoms that spread the heat, and with sides designed for beating and whipping foods without slopping."[28]

Ads for pots and pans in the seventies were, indeed, geared toward homemakers who were attracted to the colorful, modern-looking cookware sets available in hardware and department stores. The cast-iron frying pans and enameled saucepans of the World War II generation were out—and the heavily advertised and affordable sets from companies such as Regal Ware, Wear-Ever, and West Bend—were in, in decorator colors. An ad for Regal Ware, based in Kewaskum, Wisconsin, reads: "Hey, American Woman. You like bold colors in your fashions, your car, your furniture, even your bathroom fixtures. Now how about doing something about those pots and pans?" It goes on to explain that "bold colors are in and cooking is fun with Regal Mardi Gras. So don't spoil the fun with a potpourri of plain old pots and pans."[29] At the same time, as nonstick cookware came on the market, Julia acquired several examples, including a Joyce Chen–branded Teflon-coated pan for cooktop frying. Julia found space for her nonstick pans among the cast-iron and aluminum skillets already hanging on the wall near the Garland.

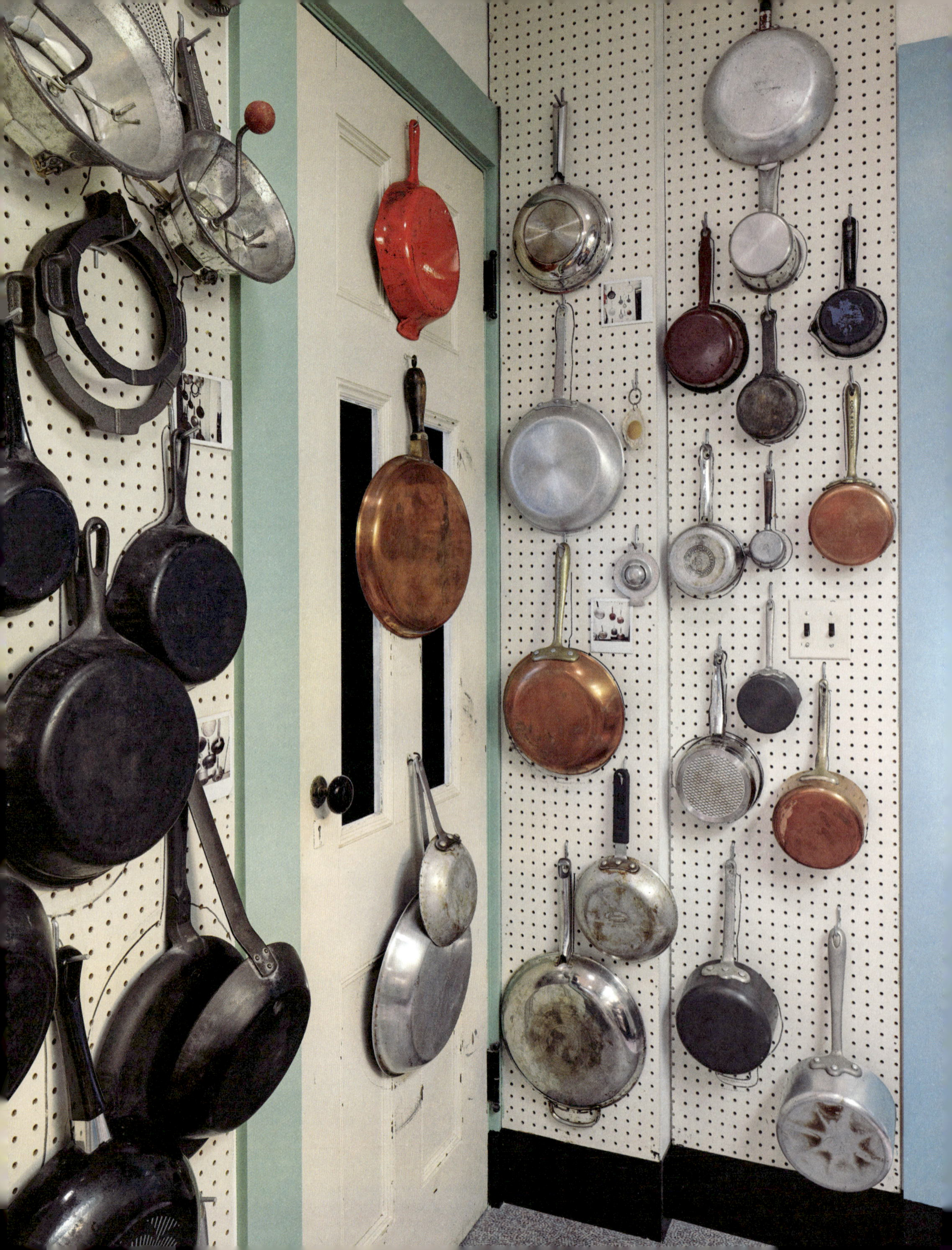

FOCUS: PANS FOR EVERY PURPOSE

Given Julia's remarkable and lifelong level of culinary activity, how does that specifically translate to the number and range of pots and pans in her home kitchen?

All told, there are some 135 pots and pans, including skillets, frying pans, straight-sided "sautoir" pans, sauté pans, crepe pans, gratin pans, baking sheets, fish pans, roasting pans, stock pots, soup kettles, saucepans, bread pans, muffin pans, and specialty cookware, stored in Julia's main kitchen. Julia fit the cookware, made of copper, cast iron, aluminum, and other materials like Calphalon, into spaces near where it would be used.

opposite: Pegboard-covered walls within reach of the Garland range hold the skillets, pans, and saucepans Julia used most often. The door opens a closet where she kept supplies and miscellaneous kitchen equipment. *left:* Julia's electric skillet

JULIA CHILD'S KITCHEN

CREPE PAN

SABAYON BOWL

MUFFIN PAN

CREPE PAN

CARAMEL-MAKING
SAUCEPAN

SAUTÉ PAN

FISH PAN

140 CHAPTER 4

JULIA CHILD'S KITCHEN

GRATIN PANS

RICE BALL COOKER

BUTTER WARMER

GRATIN PANS

GRATIN PAN

GRATIN PAN

GRATIN PANS

"EVERYBODY SHOULD LISTEN TO THE COOKS."

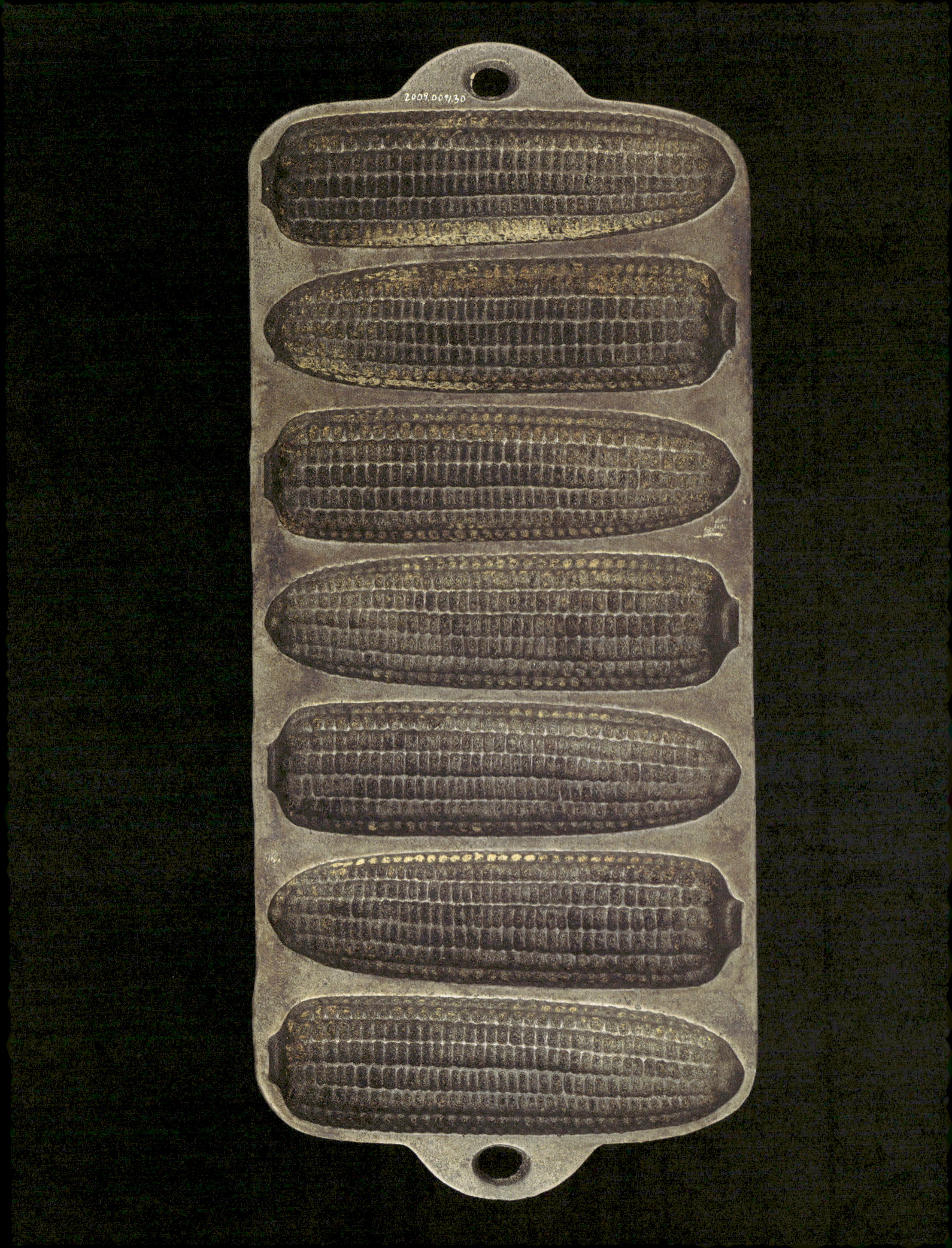
2009.009.130

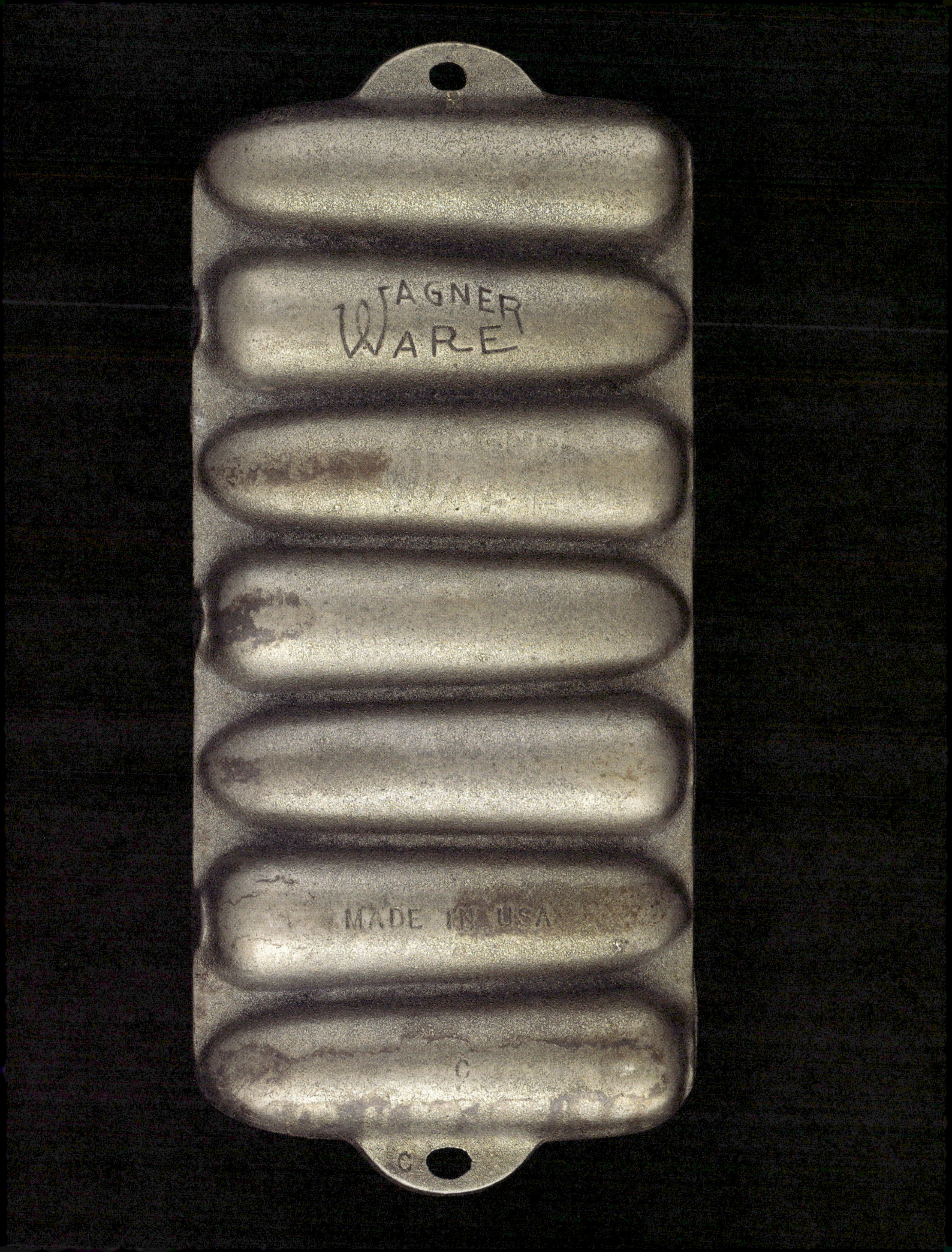
WAGNER
WARE
MADE IN USA
C
C

"GOOD ROLLING PINS ARE AWFULLY IMPORTANT."

Julia made her assessment of ordinary rolling pins sold to American consumers brutally clear. In an early episode of the *French Chef* television show, she held up a standard rolling pin and, in a dramatic flourish, tossed it to the side, calling it "a silly kind of a pin to have!"[30] The pin landed in the wastebasket, and Julia never bothered to retrieve it, as she found it utterly without merit. Instead, Julia encouraged her viewers to invest in heavier and longer pins that would help them roll out dough for pies and puff pastry. She found what she called the "Cheshire pin," because it was made in Cheshire, Connecticut, "perfect because it's heavy enough, it does half the work for you." A "typical French rolling pin" without handles was declared "nicer than most because it was [made of] olive wood." Another pin, tapered at the ends, found favor, as did the ribbed pin for making French puff pastry, because the edges break up the butter and smooth out the dough.[31]

Julia's statement about the importance of rolling pins was underscored by how she cared for and displayed them.[32] She stored her pins in a large copper stockpot, which was typically kept in the pastry pantry adjacent to the kitchen. The visual appeal of the gleaming pot holding Julia's impressive array of rolling pins and other long tools such as dowels, skewers, and long-handled forks, accounted for its movement onto countertops in the kitchen proper as a favorite backdrop for photography and television.

opposite, left to right: Thorpe Rolling Pin, Cheshire, Conn., which Julia described as "heavy enough to do half the work for you"[33] (27.9 inches long, including handles); Tutove, Rouleau Magique, is a cannelated pin designed to distribute the butter while rolling out croissant dough (25.9 inches long, including handles); wooden rolling pin with free-moving wooden handles and plastic spacers (12.5 inches long, not including handles); French-style pin without handles, made of olive wood (19 inches long); French-style wooden pin, slightly tapered and without handles (22 inches long). In *Baking with Julia*, by Dorie Greenspan, p. 21: "The French pin gives you good control over the dough and, because it's handleless, can be used for kitchen chores like butter bashing (a technique for softening butter)."

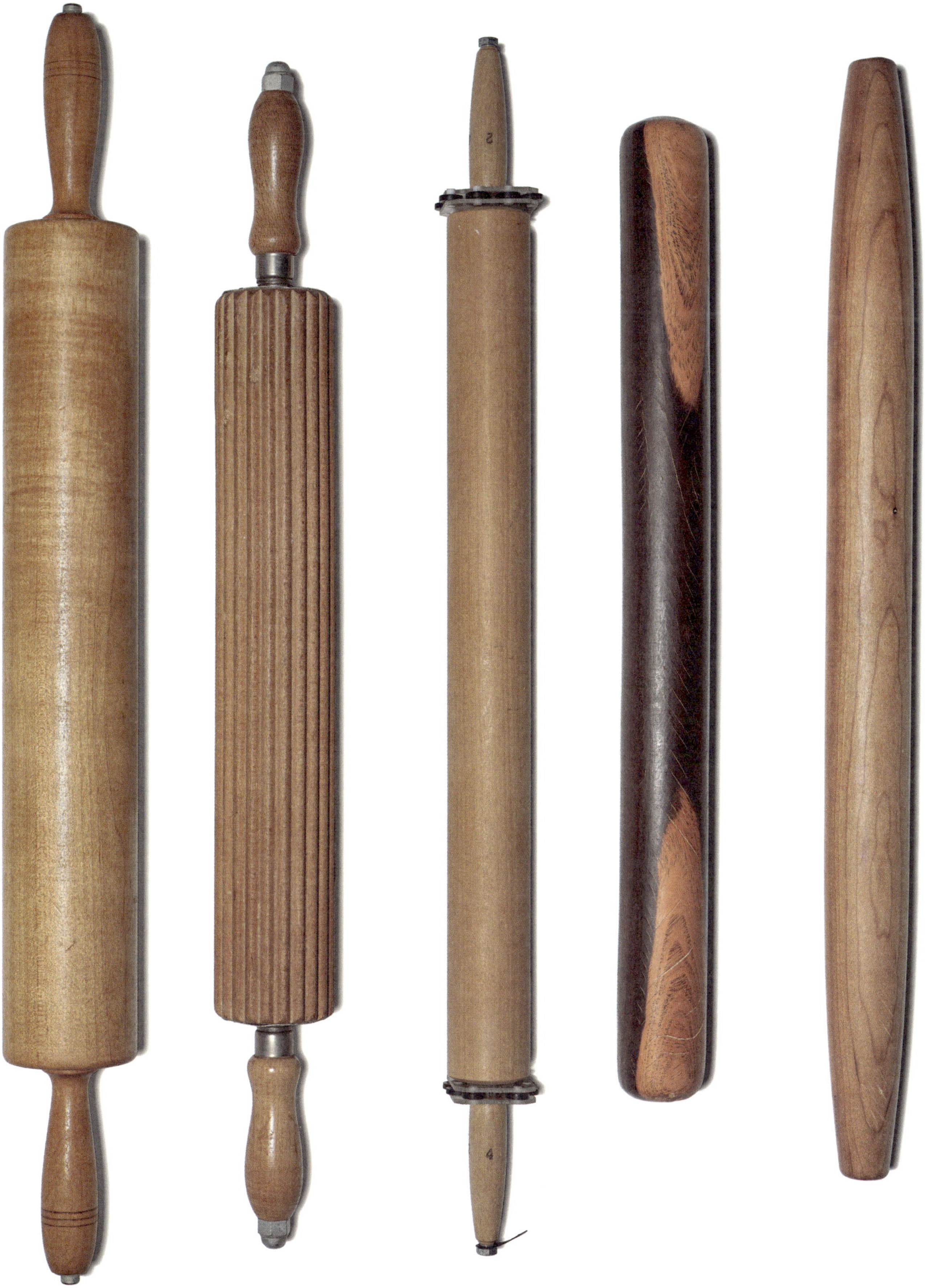

Julia stored these pastry sticks for turning lefse (Norwegian flatbread traditionally made with riced potatoes), an 18-inch ruler, an acrylic rolling pin, and a dowel in her big copper stock pot with her rolling pins.

Copper stock pot that held rolling pins and other long tools for baking

"MY TRUSTY MALLET."

In 1975, Julia went on tour for her new book, *From Julia Child's Kitchen*, a volume that provided cooks possessing different levels of experience with what they needed: a basic recipe and more complex variations. By this time, Julia was a well-known and much-beloved personality and drew hundreds of fans to her book signings and cooking demonstrations. Described in the press as "joyous, jolly, and exuberant" and as the "Girl Scout leader of gourmet cooking," Julia reinforced her message that cooking was not drudgery, but creative, joyful, and necessary. Her demonstrations in 1975 included money-saving tips, such as how to cut up a whole chicken and use every part. She told her audience in Stamford, Connecticut, "It costs to buy it cut up. Why should you pay for someone else's work when, if you know how to do it, you can save all that money for yourself?"[34]

For such book tours, Julia packed up some of her key tools from home and with help from Paul and various assistants, arrived at restaurants and department stores to "cook while talking."[35] One sturdy tool that got a workout on the 1975 tour was her "trusty mallet," a wood-handled rubber mallet she used to pound chicken breasts between pieces of wax paper to render them paper-thin. Cooks learned that this technique for flattening chicken breasts could be used for various recipes, and if they didn't have a trusty rubber mallet, they could use "a pestle, a rolling pin, a plumber's hammer, or the side of a bottle."[36]

BUFFALO IRON

Julia learned how to cook green beans without losing their vibrant color from Chef Max Bugnard, her French instructor at Le Cordon Bleu. While working aboard transatlantic steamships as a young man, he observed a chef dropping green beans into a huge cauldron of boiling water, then plunging a red-hot poker into the water to return the boil quickly. The rest of the process adhered to the classical method of blanching the beans by cooking them for two to three minutes and then immersing them in an ice bath. Julia mentioned this to Sherman Kent (the friend who had sold her the six-burner Garland range and whom she called "Old Buffalo"), and he made her the iron that she named after him.[37] The buffalo iron hangs from the hood of the range.

Julia's longtime friend and Oklahoma chef John Bennett told the story of making dinner for Julia and Paul in their Cambridge kitchen in 1962, explaining how the buffalo iron was used in creating a memorable meal using Julia's recipes. He also revealed the unfettered enthusiasm that young chefs brought to an opportunity to cook in Julia's kitchen, just when she was gaining prominence among culinary professionals. Bennett began his training in 1961 at the Culinary Institute of America, which was then located in New Haven, Connecticut. He took a job at the Mermaid Tavern in Stratford, some twenty-five miles away, where he met James Beard. On the spur of the moment, he invited Beard to speak to his classmates at the CIA and Beard arrived with two guests—Paul and Julia Child. Bennett and his friend Robert Dickson managed to score an invitation from Julia to visit her in Cambridge, and within a few weeks they arrived ready to cook from Julia's new book, *Mastering the Art of French Cooking*.[38]

> We made spinach with a buffalo iron, a large heavy piece of iron heated red-hot that's plunged into the spinach water to bring it back to a roaring boil to keep the spinach green. We then cooled the spinach, squeezed it dry, chopped it, then tossed it with shallots, garlic, and nutmeg in lots of brown butter.
>
> We prepared strip sirloin in a well-seasoned black cast-iron skillet, Diane style, accompanied by Gratin Dauphinoise potatoes...
>
> From the book [*Mastering the Art of French Cooking*, Volume One], we made Charlotte Malakoff with strawberries, homemade ladyfingers, almonds, and lots of butter generously flavored with Grand Marnier, molded and chilled to be served with a fresh strawberry sauce.[39]

One of two buffalo irons in Julia's kitchen

Paul Child wrote of the guest chefs:

MONDAY, JUN 5, 1962, TO CHARLES:

OUR TWO YOUNG CHEFS FROM THE NEW HAVEN SCHOOL SPENT THE PAST WEEK-END WITH US. THEY & JULIE WERE LIKE FABULOUS JINNS IN THE KITCHEN: SPEWING OUT LOBSTER THERMIDOR, DANISH PASTRY, SALADES COMPOSÉES, CHARLOTTE MALAKOFF, QUICHES AU ROQUEFORT, CREPES A L'ORANGE FANCIES, ETC. ETC. EAGER GUESTS DROOLING SLIGHTLY IN ANTICIPATION, POURED IN AND OUT FOR 3 DAYS, AND THE PLACE SMELLED LIKE HEAVEN ITSELF.[40]

WHISKS: "YOU SHOULD HAVE SEVERAL SIZES."

Julia was a devoted user of wire whisks for beating eggs and general mixing. For eggs she advised, "the idea is to have the largest whisk and smallest bowl—it gets the egg whites in motion at once." [41] Julia found whisks easier to use than the rotary eggbeaters that were familiar to most American home cooks because they did not require the use of both hands. She collected different sizes and shapes of whisks and popularized them in the United States through her cookbooks, television shows, and live cooking demonstrations.

She recommended that cooks have several sizes[42] and certainly practiced what she preached. Her kitchen contains thirteen wire whisks; they hang on pegboard adjacent to the Garland range or are kept in ceramic crocks above the stovetop.

right: Whisk just to the left of the Garland range *opposite:* Julia's stock pot filled with baking tools

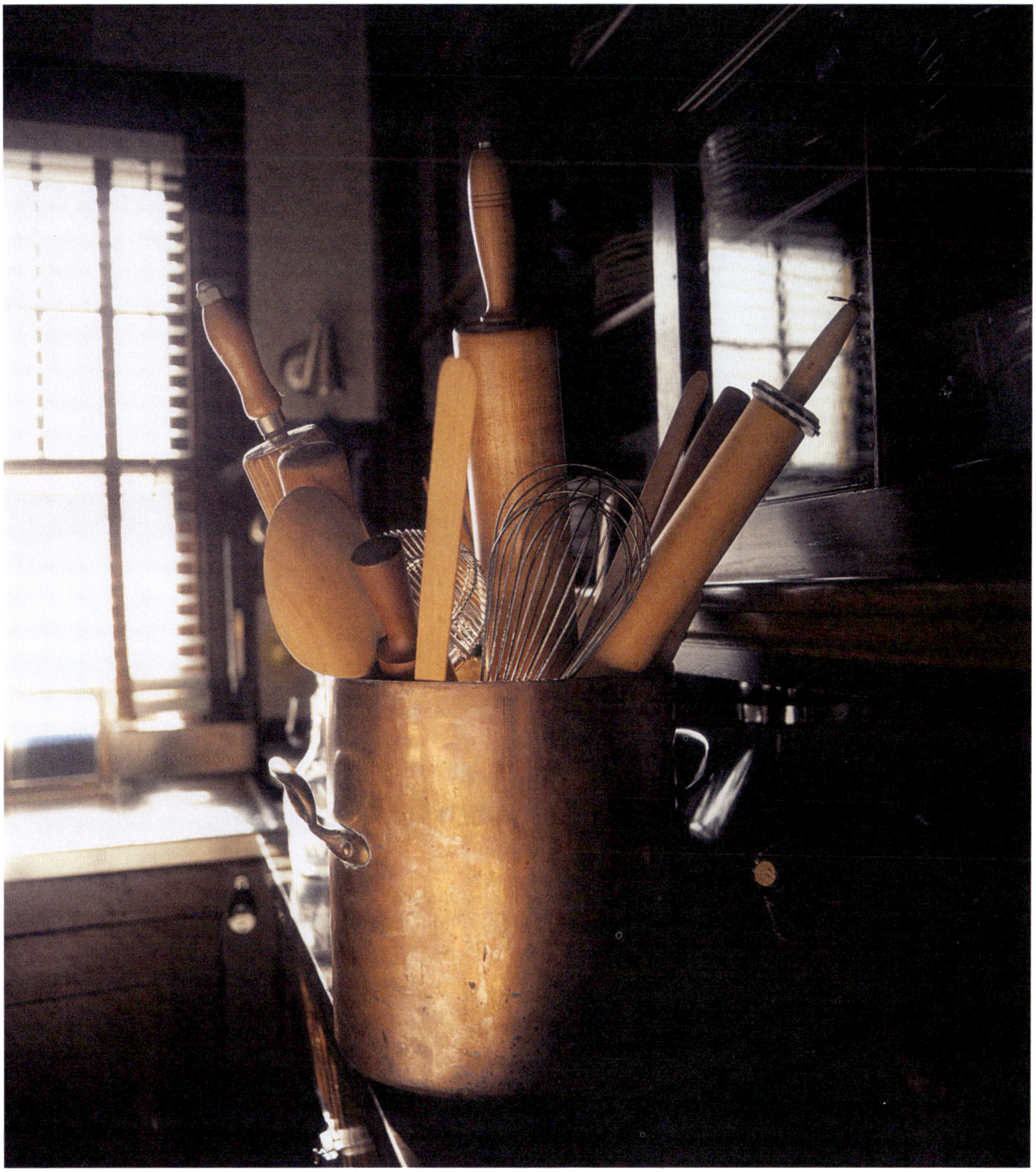

FOCUS: PROPS IN THE KITCHEN

Julia, the teacher and performer, sometimes used kitchen objects as props for comic effect on her television shows. For episodes involving fish, she frequently called on her friend George Berkowitz, founder of Legal Sea Foods, to "get me some funny fish" that would make an impact on TV. Not only did he provide her with fish, but he also showed her how to butcher unfamiliar species. Her shows on preparing swordfish and monkfish reflect that relationship as she wielded her so-called fright knife to focus attention on the task at hand.

Referring to what she called her "memorial cleaver" on another episode, she noted, "In TV you want to do things loud." Acknowledging Chef Emeril Lagasse's penchant for dramatic sound effects, she continued, "People love that, whamming noises, as we know."[43]

In another memorable program, Julia opened an umbrella and donned a yellow slicker when demonstrating the new salad spinner, a device made popular in the seventies to wash lettuce greens and spin them dry.

And she tapped one by one a lineup of whole, raw chickens—that she dubbed "the chicken sisters"—with the tip of a knife in a gesture similar to bestowing honor, to emphasize the difference between "Miss Broiler, Miss Fryer, Miss Roaster, Miss Caponette, Miss Stewer, and Old Madam Hen."

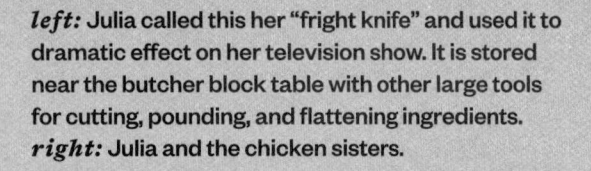

left: Julia called this her "fright knife" and used it to dramatic effect on her television show. It is stored near the butcher block table with other large tools for cutting, pounding, and flattening ingredients.
right: Julia and the chicken sisters.

JULIA CHILD'S KITCHEN

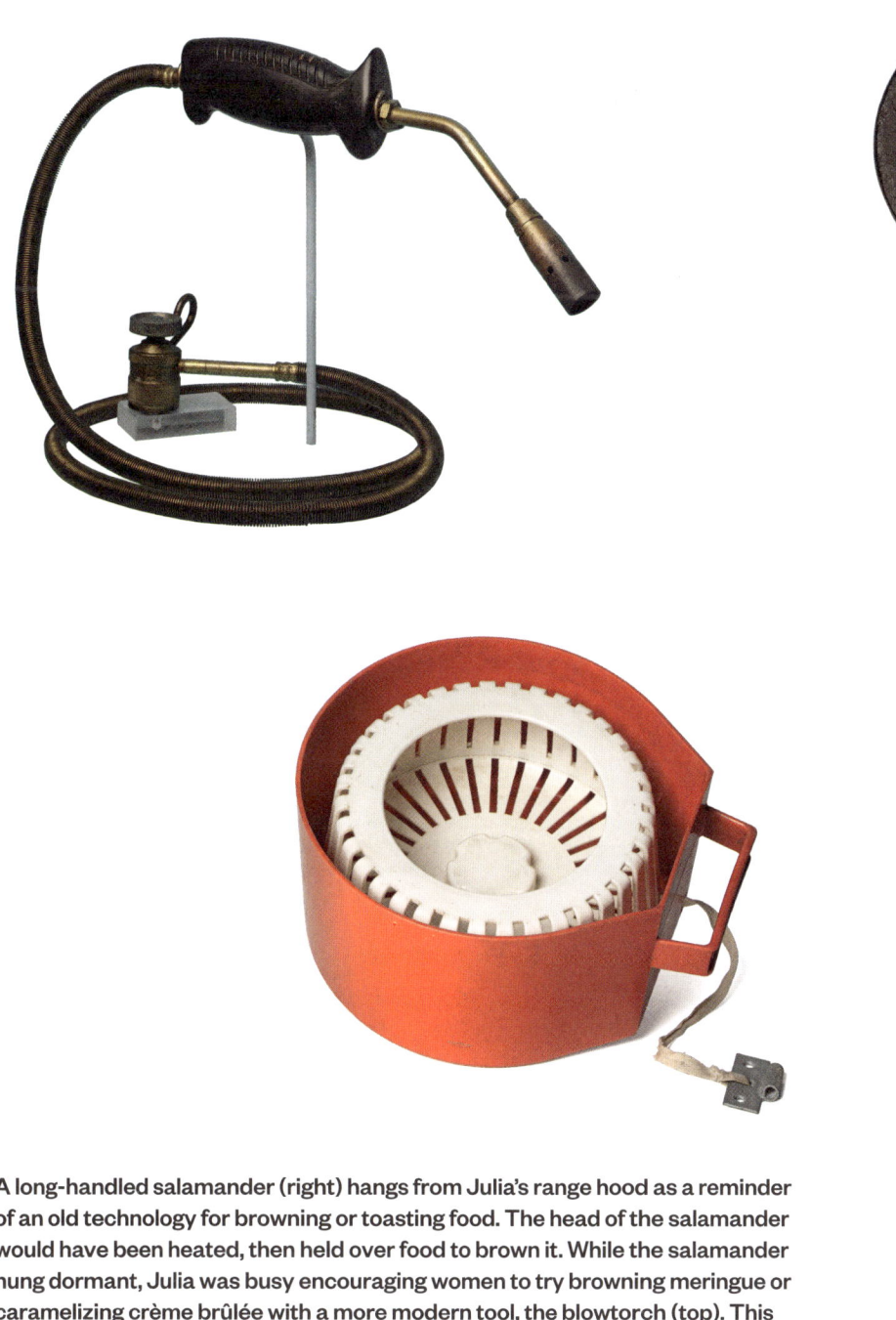

A long-handled salamander (right) hangs from Julia's range hood as a reminder of an old technology for browning or toasting food. The head of the salamander would have been heated, then held over food to brown it. While the salamander hung dormant, Julia was busy encouraging women to try browning meringue or caramelizing crème brûlée with a more modern tool, the blowtorch (top). This blowtorch was made by the Bernzomatic Corporation in Germany, and Julia used it with a separate fuel canister that was not collected by the museum. Smaller, specialized cooks' blowtorches are widely available now and do not require separate fuel tanks. Julia's red salad spinner (above) has a hinge at the end of the pull, presumably to provide a sturdy grip.

"EVERYBODY SHOULD LISTEN TO THE COOKS." 153

"I've always been a gadget freak

and some things are just *wonderful!*"

JULIA CHILD'S KITCHEN

FOCUS: GADGETS

"I've always been a gadget freak and some things are just wonderful!"

When Julia made this confession,[44] she was referring to an array of hand tools designed for specific tasks. She kept most of these gadgets in drawers that were easily accessible to work surfaces such as the countertops, the Garland range, and the kitchen table. Julia collected different designs of certain gadget categories, such as knives for opening shellfish, and acquired many others in the spirit of experimentation. She also received gifts of gadgets, some of them homemade, from friends and admirers alike. A full four drawers in the kitchen contained gadgets to cut, shape, open, clean, pull, and grab—all necessary in kitchen work.

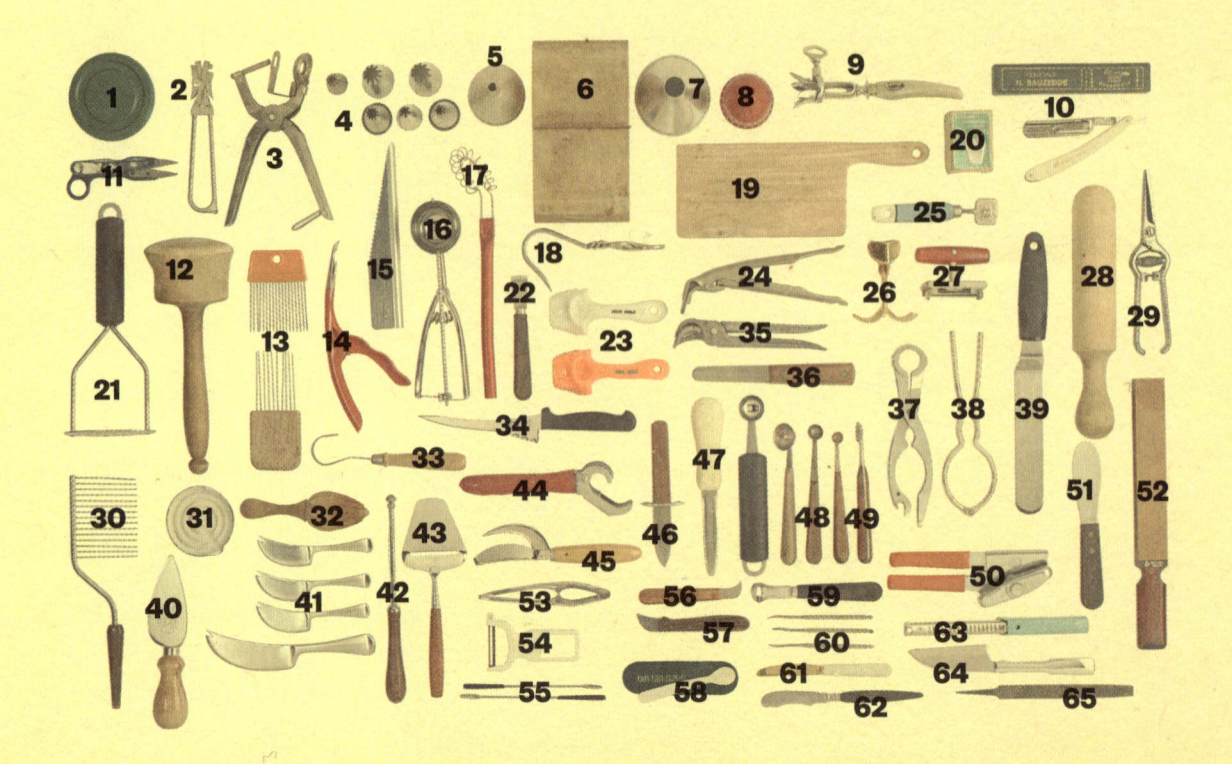

#	Item	#	Item	#	Item
1	LID FOR CONTAINER	21	MASHER	43	CHEESE PLANE
2	KNIFE SHARPENER	22	ZESTER	44	JAR OPENER
3	CHERRY PITTER	23	FISH SCALERS	45	SHELLFISH OPENER
4	PASTRY TIPS	24	POT GRABBER	46	OYSTER KNIFE
5	FUNNEL	25	ZESTER	47	OYSTER KNIFE
6	SCRAPER	26	HINGED GRIPPER	48	MELON BALLER
7	FUNNEL	27	JAR OPENER	49	GARNISH TOOL
8	FUNNEL	28	POUNDER	50	CAN OPENER
9	MANCHE A GIGOT LAMB BONE HOLDER	29	SHEARS	51	SPREADER
10	RAZOR AND BOX	30	CAKE BREAKER	52	RAZOR SHARPENER
11	SNIPPERS	31	BOIL CONTROL DISK	53	LOBSTER CRACKER
12	SIEVE PUSHER / CHAMPIGNON	32	CITRUS JUICER	54	VEGETABLE PEELER
13	PASTRY DECORATING TOOLS	33	BUTTER CURLER	55	MARROW SCOOPS
14	SHRIMP DEVEINER	34	SHRIMP KNIFE	56	CHESTNUT KNIFE
15	SHRIMP SHELLER	35	POT GRABBER	57	CHESTNUT KNIFE
16	ICE CREAM SCOOP	36	KNIFE SPREADER	58	CAVIAR SPOON
17	WHISK	37	JAR OPENER	59	ZESTER
18	MEAT HOOK	38	JAR OPENER	60	NUT PICKS
19	SPREADER	39	SPATULA	61	SPREADING KNIFE
20	CHAMPAGNE STOPPER IN BOX	40	PARMIGIANO REGGIANO CHEESE KNIFE	62	SPREADING KNIFE
		41	CHEESE KNIVES	63	JAR OPENER
		42	CHEESE SLICER	64	CHEESE KNIFE
				65	FILE

FOCUS: ARTFUL ANIMALS IN THE KITCHEN

Paul Child's first photographs of the kitchen after the renovation show the basic floor plan and equipment layout, but to the eyes of anyone who has seen Julia's kitchen on television or at the National Museum of American History, the images seem eerily stark and empty. The now familiar layers of cookware and evidence of an active culinary life are clearly missing, as are the objects of art and items of whimsy that have caught our attention over many years. Julia was like the rest of us—she wanted to be surrounded by things that made her happy, and from what we can tell by exploring the kitchen (and reading her writings), Julia adored cats. And chickens. And the occasional fish. A roundup of Julia's animal companions includes:

top: This ceramic fish is mounted above the doorway connecting the kitchen and the food pantry.
bottom: Refrigerator magnets

158 CHAPTER 4

Ginger cat cutout on wood

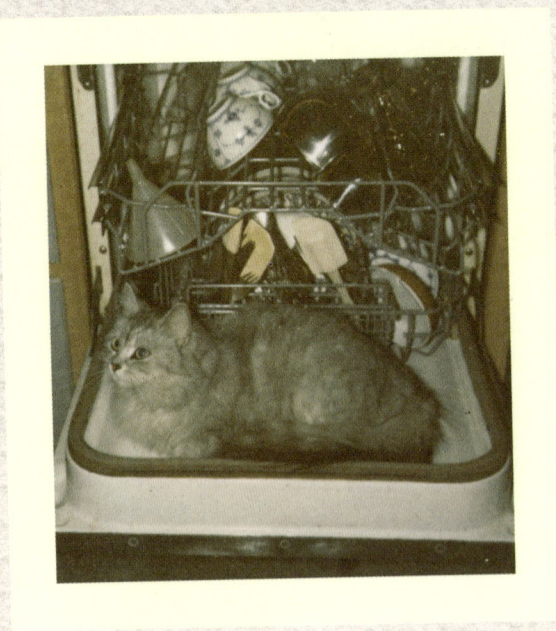

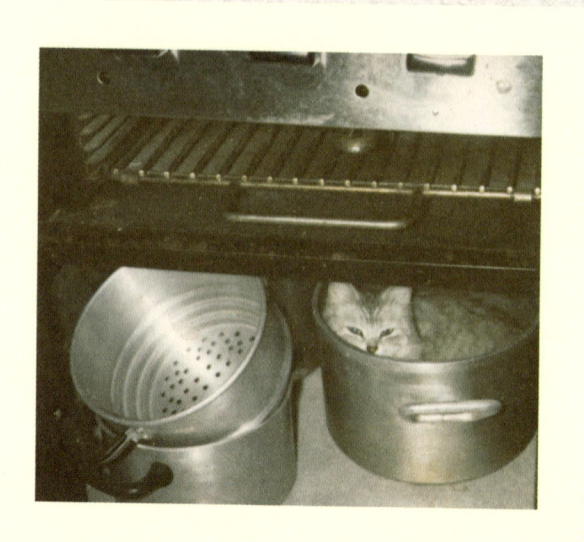

Julia's real cats making themselves at home on the dishwasher door and inside a stock pot in the kitchen

Painting by Julia's friend
Rosemary Manell

FOCUS: BLUEFISH AND ROCK COD PRINTS

Above the doorway connecting Julia's kitchen and the pastry pantry hangs a large print of a fish. Measuring 40 × 12 inches, the print is made of paper, ink, and wood. Julia's longtime friend Pat Pratt explained the story of the print, which confirms that Julia was a friend, ever-curious cook, and intrepid angler:

"I made the print of the bluefish on the day when Julia caught it off our Herreshoff 12½ foot sailboat while sailing in Saco Bay near Prouts Neck [Maine]. Julia and I were with my husband, Herbert Pratt, at the tiller. It was the morning of August 31, 1975. Julia and I were fishing for mackerel with the usual small-hooked, multicolored mackerel rigs, holding the lines by hand over the sides of the gunwales. Suddenly Julia yelped that she had a huge bite. With considerable pulling, she got what we thought would be multiple mackerel wiggling on the line. Instead, to our amazement, it was a big fish. When we got it into the cockpit and onto the deck, we realized it was a bluefish—the first one we had ever caught, or seen, in Maine. We were all astounded.

"Julia said with glee that she had been eager to cook a whole fish in a new way. We went ashore and showed it to Paul. I had been making fish prints in the Japanese manner that summer, using my regular Winsor and Newton watercolors, so I had all the equipment to make one [fish print] of the bluefish. I cleaned and dried the exterior of the fish and laid it on a flat surface. I covered it with Payne's Grey [paint color] using my 2-inch flat brush. Then I placed a sheet of rice paper over the fish and carefully rubbed it to get all the details of the fish, including the fins and tail. I carefully lifted the paper off to have a nice clean image of the fish.

"Our dining room table was made of Cypress wood and through the years of being scrubbed it had a nice, raised grain. Paul said, 'Why not make the fish look as though it

Bluefish print by Pat Pratt, 1975

were in water by making a rubbing of the grain in greens and blues with wax crayons?' We placed the dried print on top of the table and with a whole Caran d'Ache crayon, stripped of its paper wrapping, we lightly rubbed over the print. 'Voila!' said Julia, 'It looks alive.'

"While Julia and I prepared the fish in her new way, Paul and Herbert set the table and chose the white wine for lunch. The new way was: place the cleaned but not scaled fish on a baking sheet. Oil the fish. Bake in a 400-degree oven for about 20–25 minutes. Skin the fish and place the cooked fish on a platter to serve.

"Licking our chops in delightful anticipation, we sat at the table with a wide view of the sea from which the fish came. Julia served our plates and just before taking the first bite, we raised our glasses in joy. We all took our first bite and, to our horror and dismay, the fish was tough as leather. It was basically inedible! We were utterly disappointed, as we had thought what perfection it would be to have a spanking fresh fish. We had no idea what was wrong.

"At eight o'clock one morning ten years later, Julia called me. 'Pat, Pat,' she said, 'I just found out why our bluefish was so tough. I've just been talking to John, in Seattle, who deals with all sorts of fish big time at the fish pier ... He said it is very important that fish be out of rigor mortis when you cook it, otherwise it will be 'tough as leather,' it may be a matter of days for big fish like salmon and tuna.' Julia was a bird dog in always wanting to find answers to questions and problems. This time, it took ten years!"

If Julia and Pat had put the fish back on ice and waited a few hours, it would have passed through rigor, at which point the muscles would have softened again and the fish would have been edible when cooked.[45]

A second fish print hangs above the refrigerator and is partially obscured by a menagerie of wooden cats, chickens, and kitchenware. At 25.5 × 17.7 inches, this print is signed by Paul Child. While we do not know the exact date for Paul's fish print, we know that he used the same techniques described by Pat Pratt. She speculates that Paul made the wavy water by hand "as he was not near our dining room table for the raised grain."[46]

"A REVELATION TO COOK IN JULIA'S KITCHEN."

Beginning in 1965 and lasting into the eighties, Julia and Paul typically spent the months between May and October, and sometimes longer, traveling or at their second home, La Pitchoune in Provence. While away from Cambridge, they relied on house sitters to mind the property, and with Irving Street's proximity to Harvard University, they were assured a steady supply of candidates for the job. Interviewing for the position gave prospective sitters a glimpse into the Childs' relationship and the way their lives revolved around the kitchen and food.

In 1980, Sherrod Reynolds and her soon-to-be husband, Alan Sturrock, had just completed their graduate work at Harvard when another couple recommended them for the house-sitting position. They were vetted by a trusted intermediary before receiving an invitation from Julia for an interview over lunch at the residence.

Sherrod's expectations for lunch were only that they would be "wowed," and Julia didn't disappoint. As they entered the kitchen at the appointed hour, they found Julia standing at the stove. Sherrod recalled, "We sat at her table in the kitchen while she cooked one single perfect burger in a sauté pan. She managed to make hamburger into something else altogether. Seeing her flip it with a twist of her wrist and bathe it in red wine was a teachable moment right there." To serve, Julia cut the burger into wedges and plated it with a side of corn chips. During lunch Paul regaled them with stories about the kitchen, taking great pleasure in pointing out the details of the design.

The Childs spent longer than usual staying abroad or traveling, and the young couple got to live in the house for most of a year. With Julia's encouragement, they made themselves at home, playing the piano, browsing the bookshelves, and, of course, using the kitchen. The countertops that suited Julia's six-foot, three-inch frame were definitely too tall for Sherrod, who, at five feet, one inch, had to make do.

Years later, Sherrod wrote that it was a "revelation" to cook in Julia's kitchen. Just by finding her way around the room, she learned how to set up a kitchen and to cook. Awed by the fact that Julia had multiples of every possible thing you could need or want, Sherrod also availed herself of Julia's library upstairs, which contained cookbooks and recipes for an astonishing array of world cuisines.

She recalled that the area for making bread and working pastry dough had a marble surface to prevent overheating of the dough, and that all the measuring cups and spoons were right at hand. The idea of having more than one set of measuring spoons was "mind-blowing." And the area for vegetable preparation was near the sink, with the knives on magnets just above the sink. "I learned so much about how to organize a kitchen from cooking there. It was a fabulous opportunity."

What's more, she experienced the phenomenon of Julia receiving all kinds of calls from random people because her phone number was listed in the Cambridge directory. Sherrod took calls from people badly in need of advice, including one tearful woman who was cooking a lobster and was terrified by the creature banging around in the pot. Another caller, frustrated while trying to cook potato baskets, rang to ask how to prevent them from falling apart.[47] Had she been there, Julia would certainly have walked the callers through the culinary crises. Other calls and correspondence also came in, including some that were critical of Julia's support for Planned Parenthood. These inquiries were handled by Julia's assistant but made an impression on Sherrod about how being a principled, outspoken celebrity on a divisive issue like abortion rights left Julia and her home sanctuary vulnerable to angry communications and voices on the other end of the line.[48]

opposite: A set of ceramic measuring cups in Julia's kitchen. *right:* Julia kept her thermometers and basting brushes all together in a crock.

Julia

CHAPTER 5

"Welcome to my house and to my kitchen."

previous spread: One of Julia's aprons *left:* Julia's kitchen in 1993 at the time of filming *In Julia's Kitchen with Master Chefs* *opposite:* Julia during filming of the show

When Julia Child turned eighty on August 15, 1992, she wasn't thinking about retiring. Instead, she was considering another go at cooking on TV, this time with a new producer, Geoffrey Drummond, who cofounded A La Carte Communications with producer Natan Katzman in 1990. Drummond had cut his cooking-show teeth on *New York's Master Chefs*, a 1985 documentary series for PBS that featured thirteen chefs who represented many of New York's finest restaurants.[1] The lineup was impressive: Lidia Bastianich (Felidia), Seppi Renggli (the Four Seasons), Stanley Kramer (Grand Central Oyster Bar), Larry Forgione (An American Place), André Soltner (Lutèce), and others. Although the series was nominated for an Emmy, it came up short for an award. According to Drummond the consensus was that the program was sorely in need of a host.[2]

Drummond worked on other projects while searching for the perfect cooking show host. When his neighbor Jacques Pépin suggested Julia Child, Drummond hesitated and asked, "Isn't she retired?" Setting the record straight, Jacques pointed out that Julia was still teaching and would likely embrace the opportunity to connect with the next generation of chefs. Jacques knew his friend Julia very well, indeed, and when Drummond reached out to her, she enthusiastically responded that she was curious to learn more about what Drummond had referred to as "Masterpiece Cooking." Likening the program he had in mind to PBS's *Masterpiece Theatre*, famously hosted by Alistair Cook, Julia quipped, "Oh, then I could be the Alistair Cookie of *Masterpiece Cooking*!" Although it was a fine idea, Julia would never have fit the mold of erudite host broadcasting from a comfy chair and far removed from the action. As Julia had described herself decades earlier, she was like a sheepdog, wanting to be in the middle of everything, including cooking with guest chefs.[3]

Drummond's introduction to Julia took place at a Boston University event and was facilitated by Jacques and Rebecca Alssid, Julia's cofounders of the Culinary Arts Certificate program at the university. Keen to learn more, Julia invited Drummond to 103 Irving Street, suggesting he arrive around 8:30 the following morning. Arriving right on time, he noted the "wonderful, professorial" presence of the house as he rang the bell at the back door. Julia, still upstairs getting ready for the day, buzzed him inside through an intercom system. Drummond recalls that he ascended the back stairs slowly and upon entering the kitchen, he heard Julia's distinctive voice from above, "Oh, dearie, I'll be down in a minute, why don't you start breakfast?" Of all the things he expected from the meeting, making breakfast for Julia Child in her home kitchen was not on the list. However, he immediately got down to business and located bacon, eggs, and an omelet pan. He wondered, briefly, if he was being tested, but also realized that the kitchen was set up so intuitively that even a stranger, someone who had never set foot in the house before, could walk in and begin cooking breakfast without delay. Julia soon appeared, and together they finished cooking the meal before sitting down for breakfast at the kitchen table as if they were old friends. On reflection years later, he concluded that cooking was not a test, but Julia's way of welcoming him into her home, her kitchen, and her life.[4]

This breakfast beginning led to Julia's extraordinary last decade of television cooking shows in the nineties. The first, *Cooking with Master Chefs* (which aired 1993–94), took Julia into the kitchens of sixteen professional chefs, including Emeril Lagasse (New Orleans), Michel Richard (Los Angeles), Charles Palmer (New York), Patrick Clark (Washington, DC), Robert Del Grande (Houston), Jean-Louis Palladin (Washington, DC), Susan Feniger and Mary Sue Milliken (Los Angeles), Jeremiah Tower (San Francisco), Nancy Silverton (Los Angeles), Jacques Pépin (Connecticut), Alice Waters (Berkeley), and others.[5] Julia introduced each episode from her Cambridge kitchen, then sometimes stood side by side with the chefs in their restaurant or home kitchens, asking questions, tasting, and helping with certain culinary tasks. The program required a significant amount of travel and proved to be both costly and exhausting.

The series, however, inspired Drummond and Julia to consider flipping the script and making her kitchen the setting for future episodes. Instead of crisscrossing the country, why not bring everyone together in Julia's favorite kitchen, her own, in Cambridge? With Paul's long decline and his death in 1994, the idea of having chefs come to her was an appealing prospect. Plus, in Cambridge, she could truly

While working on the series *Cooking with Master Chefs*, Julia was fully involved, even if she wasn't on camera. In this photo, taken during filming while Chef Michel Richard makes hot chocolate truffles and a chocolate dome with raspberry sauce in his home kitchen in Los Angeles, Julia is seated in an adjacent room and watches live as well as the director's feed on video monitors, taking notes on an early Toshiba laptop, and speaking on a giant cordless phone, probably with cookbook editor Judith Jones. Julia would have been noting details about the recipe and techniques for the companion book, *Cooking with Master Chefs*, published in 1993. The program's producer, Geoffrey Drummond, noted Julia was always an early adopter of technology, as surely evidenced in this snapshot.

engage in the banter that takes place when people cook together. Some key elements of the show, as established with *Cooking with Master Chefs*, would remain—the guest chefs would be the center of attention, while she would be the gregarious and generous host/student, which fit her style and personality. Thus, it was decided to tape the next series at home. *In Julia's Kitchen with Master Chefs* (which aired in 1994) brought twenty-six nationally recognized chefs into the Irving Street kitchen: Daniel Boulud, Leah Chase, Charlie Trotter, Jim Dodge, Madhur Jaffrey, Jimmy Sneed, Roberto Donna, Rick Bayless, Zarela Martinez, Jasper White, Gordon Hamersley, Jody Adams, Reed Hearon, Dean Fearing, Johanne Killeen, Jacques Torres, Jean-Georges Vongerichten, Lynne Rossetto Kasper, Carol Field, Christopher Gross, Michael Lomonaco, Monique Barbeau, Mark Militello, Alfred Portale, Joachim Splichal, and George Germon. She introduced each show with a cheerful, "Hello, I'm Julia Child! Welcome to my house and to my kitchen, and to another culinary adventure with one of America's master chefs."[6]

above: Daniel Boulud, born in Lyon, France, moved to the United States in 1980. In 1986 he opened his own restaurant, Daniel, in New York City. On an episode of *In Julia's Kitchen with Master Chefs* he made green pea soup and roasted veal chops with sweetbreads, with Julia at his side. *below left:* New Orleans chef Leah Chase in Julia's kitchen, 1993

Julia's intent was to feature contemporary cooking and—as proclaimed on the companion book's cover—"the exciting new flavors of American cooking today." One of the shows focused on traditional flavors that might have seemed new to some of Julia's viewers: a style of cooking that melded tradition and skill and drew on the foodways of the southern kitchen. Chef Leah Chase of New Orleans's Dooky Chase restaurant prepared fried chicken, biscuits, and sweet potato pie, deftly moving through all the culinary steps while sharing wisdom from her Louisiana upbringing. She spoke about her mother's breakfasts of biscuits and jelly that sustained her as

Zarela Martinez cooking with Julia, 1993

a child in school, and about how recipes are ideas that you then put in a little of yourself to make better. When she slid the sweet potato pie in the oven, she said, "You put it in, look at the temperature, and say a little prayer," a sentiment that surely resonated with Julia's viewers.[7]

The programs by Madhur Jaffrey and Zarela Martinez also provided Julia and her viewers with recipes and culinary journeys—from India and Mexico, respectively—that were perhaps less familiar than the cuisines of Europe. Madhur Jaffrey's roasted curry powder, shrimp in a spicy coconut sauce, tamarind paste, basmati rice, and other dishes brought aromas to the kitchen that Julia described as "magical." Similarly with Chef Zarela Martinez's poblanos rellenos, mole verde, puerco cocido, and tamales. By introducing Julia's viewers to the flavors of Mexico, Chef Zarela was opening up a world of dishes and techniques that went far beyond the more familiar Tex-Mex dishes that were appearing with increasing frequency on the American restaurant scene. In the years following their appearances on *In Julia's Kitchen with Master Chefs*, both Madhur Jaffrey and Zarela Martinez produced cookbooks and continued their culinary careers.[8]

The series was popular with viewers and recognized by the industry as a winning formula for television. In 1996, three years after the show aired, Julia was awarded an Emmy for Outstanding Service Show Host for *In Julia's Kitchen with Master Chefs*.

The shows featuring chefs in Julia's kitchen were so successful that two other series followed: *Baking with Julia* (in 1997) and *Julia and Jacques Cooking at Home* (in 1998–99).[9]

Julia and Geoffrey Drummond celebrate receiving the Emmy for In *Julia's Kitchen with Master Chefs*

The kitchen became the perfect backdrop to foreground Julia's new approach to television cooking—welcoming guest chefs into her home kitchen and sharing the stage, allowing them to teach her massive and loyal television audience, and Julia herself, about a dish, a culinary tradition, and something about themselves. Her guest chefs would be the stars; she would step ever-so-slightly to the side, to make that clear. For two of the three programs taped in her kitchen—*In Julia's Kitchen with Master Chefs* and *Baking with Julia*—she played the roles of both mentor and student, while her kitchen played the roles of television show setting and in-real-life culinary workspace. The kitchen, always a teaching and learning space, was now an even more lively and inclusive classroom. Julia gleefully announced at the beginning of each episode of *Baking with Julia*, "Welcome to my home, what fun we're going to have!"

"SHE WAS ENCOURAGING, MENTORING, AND LEARNING."

At this point in her long career, Julia was fully engaged in her role as a mentor, while her kitchen, as described by Geoffrey Drummond, became her ashram, the space where students of all ages, genders, and backgrounds could strive toward culinary competence and joy.[10] Chef Nancy Silverton recalled that "she was encouraging, mentoring, and learning."[11] Julia's commitments to the support of culinary education ran deep and were continuously demonstrated in her work on behalf of organizations such as the American Institute of Wine & Food (AIWF), the International Association of Culinary Professionals, the Boston University culinary arts and gastronomy program, Les Dames d'Escoffier, the Culinary Institute of America, as well as Smith College and Planned Parenthood.[12] As Americans had struggled through the tumults of the Civil Rights and Women's Rights movements, Julia came to realize how industry biases worked against entire groups of people. She changed her mind about comments she had made early in her career about gay men in the industry and about women's places in professional kitchens. When asked by a reporter in 1970 about "women's lib," she replied, "You know it wasn't until I began thinking about it that I realized my field is closed to women! It's very unfair. It's absolutely restricted! You can't get into the Culinary Institute of America in New Haven! The big hotels, the fancy New York restaurants, don't want women chefs… You know, people with skills are becoming scarce. If they need people who are earnest, intelligent and dedicated, they're going to have to allow women in."[13]

She became an advocate for broad access to industry jobs and respect for workers in food. She genuinely wanted to meet and show support for people in all levels of restaurant work, which led to her habit of barging into restaurant kitchens wherever she was dining out to chat up the line cooks and staff. And her support for women working in various food sectors never wavered but only grew.

At the same time, Julia also understood how food in the United States had changed since her early years as TV's *The French Chef*. Reflecting the changing demographics of American society and the expanding diversity of cultures among the populace, Julia's interest expanded as well, to include ingredients and dishes representing American regions, culinary traditions, and ideas about the importance of fresh over processed foods. Naturally drawn to young people, she was quick to welcome new generations and their culinary expertise to her home kitchen, where she shared her big television audience with dozens of up-and-coming chefs.

THE NIGHT BEFORE FILMING

Geoffrey Drummond described how A La Carte Communications organized and carried out the complicated choreography of taking over the 103 Irving Street house to tape the cooking shows in Julia's kitchen. For *In Julia's Kitchen with Master Chefs*, Julia typically invited the chefs to come over the night before to cook a meal together as a way for everyone involved in the production to get to know each other. Present in the kitchen would be Drummond, the culinary producer Susie Heller, and a few others who gathered to cook and socialize before the next day's taping. It is important to note that this was in 1994, shortly after Food Network was launched and up-and-coming chefs did not have the many role models or opportunities for TV cooking that exist in the twenty-first century. Julia's shows and her reputation were such that many guest chefs were intimidated by the prospect of appearing by Julia's side on television. If they were anxious when they arrived the night before, "her kitchen and her presence" put people at ease and "all of a sudden it became a fun adventure."[14] In general, the night-before meals were not formally organized; sometimes the menu would reflect what would be cooked for the next day's taping, and other times they would cook from Julia's fridge and pantry. One memorable evening they cleaned, prepped, and cooked two bluefish that Boston's Gordon Hamersley had caught that afternoon.[15]

TRANSFORMING THE KITCHEN FOR TV

Julia thrived in the controlled culinary chaos that descended on her home during taping sessions. She reveled in how the sprawling house absorbed the television equipment and the crews of technicians, culinary assistants, and producers who made the magic happen. She had her personal retreat on the second floor, but during taping the first floor was considered public space. The dining room's windows were blacked out to accommodate a bank of monitors and sound mixing boards; the library became a greenroom for special guests to view the taping; and the living room was fitted out for food photography. Even the basement was put into service as a secondary kitchen, prep area, and place to store dishware and ingredients.[16]

Yet it was the main kitchen that underwent the greatest transformation. The crew removed the kitchen table and put it in storage. They built a cooking island in the middle of the room, fitting it out with a cooktop with gas burners, which involved some negotiations given fire regulations in the historic neighborhood. They installed two-inch steel pipes on the ceiling, one of which is still visible in the kitchen at the Smithsonian, and created a grid to hold the television lights needed for the taping.

Julia in the basement kitchen where dishware for the television series sat beneath Paul's jars of nails, bolts, and other home repair items

"WELCOME TO MY HOUSE AND TO MY KITCHEN."

JULIA CHILD'S KITCHEN

178 CHAPTER 5

JULIA CHILD'S KITCHEN

The crew used four cameras, which just fit in the kitchen and required the cameramen to be especially agile as they moved in and out of the room. Perhaps the most permanent change was to a neighbor's house, which was visible through the kitchen windows and, potentially, to television viewers. Its gray siding absorbed light, and Drummond determined that the cameras needed a color that would reflect light instead. As a supreme act of generosity, Julia's neighbors agreed to have the production company paint the side of their house that faced Julia's kitchen window a warm yellow. With that problem solved, the episodes were further enhanced with greenery temporarily placed outside the kitchen window. The set was also visually warmed with colorful window treatments that replaced Julia's ordinary, tan venetian blinds.[17]

For filming, the crew kept Julia's tools and equipment in their rightful places inside the kitchen, but for each episode, Julia and her guest chef selected certain knives and pans they wanted to use to prepare the featured dishes. Occasionally, the set assistants would move a particular object to the counter behind the cooking island, so as to be in the camera's view. For example, Julia's big copper stockpot filled with rolling pins was often set on the back counter and various works of art, usually paintings and images of cats, were staged for effect. A wooden cutout of a ginger cat sitting tall became an "Alfred Hitchcock–like" presence in many episodes.[18]

All told, there were twenty-seven people working in the house for taping the Julia and Jacques series, including three cameramen, audio and video engineers, line producers and editors, hair and makeup artists, and the culinary producer, Susie Heller. The culinary coordinator, two food assistants, and one kitchen assistant worked in the cellar's prep kitchen, where they twinned all of the dishes—making multiples to be sure the recipe worked and to have ready to show at various stages of completion during a program. Through it all was Julia's trusted assistant, Stephanie Hersh, who "was everywhere, all the time," according to Drummond. "She was terrific. Definitely a fixer."[19]

opposite top: The camera setup for *Julia and Jacques Cooking at Home*, 1998. *opposite bottom:* Jacques Pépin and Julia (with Louise Miller checking makeup) as they prepare for taping an episode of the show in 1998. Note the window treatments and the cat figure behind Julia's shoulder. *above:* Stephanie Hersh in the basement kitchen

"WELCOME TO MY HOUSE AND TO MY KITCHEN."

"YOU WON'T BE IN THE KITCHEN."

Julia Child hired Stephanie Hersh to work in her home office in 1989. Hersh, whose first cooking experience was as a precocious six-year-old with an Easy-Bake Oven, had completed a BA degree in theater, English, and anthropology from Franklin and Marshall College in Pennsylvania before graduating from the Culinary Institute of America in Hyde Park, New York. She moved to Boston and worked in hotel kitchens before running a pastry and catering company. Lacking the office skills that would have helped her operate her business, Stephanie enrolled in secretarial school for a one-year program. In a plot twist worthy of a Hollywood rom-com, she learned on the day before her graduation ceremony that Julia Child had contacted the school looking for an assistant. It had to be someone who possessed secretarial skills and at least some rudimentary culinary knowledge. As no other student in the program fit that description, the school forwarded Stephanie's résumé to Julia for review.[20]

When word came back that Julia was not interested in hiring her, Stephanie naturally wanted to know why. Badly. The school's administrators were reluctant to call Julia but Stephanie insisted. When they reached Julia, Stephanie learned that her culinary credentials were so impressive that Julia didn't think she would be satisfied doing office work. Stephanie insisted that there was nothing in the world she wanted to do more than work in Julia's home office, and finally Julia agreed to a trial period of one week. Before ringing off, Julia reminded Stephanie, "You won't be in the kitchen" but would be handling correspondence and administrative tasks in the upstairs office.[21]

When Stephanie turned up at 103 Irving Street the following day, she found "total mayhem." Julia had forgotten that the CBC—Canadian television—would be filming a program about Julia that day. Following the sound of Julia's famous voice, Stephanie found her and the crew in the formal dining room. Julia took Stephanie aside and quickly informed her that she had agreed to be filmed making lunch in her kitchen. Specifically, Santa Barbara Fish Stew from *The Way to Cook*, Julia's 1993 cookbook that distilled her knowledge of classical techniques and updated ideas about a more freestyle approach to cooking.[22] Without missing a beat Stephanie confidently walked into the kitchen for the first time, assessed the ingredient situation, and was relieved to see a variety of fresh fish. She set out preparing the dish to various points so that Julia could jump in and finish the stew with the cameras rolling. The knot that had been tightening in Stephanie's shoulders disappeared when Julia entered the kitchen, smiled, and declared, "Now I will make myself some lunch!"[23]

Stephanie continued working for Julia, earning the title "Executive Personal Assistant," until Julia's death in 2004. Their strong personalities seemed to mesh and, as Stephanie recalls with deep and genuine fondness, they had many adventures over the years. Stephanie's introduction to Julia's home kitchen, like Geoffrey Drummond's, required her to hit the ground cooking, albeit with much higher stakes. And while Stephanie was hired to do administrative work, she was definitely invited into the kitchen to cook with and for Julia for the duration of her employment.

"OH, MY, I JUST BURNED JULIA CHILD."

When Chef Nancy Silverton was invited to appear on an episode of *Baking with Julia*, she didn't exactly jump at the opportunity. Silverton, a pastry chef, bread baker, and cofounder of La Brea Bakery in Los Angeles (in 1989), had experience with baking on television and no desire to repeat it. She had appeared in the first season of *Cooking with Master Chefs*, the season that was *not* filmed in Julia's home kitchen, and for which Julia assumed more of a host and producer role. Silverton recalled that for the bread baking episode, Julia was not standing by her side, but appeared at transitions in the show from her home kitchen and spoke from a script. There was no sense of dialogue in the production; nor was there a sense of an unseen audience. She recalled, "Teaching bread baking is difficult. They were producing [the show] in a way that wasn't natural. [There were] a lot of retakes. It wasn't a pleasant experience." Still, in the two-year history of the series, Silverton's bread program was incredibly popular with viewers and provided the impetus for the *Baking with Julia* series that followed. What's more, "Julia realized that the whole [series] would be more successful if she was in [the program]," and with Julia in the frame, Silverton was persuaded to appear on the third season of *Baking with Julia*, in 1997.[24]

Silverton recalled what it was like to cook next to Julia while she demonstrated how to make a crème fraîche brioche tart with fresh fruit poached in white wine sauce.

"[It was a] completely different experience, having the dialogue with her next to you. But what was so beautiful about her kitchen was how humble and how useable and how worn it was. And it was Julia. Julia would talk about many things on her show besides loving butter and fixing one's mistakes. The fact was, that she did not use or care about fancy kitchen tools and fancy kitchen ingredients. She was exactly who she was. It wasn't the television Julia and the real Julia; this was Julia. And I loved just cooking next to her because it made the whole experience not only that much easier as the cook/teacher but the idea of not talking to a screen or camera, but I was talking to her and she was so engaged, so interested in what I had to say and teach. I know that with everyone else that she invited to cook with her, they were the stars, they were the teachers, and she was the student."[25]

Unlike some guest chefs, Silverton did not arrive the night before to cook with Julia and get comfortable in the kitchen. She jumped right in, having been told that Julia wanted to shoot in real time as much as possible and preferred not to rely on editing to make the program:

> So, the only thing she said [was that in the] last few minutes when you're going to let me taste, I'll tap you on the hip when we have three minutes left.[26]
>
> I got that tap just before I threw the fruit that I was going to be warming in this very, very hot wine syrup. But I had three minutes. So, I cooked the fruit, I put it on the tart, I put on the sabayon, I cut a bite, and [she put] it in her mouth. I saw [her] tears and in my head was, 'Oh, my, I just burned Julia Child,' because the syrup was so hot."

As viewers of this memorable episode of *Baking with Julia* will attest, Julia's tears and her comment, "It's a dessert to cry over!" could not have been more real. At the time, Silverton was so relieved that Julia was all right, she didn't realize that she had just received the highest compliment imaginable for her craft—her beautiful crème fraîche brioche torte with fresh fruit poached in white wine sauce.[27]

"THE RECIPES WORKED."

The baker and pastry chef Dorie Greenspan was already a published author and a first-generation chef on Food Network when she met Geoffrey Drummond in the mid-nineties. She declined his invitation to work on the *Baking with Julia* series but several months later changed her mind. Their first trip to Cambridge to meet Julia was similar in important ways to the experiences of many others. "We came in as everyone did and the first thing you see after Julia hugs you—that amazing stove." But it wasn't just the Garland that drew Dorie into the kitchen, it was the beehive

Julia's guests chef Nancy Silverton (left) and Martha Stewart (right) in the kitchen for the *Baking with Julia* series

of activity surrounding it. Stephanie Hersh and culinary assistants were standing by and monitoring several saucepans on the stovetop. With timers around their necks and clipboards in hand, they were testing for the ideal timing for cooking eggs. Dorie picked up on a "Santa's elves" vibe and realized she was "in a workshop where everything is buzzing."[28]

For Dorie, however, the best part was seeing "Julia ... sitting at that table, making a tuna sandwich for lunch that she asked me to work on. I think my job, the only thing I did, was to cut the celery. I thought it had to be perfect. Julia didn't care but I wanted it to be just so." After taking the time to cut perfect celery slices, Dorie looked up to find Julia watching her and asking, "Done?" Thus began a friendship that grew stronger the more the two worked together on the big book project based on the TV series *Baking with Julia*. They shared an approach to recipes—clear, detailed, accessible—and the overarching goal for their work. Dorie remembered, "When she would call me from the road [during book tours and cooking demonstrations], Julia never said, 'Oh, we had a huge crowd' or 'I signed a lot of books.' The first thing she would say, 'The recipes worked.' The thing that made her happiest, was that the recipe worked and [knowing that] anyone who made the recipe would be successful."[29]

Baking with Julia was filmed over four seasons, from 1996 to 1999, and was as ambitious as the previous series, *In Julia's Kitchen with Master Chefs*. Julia welcomed twenty-seven bakers who represented different backgrounds, skills, and phases of their careers into her kitchen. In addition to Nancy Silverton, the chefs included Charlotte Akoto, Mary Bergin, David Blom, Flo Braker, Lora Brody, Marion Cunningham, Marcel Desaulniers, Naomi Duguid and Jeffrey Alford, Markus Farbinger, Danielle Forestier, Gale Gand, Lauren Groveman, Johanne Killeen, Craig Kominiak, Norman Love, Leslie Mackie, Nick Malgieri, Esther McManus, Alice Medrich, David Ogonowski, Beatrice Ojakangas, Joe Ortiz, Michel Richard, Martha Stewart, and Steve Sullivan. With Julia by their sides, they created breads, cakes, and pastries, and managed to demonstrate the strength required for working bread dough and the delicacy needed for decorating baked works of art. Perhaps one of the most memorable episodes (in addition to Nancy Silverton's) was Martha Stewart's construction and decoration of what was called "A Glorious Wedding Cake" in the book by Dorie Greenspan that followed the series. As Martha expertly built the three diamond-shaped tiers and carefully shaped and painted the marzipan fruits and leaves, Julia gamely followed along, asking questions, and enjoyed the grand finale—tasting Martha's perfectly built masterpiece.[30]

WHO IS ON JULIA'S SPEED DIAL?

Julia's kitchen telephone—an AT&T, twenty-four-button unit—sat at the end of a counter, out of the way of cooking traffic. She kept a kitchen stool nearby for perching on while using the phone to make appointments, help home cooks avert disasters, and catch up with family and friends. Long before smartphones and handy directories of contacts, landline units had buttons that could be programmed for dialing frequently used numbers quickly by pressing a single button. Julia's speed-dial roster included her longtime friend and culinary associate Rosemary Manell, the American Institute of Wine & Food (AIWF), her producer Geoffrey Drummond, the limo and yellow cab companies, her hairdressers, her niece Phila Cousins, her assistant Stephanie Hersh, and Dorie Greenspan. Dorie revealed that she and Julia spoke by phone every morning for years, a habit they developed while working together on the book *Baking with Julia*, the award-winning volume based on the television series.[31] No wonder, then, that her name was attached to button #21 on Julia's kitchen phone.

Julia's phone corner included a Rubik's cube, notepads, a globe light, and a thermometer.

JULIA CHILD'S KITCHEN

"WELCOME TO MY HOUSE AND TO MY KITCHEN."

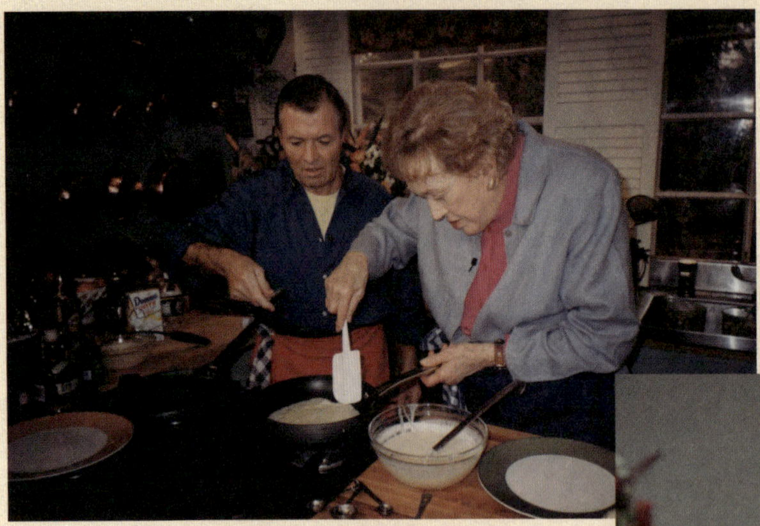

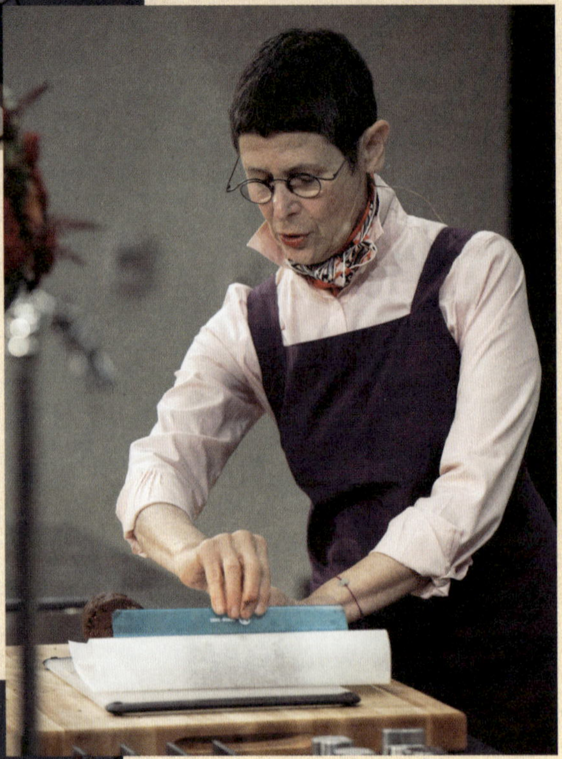

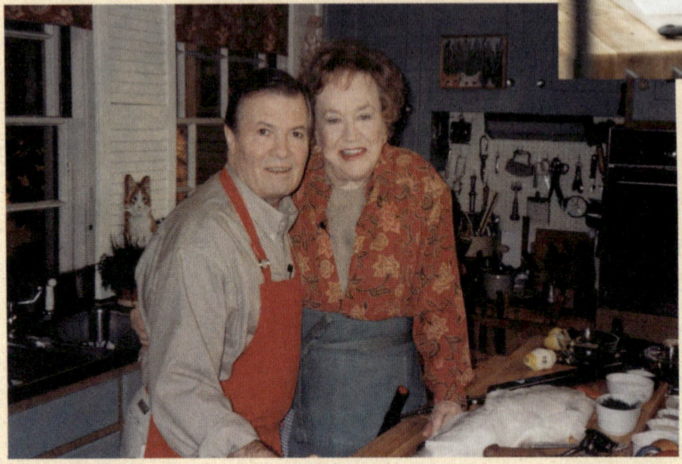

"WHAT DID WE TEACH TODAY?"

Of all the chefs who cooked with Julia in her home kitchen, Jacques Pépin stands out, for it was he who joined her for her last cooking series in the Irving Street kitchen. *Julia and Jacques Cooking at Home* featured the two friends and much-beloved television chefs cooking side-by-side in Julia's kitchen. The series was taped in 1998 and aired on PBS during the 1999–2000 season. Reruns on PBS continue to be scheduled and, like all of Julia's television shows, are perennial, sentimental favorites among viewers.

By the nineties, Julia and Jacques had an easy familiarity and obvious affection for one another. They had met back in 1960 and become friends as their worlds overlapped around work and culinary events in New York and Boston. Together with Rebecca Alssid, they started the Boston University program in gastronomy, and over many years when Jacques was teaching at BU they would socialize, often with Jacques's wife, Gloria, in Boston. They began presenting live cooking demonstrations together, and their personal chemistry and mutual professional admiration became apparent to audiences and producers alike. They agreed on many aspects of cooking, including, "taste over appearance, simplicity in recipes, using the proper techniques, using the best-quality ingredients, following the seasons, keeping an open mind to new food preparations, and…sharing both wine and food with family and friends."[32] Yet they didn't always agree on all culinary matters and therein lay an important aspect of the program's appeal. The two would joke with each other in a way that audiences found genuine and irresistible. In the cookbook by David Nussbaum that resulted from the series, Jacques wrote, "We agree about some dishes and disagree about others, but always in a spirit of camaraderie and curiosity."[33] He recalled that as they were developing the series, Julia "said, 'What do you want to do?' And I said, 'I don't know,' and she said, 'Why don't you write down 100 things that you want to do and I'll do the same thing.' I think that maybe three of mine made it in the show!"[34]

opposite top: Julia and Jacques making crepes, 1998 *center:* Dorie Greenspan demonstrating a cookie recipe at the Smithsonian's 2016 Food History Weekend *bottom:* Julia and Jacques, 1998

Jacques recalled another element of the show that appealed to him: "The fascinating part of cooking is that there is invariably another way of doing a particular technique or preparing a recipe that makes it better, or at least different. You are always an apprentice, and the learning is continuous if you keep an open mind."[35] On their shared interests, Julia wrote, "Food is not only our business but our greatest pleasure, and we think its preparation should be a joyful occupation."[36]

In all, twenty-two episodes of *Julia and Jacques Cooking at Home* were filmed in Julia's home kitchen. As with the other shows taped in the kitchen by A La Carte Communications, Geoffrey Drummond and a supporting cast of some twenty-seven individuals took over the house for a solid month to tape multiple episodes. Drummond recalled the special dynamic between Julia and Jacques: "Julia was a master of surprises. Jacques comes out of the restaurant world where everything is boom, boom, boom, and Julia comes out of [TV's] 'shock 'em if you can' and what Jacques was able to do—a combination of intelligence and being one of the most technically skilled chefs ever, and a deep love and respect for Julia. There was really a magic between them . . . and the kitchen was comfortable for them. They really got to know and live in the space."[37]

The success of *Julia and Jacques Cooking at Home* was in the comfort and camaraderie the two stars exuded, effortlessly, on the screen. The familiar kitchen in the background, coupled with the range of cooking tools and equipment borrowed from Julia's personal "batterie de cuisine," reinforced the notion that viewers could try this at home and likely succeed. Jacques recalled the taping sessions: "Cooking together was fun, to share food. You cannot cook indifferently. We got involved in cooking and discussing. After that we would have dinner and discuss our recipe." And at the end of each show, they would say to each other, "What did we teach today?" Throughout all the fun and friendship, the main goal was always sharing knowledge with aspiring cooks.[38] The resulting cookbook written with David Nussbaum and with photographs by Christopher Hirsheimer captures the two approaches taken by Julia and Jacques for each recipe. With Julia's thoughts on the left of the page and Jacques's on the right, readers can learn from both masters at the same time, just as they did on the television show. This format also makes clear an important point about cooking in general: There's more than one way to make a dish.[39]

Jacques, Geoffrey Drummond, and Julia, 1998

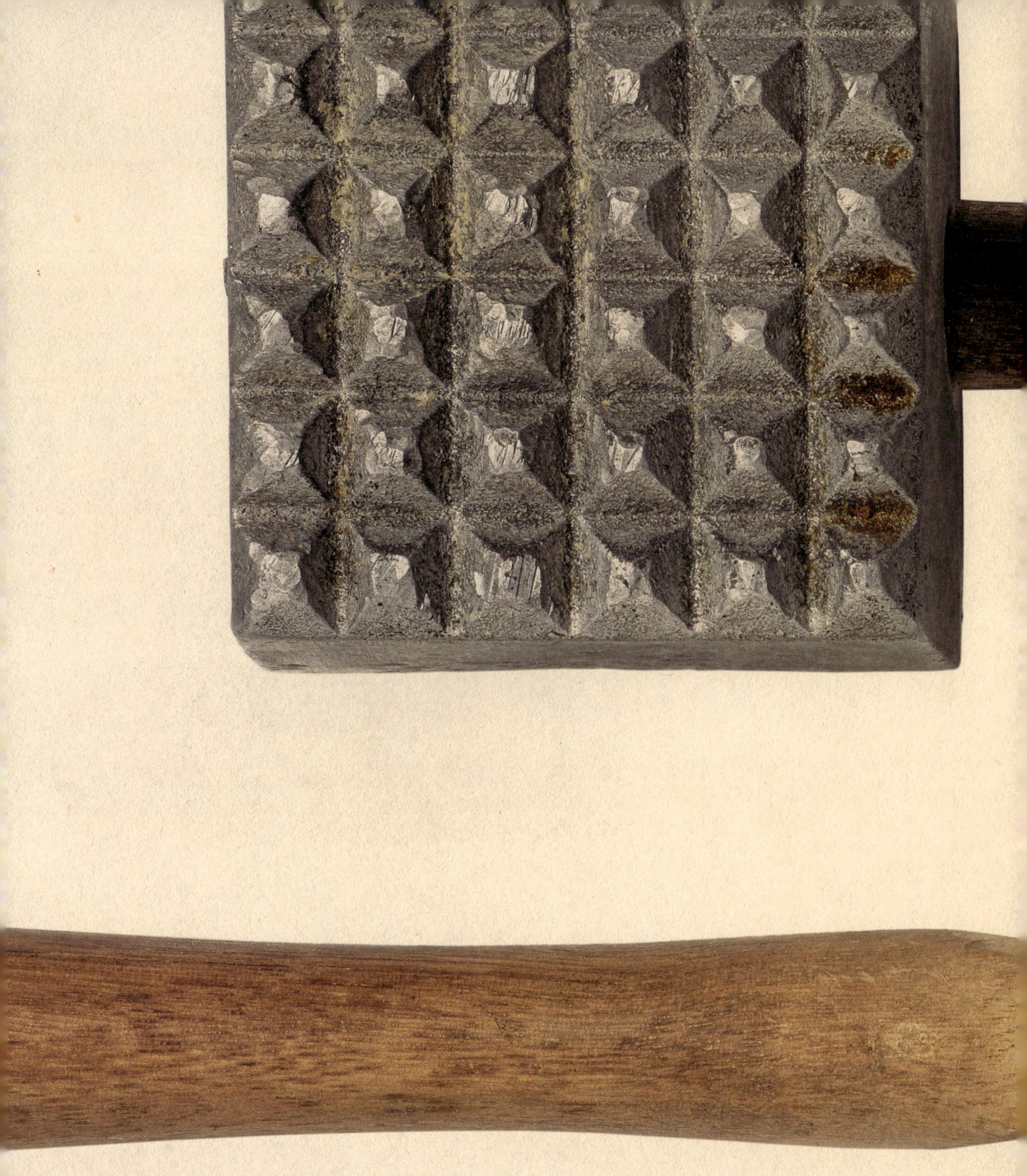

CHAPTER 6

"I'm absolutely delighted that the Smithsonian is taking my kitchen."

Curator Rayna Green answered her office phone at the National Museum of American History on an August morning in 2001 and was greeted by a familiar voice. Carolyn Margolis, a Julia devotee and colleague at the National Museum of Natural History next door and, like Rayna, a member of the American Institute of Wine & Food (AIWF), wanted to talk about the recent article in the *New York Times* announcing Julia Child's decision to leave her longtime home in Massachusetts to return to her home state of California.[1] At age eighty-nine, Julia was ready to leave New England winters behind and settle into Santa Barbara, a place she had loved since childhood and where she and her husband had resided part-time since 1981. By way of describing Julia's legacy, the article revealed that she would be lending her famous French copper pots to an organization founded by her dear friend, the winemaker Robert Mondavi, for his new venture, Copia: The American Center for Wine, Food & the Arts, in Napa, California. This detail raised the question "What about the rest of the kitchen?"—a question that was already on the minds of culinary professionals and Julia's associates.

previous spread: Two of Julia's well-used meat tenderizers

Rayna mustered the troops, her colleagues in the American Wine History project: Nanci Edwards, a museum specialist and project manager at the museum and a member of the AIWF; John Fleckner, head of the museum's Archives Center; and me, a curator in the Division of Work and Industry. The three of us had been working together for several years on documenting the history of American wine and had been discussing ways of adding more food history research and collecting to the project plan. Museum curators typically create collecting plans and most maintain an ongoing mental list of objects and stories that would be especially important to pursue if an opportunity arose. For us, that list included material reflecting the big changes in food and beverage history in the late twentieth century—a critical period of transformation in terms of technology and culture. At or near the top of that list was Julia Child, the influential and much beloved cookbook author, hilarious and knowledgeable television cook for nearly forty years, and cultural icon who inspired millions of people in multiple ways over her long public life. The question about her kitchen hit home; we decided to ask Julia for an interview in her kitchen before she packed up to head west. Perhaps we would ask her to donate an emblematic object. A balloon whisk? A copper pan? More? A whole lot more? Of course, we weren't aware of what she was thinking in terms of gifting objects to family members—perhaps decisions had been made already, and who were we to mess with the intentions and expectations of Julia and her nearest and dearest? However, we were keenly aware of

left: Nanci Edwards and Paula Johnson arriving at 103 Irving Street with Rayna Green, who snapped this view of our arrival at the back entrance. A note about the photographs of the Smithsonian team in 2001: these were taken with an ordinary digital snapshot camera to document our work in the field. We fervently wish we had traveled with one of the Smithsonian's excellent professional photographers, as the quality of our shots in the field doesn't measure up to the significance of the endeavor. *right:* Rayna Green and Nanci Edwards performing the original inventory of Julia's kitchen in August 2001

the long-term financial, storage, and staff responsibilities of accepting a large and complex object or group of objects into the national collections *for perpetuity*, a fact of museum work that had to be considered as we contemplated the depth and breadth of what we might encounter in Cambridge.

Rayna, who had last seen Julia at an event in Napa, California, the previous year, made the call. Julia picked up the phone and upon hearing our request for an interview, urged us to "Come ahead!" to Cambridge.

Two days later, we arrived at 103 Irving Street and crossed the threshold into Julia's famous kitchen. As we greeted our host, we couldn't help noticing that the kitchen itself was practically alive with things—every surface was covered with culinary tools, books, papers, artwork, and personal items, yet the overall effect was one of order and accessibility and expertise, with a dash of whimsy thrown in. The three of us had what can only be called a curatorial mind meld as we silently realized that a balloon whisk or copper pan wouldn't do justice to Julia. The whole kitchen was the artifact, the treasure.

We took seats around the kitchen table and spoke with Julia about her plans and about the Smithsonian's work in food and beverage history. As Julia gestured around her kitchen, she started telling us the history of this object or that, a memory about a saucepan or a painting, why this knife was perfect for this task and not that, why there were little notes on Dymo labels and masking tape near various surfaces. As she spoke, we recognized that the handful of colleagues and culinary professionals who had boldly argued that the kitchen "belonged" at the Smithsonian had a valid point, even though they had no clue about what that would entail.

After taking a brief break, during which we confirmed among ourselves that we wanted to make the ask for the entire kitchen, we did just that. Julia was only slightly taken aback, since her longtime assistant, Stephanie Hersh, possibly in collusion with others, had already suggested to her privately that the Smithsonian had a history of collecting big and complex objects. As we spoke about the practicalities and the larger goals of taking on the entire kitchen, she understood that our interest was not solely focused on the celebrity side of her history, but in the stories she had just been telling us about this knife, that pan, the big Garland range, and the very table where we were sitting. Her stories reflected the major phases as well as details of her life, but also revealed a more expansive history about the second half of the twentieth century—of attitudes toward cooking and food; of shifting ideas about gender roles, kitchens, and what it took to create a different path; of broader notions about the relationship between new technologies and traditional culinary techniques; of the powerful movements around education and food, and so much more.

When Julia excused herself to phone her family members, notably her niece Phila Cousins, we assessed the task at hand and developed a plan for documenting the objects and their locations. This information, we knew, would be crucial to successfully justifying to the museum that this complex artifact would, indeed, be worth acquiring for the national collections and for the benefit of the American people.

"WE'LL HAVE TO ASK JULIA."

When Julia returned to the kitchen, she gave us a nod and the official go-ahead. Yes, she would be delighted to donate her kitchen (as long as we didn't destroy the house by taking the walls and the window glass, too). As she had work to do in her second-floor office, she left us to begin the inventory. Having had some experience documenting buildings and boats in my early museum career, I set up a system to draw a floor plan and number each wall, with each cabinet, drawer, and large object numbered and keyed to its appropriate wall location. We set up a laptop, a camera, and a video recorder, and began counting and identifying everything we encountered. The temptation to revel in the excitement of what we were doing was almost overpowering ("Look at Julia's aprons in this drawer!" "How many baking sheets does a cook need?" (twenty-four, in Julia's case); "Here's a gift from James Beard—a champagne stopper in its original box!"; but we managed to stay focused and made great strides.

A gift from James Beard: a French champagne bottle stopper

JULIA CHILD'S KITCHEN

Every so often, one of us would encounter a mystery that required a pause and some conversation. As Rayna opened one of the cabinet doors, something jangled. She looked up to see a round mirror hanging from a nail on the inside of the door and said something like "huh?" Later, when we got around to inventorying the contents of the drawer just below that cabinet, we found a lipstick and realized the mirror was for getting ready to greet visitors to the kitchen. The mirror, to suit Julia's height, was literally way above our heads.

This re-created view of encountering Julia's makeup mirror shows intern Reeza Baldonado (Smith College, class of 2025) opening the cabinet door. At just under five feet tall, she had a reaction similar to Rayna's and mine.

FOCUS: MYSTERY OBJECTS

Throughout the day we would be flummoxed by an object and hold it up to ask if anyone knew what it was. The drawers filled with gadgets were especially challenging, and we soon started a pile of "we'll have to ask Julia" things. (Yes, we kept track of where to put them back.) Every so often we would hear Julia descending from her office and quickly arrange the pile of curiosities for her perusal. Among the mysteries she solved were a manche à gigot (holder for lamb bone when carving), a handmade device for taking the kernels off ears of corn, and a stone-crab claw cracker.

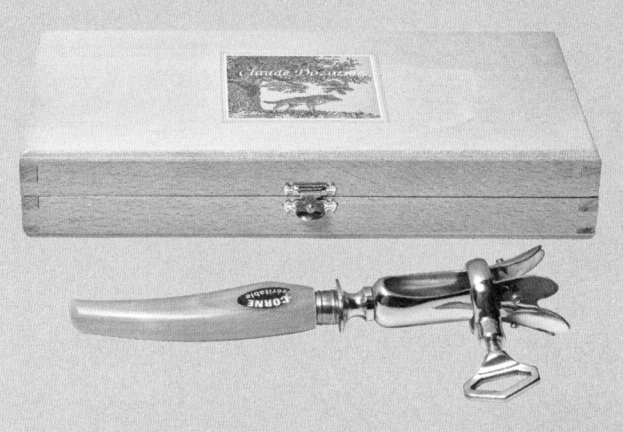

MANCHE À GIGOT

"This is if you're carving a leg of lamb, you put the end of the leg bone right in there and then you have something to hold on to. That's why it's useful to go over to Europe and see that they've been carving legs of lamb for generations until somebody invented this idea of how to hold the legs. I wish that we carved more legs of lamb at the table... it's very convenient to be able to hold it."[2]

CORN CUTTER

"I never used to consider recipes that called for grated fresh corn. It was just too much work to run a knife point down every single row on the ear and then to scrape out the milk and pulp with the back of the blade. Then my brother-in-law [Charles Child] gave me a wooden corn scraper one Christmas, and, mad to use it, I discovered that fresh corn was available almost all year round. I confess I had never looked at it before—dismissing it as inedible out of the summer season. But I found it delicious when scraped off the cob with my new grater and turned into cream-style dishes."[3]

"I'M ABSOLUTELY DELIGHTED THAT THE SMITHSONIAN IS TAKING MY KITCHEN."

STONE-CRAB CRACKER

Julia spent a day with the Florida chef Allen Susser, who in 2009 recalled her enthusiasm for experiencing the harvest of stone crabs, a Florida delicacy: "When Julia came to Miami on one of her many visits, she insisted that I take her out stone crabbing. She wanted to know firsthand all about our delicious stone crabs. Julia was funny though; she seemed large for the little boat. She had to personally pull the traps and break the claws from the crab. Then after our sojourn down to the Keys she became very excited to throw the just-caught claws into a pot of boiling seawater to cook them... We devoured the lush stone-crab meat. I remember Julia saying, 'This is what life is about' while she licked her fingers clean."[4]

The initial object inventory took the rest of the day and most of the next. The atmosphere was electric with our excitement at the possibilities that lay ahead. We knew we were about to embark on a major campaign to convince our colleagues and leadership that collecting Julia Child's home kitchen was an initiative worthy of the museum's support. As we packed up to leave Cambridge, we made plans to film an interview with Julia in a few weeks' time to be sure we recorded her stories in her own voice and in the marvelous kitchen surrounded by her culinary treasures.

"WE HAVE A JOB TO DO."

The morning of the interview exuded promise with clear skies and abundant sunshine. We three had checked into a hotel the previous night and had purchased supplies for our shared breakfast with the crew, keeping the perishables cold in a bathtub filled with ice. That morning we picked up fresh bagels and coffee, then headed to Irving Street, where we would meet Geoffrey Drummond of A La Carte Communications, who had produced Julia's three television series from the kitchen, as well as his New York crew and a sound team from Boston who would film our interviews. As we were setting up the kitchen table where Julia would sit, we marveled at the beautiful day and the downright honor we felt at being able to interview Julia Child in her kitchen before it would be packed up for transport to Washington, DC.

Julia was upstairs getting her hair and makeup done. While we waited, her electrician was tinkering with the TV that Julia kept on a wheeled cart just inside the adjacent food pantry. We didn't know exactly why the electrician needed to be in the space just then, but Geoffrey Drummond later told us that Julia was keen to watch *The Sopranos* on HBO and had asked the electrician to stop by.[5] As he finished up, he turned on the TV to be sure it was working properly. Time stood still as all of us standing by in the kitchen realized that the airplane hitting the side of the World Trade Center in New York was real. It was September 11, 2001, and terrorist attacks on the United States were underway.

At that moment, we heard the elevator bringing Julia downstairs to the kitchen. The electrician turned off the TV and rolled it back into the pantry. We must have looked like deer in headlights as Julia entered the kitchen. She surveyed the scene and looked at each of us while saying something like, "I've been listening to the radio, and I know what's happening. It may seem strange for us to be talking about kitchen utensils when the world is changing, but we have a job to do." Julia

Julia and Paul Child, 1977. Photograph by Hans Namuth

had assessed the situation and realized that no one would be leaving Boston that day, concluding that we might as well do our work. She could tell we were all anxious about our families and friends in New York, Washington, and Boston and tried easing those worries by promising to take frequent breaks, as many as we needed. Perhaps we could get through to our loved ones for news, somehow. In that moment she demonstrated that, at eighty-nine, she was thinking with laser clarity as well as steely resolve and genuine compassion. At some point she mentioned that the day felt awfully like the day that President John F. Kennedy was assassinated. On November 22, 1963, she, Paul, and their neighbors, the Galbraiths and the Schlesingers, had sat around the very same table, trying to comprehend the national and global dimensions of such overwhelming, shocking news.

Our interview with Julia proceeded and ultimately generated the stories she wanted us to know and to share with the public. Perhaps my memory is clouded by the confusion and the strain of that day, but I had the sense that she was speaking not only to us but also to future visitors to the museum.

As promised, that day we took many breaks, including one for lunch. At some point during that morning, Julia's longtime assistant Stephanie Hersh had put a pot of veal stew on one of the Garland's back burners. The aroma wafted through the house and perhaps even helped calm our nerves, so that by the time we left the kitchen for lunch in the formal dining room, the sight of the stew, crusty bread, and a simple salad arranged on the table brought a wave of comfort, and a sense of normality and being cared for. We discovered that, true to what we

left: Julia gesturing toward the pot of veal stew and Geoff Drummond while taking a break from our interview on September 11, 2001 *right:* Paula Johnson and Rayna Green interviewing Julia in September 2001

were learning about Julia and the many cooks that prepared food in her kitchen, the stew had been made by several chefs from the local chapter of Les Dames d'Escoffier, who had created a special dinner in honor of Julia in her kitchen the previous evening.

As the long day faded, we wandered back to our hotel, where we tried to focus more on the extraordinary conversation we had just recorded with Julia Child and less on the harrowing details that were emerging about the day's historic events. For the next two days, unable to travel back to DC with the security shutdown that followed the attacks, we took long walks around Cambridge, read whatever we could put our hands on, reflected on what we had learned about Julia, and tried to find a way home. Eventually we were able to rent a car and drive back to Washington, feeling the shock of loss and raw fear as we passed close enough to Manhattan to note the missing towers.

PERMISSION GRANTED

Because the National Museum of American History collects objects for perpetuity, a great deal of care is taken in acquiring artifacts that are especially large, valuable, and complex. Curators must prepare written justifications articulating the historical and cultural significance of a proposed collection and detailing the plans for packing, shipping, processing, storing, conserving, and exhibiting the objects. Such information is determined through discussions with staff members who have years of experience in overseeing complex acquisitions of historical material.

In the case of Julia Child's kitchen, Rayna Green wrote the formal memo seeking approval from the museum's collections committee. She wrote:

> We feel that, with her complex, interesting kitchen, we would acquire an incomparable "object," a complete contextual setting that stands for Child's considerable and singular influence on the way Americans think about their food and its history. Child is herself a complex phenomenon—a beloved media star with a unique and definable style that has passed into American oral tradition, an accomplished, prolific author with many influential books continuously on bestseller lists, a self-described and much-revered educator who has garnered respectability for her profession and field of accomplishment while actually defining standards in those fields.

The kitchen is a symbol for the notable achievements of Child, herself an American icon, and when it comes to the Museum, it will join other American icons, offering a rich context for explaining and discussing the significant changes in American foodways, indeed the changes in public and domestic life in the 20th century.[6]

And thus, on September 18, 2001, after some deliberation, the museum's collections committee recommended approval of the acquisition, which was then endorsed and officially approved by the museum's leadership. As a member of the committee at the time, I recall a lively discussion about the museum taking on

Painting by Rosemary Grimes Menell of a giant artichoke with a yacht race and flag of France in the background. The painting, made in 1978, hangs in Julia Child's kitchen.

top left: The dishpan hands crew: from left, Steve Velasquez, Alexis Bierman, Cindy Ott, Rayna Green. Cedric Yeh is in the foreground. *above*: Curator Rayna Green loading the dishwasher prior to packing up the small items. *left*: Intern Alexis Bierman and collections manager Steve Velasquez ensuring inventory control while packing

such a large and complex object and the testimonials of several other committee members as to Julia's importance in American history. A check of my notes for that day reveals a lot about the National Museum of American History's amazing collections and the breadth of history they represent. Three outgoing loans to other museums involved the Stradivarius violins and cello; the scarecrow costume worn by Ray Bolger in *The Wizard of Oz*, and the compass carried on the Lewis and Clark Expedition. Acquisition cases that day included archives from a New York advertising firm and a home products company, examples of Crayola crayons and Silly Putty, and a Votomatic card-punch voting device and reader from the state of Florida. Julia Child's kitchen was clearly in remarkable company during that meeting and vice versa. Once the official Deed of Gift was signed by Julia on October 15, the path was clear to begin the process of packing and shipping the kitchen from Cambridge to Washington, DC.

TEAM ONE: "DISHPAN HANDS"

Julia's plan was to leave her Irving Street home for the last time on November 10 or 11, 2001, and we were told to have everything removed by December 21. After that the house itself would become the property of Julia's alma mater, Smith College, a gift from one of their most famous alumni.[7] It was expected that Smith would sell the property, which indeed happened within a few months.

The museum team discussed next steps under the leadership of the project manager, Nanci Edwards. Given the size of the undertaking, it was determined there would be two teams, the first to pack the small objects (small appliances, tools, gadgets, dishes, and so on) and the second to remove the cabinetry and large appliances, which would be much easier to accomplish with the smaller material out of the way.

Team one, led by Rayna Green, included Steve Velasquez, the collections manager for the Division of Cultural History, Cedric Yeh, a collections manager from another curatorial division, volunteers Cindy Ott and Alexis Bierman, and Smithsonian photographer Hugh Talman. As Rayna noted in her project diary, they made room for Hugh to set up his camera gear and lights shortly after arriving so he could photograph the kitchen just before it would be packed up. Hugh's photos, along with the original inventory, would be critical to our putting everything back where Julia had intended it to be. Rayna's diary also conveys a sense of the emotional swirl and excitement that characterized their efforts:

NOVEMBER 11-12, 2001:

JULIA'S HOUSE IS HUMMING. STEPHANIE [HERSH], PENNY, AND CHERYL, JULIA'S ASSISTANTS, ARE PACKING THINGS UPSTAIRS. EVERYTHING HAS TO BE FINISHED IN DECEMBER. JULIA LEFT THE HOUSE FOR CALIFORNIA ONLY ON SATURDAY. NATURALLY, ALL OF "TEAM JULIA" DOWNSTAIRS REALLY, REALLY WISHES JULIA WAS STILL THERE; IT FEELS STRANGE TO BE RUMMAGING THROUGH HER HOUSE AND KITCHEN WHILE SHE'S AWAY. THE PHONE RINGS CONSTANTLY. DELIVERY MEN BRING OUR PACKING SUPPLIES AND THE CHIEF DELIVERY MAN BEGS TO COME IN AND SEE JULIA'S FAMOUS KITCHEN.

OTHER OLD FRIENDS AND COLLEAGUES OF JULIA SHOW UP AT THE DOOR, COMING BY THE HOUSE TO PICK UP OR DELIVER ALL SORTS OF THINGS. RUSS MORASH, THE PRODUCER OF [PUBLIC TELEVISION'S] THIS OLD HOUSE AND THE VICTORY GARDEN AND OF JULIA'S FIRST AND FAMOUS COOKING SHOW, THE FRENCH CHEF, COMES TO THE DOOR TO TALK WITH STEPHANIE. HE TELLS US SOME STORIES WHILE WE WORK AND OFFERS HIS SUPPORT FOR OUR COLLECTING THE KITCHEN.

CINDY, ALEXIS, AND I BEGIN TAKING THINGS DOWN TO INSPECT, WIPE, WASH, AND TAG EACH ONE. WE'RE FOLLOWING THE ACTUAL INVENTORY PLAN PAULA, NANCI, AND I DEVELOPED IN AUGUST. . . CINDY WASHES, I DRY, ALEXIS TAGS AND TAKES TO STEVE AND CED, WHO BAG, WRAP, COUNT, AND PACK, CHECKING EVERYTHING OFF AND MAKING CORRECTIONS TO OUR LIST AS THEY GO. ON TO [NUMBERED DRAWER] AD3 (STEAK KNIVES, PASTRY TIPS), 4 (JARS AND PLASTIC WARE, OF WHICH WE CHOOSE A FEW), 5 (POT AND PAN LIDS), 6 (CHERRY PITTER, OLIVE PITTER, MARROW SCOOPS), 7 (A DRAWER WHERE TREASURES ABOUND, A CHAMPAGNE CORK JAMES BEARD GAVE HER, HER SIGNALING MIRROR FROM WORLD WAR II), 8 (DISHTOWELS), 9 (APRONS), 10 (MISCELLANEOUS JUNK DRAWER—YES, JULIA HAS ONE, TOO). OFF TO THE INTERIOR OF THE UPPER CABINETS WITH CUPS, GLASSES, GRATIN PANS, EGG CUPS AND TEAPOTS, THEN SPICES (WHERE I INVENTORY AND MOSTLY THROW AWAY). AS WITH WASHING THINGS, WE HAVE TO MAKE SURE NO ORGANIC MATTER ACCOMPANIES US BACK TO THE MUSEUM. AND SO IT GOES THROUGH THE DAY. WE SWITCH JOBS FROM TIME TO TIME. WE HAVE TO ASK STEPHANIE HUNDREDS OF QUESTIONS. I AM GETTING DISHPAN HANDS.[8]

Containers holding silverware, chopsticks, rulers, small graters, and brushes share a corner with a few oils, vinegars, and small mortars and pestles. Everything was carefully inventoried prior to packing.

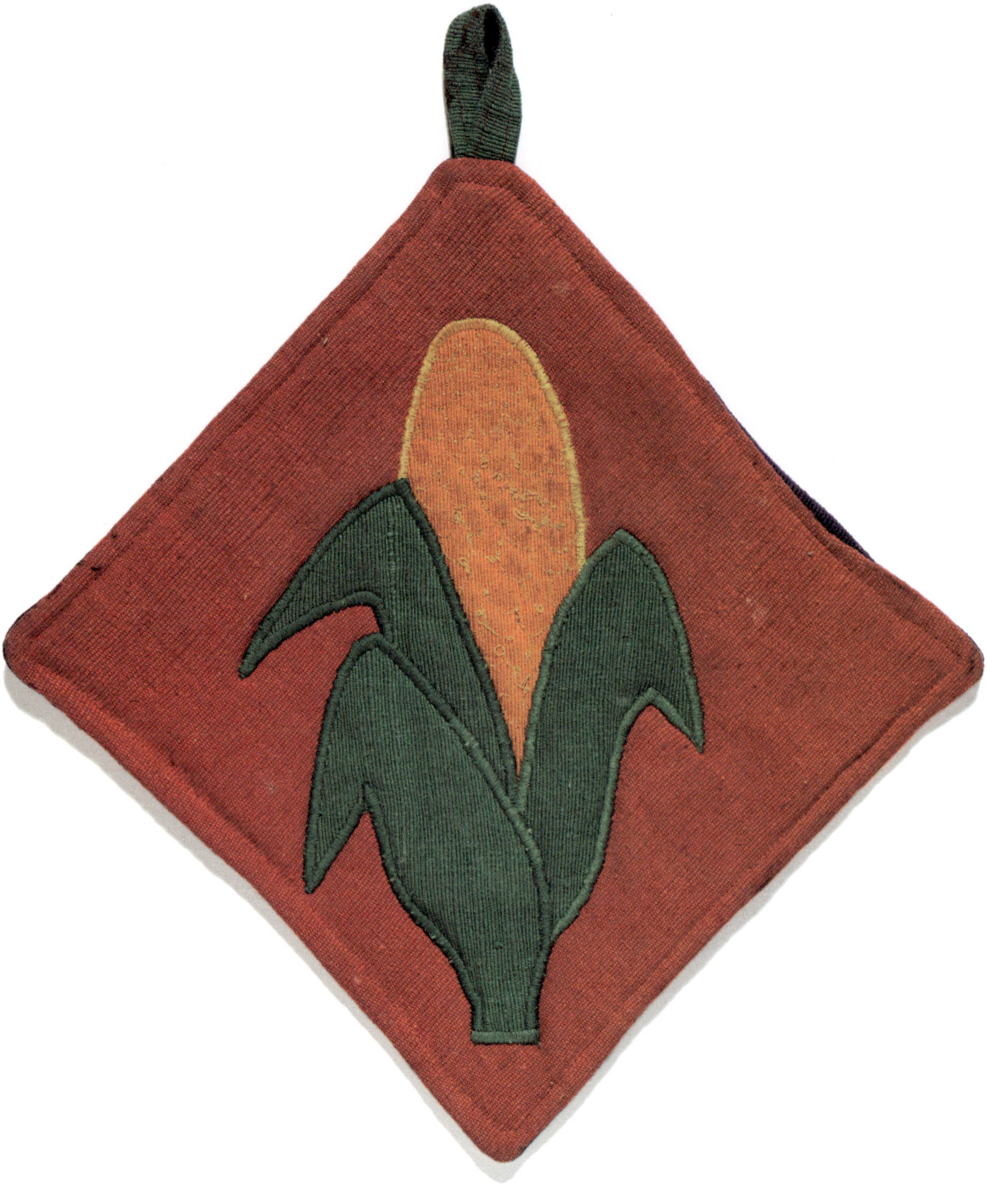

ON NOVEMBER 13, RAYNA NOTED:

ARCHIVISTS FROM THE SCHLESINGER LIBRARY AT RADCLIFFE ARRIVE TO TAKE AWAY BOXES OF PAPERS AND BOOKS JULIA HAS GIVEN THEM. "HI, SCHLESINGER!" "HI, SMITHSONIAN!" WE WAVE AND HAPPILY CONTINUE THE PACKING FRENZY.[9] I WASH. I WASH. I WASH. I'M WASHING BECAUSE I'M JUST A CURATOR WHO DOESN'T HAVE THE OBJECT CARETAKING SKILLS THAT THE COLLECTIONS MANAGEMENT PEOPLE HAVE. THEY WOULDN'T (AND SHOULDN'T!) TRUST ME TO PACK THINGS CORRECTLY. BUT HAH!!!!!!! I KNOW A LARDING NEEDLE FROM A TRUSSING NEEDLE, AND I CAN MAKE THE BIG DECISIONS, LIKE HOW MANY OF JULIA'S DISHTOWELS AND POT HOLDERS WE SHOULD TAKE. A TEAM DINNER IN A TERRIFIC ITALIAN RESTAURANT IN BOSTON'S NORTH END GIVES US SUSTENANCE TO PUSH ON.

One of Julia's potholders

NOVEMBER 14-15, 2001:

   WE ARE PROGRESSING THROUGH THE KITCHEN. EVERYTHING FROM WALL A IS PACKED. JULIA'S FAVORITE ALUMINUM POTS, ALL THE CROCKS (LABELED "SPOONERY," "SPATS," "FORKERY") FROM THE STOVE SHELF, THE POT LIDS FROM BEHIND THE SHELF, AND ALL THE BIG METAL UTENSILS HANGING FROM THE HOOD AND STOVE ARE BAGGED AND BUBBLE-WRAPPED. WALL B FALLS TO OUR HANDS. JULIA'S REFRIGERATOR MAGNETS, GLASS CATS AND ROOSTERS, POTS DE CRÈME, TIN FISH MOLDS, COOKBOOKS, AND VIDEOS OF HER COOKING SHOWS ARE IN BOXES. WE HAVE EATEN OUR WAY THROUGH BAGS OF PIZZA AND SANDWICHES, BOXES OF JULIA'S FAVORITE SNACK, GOLDFISH CRACKERS, A CRATE OF CLEMENTINES, AND TONS OF TERRIFIC COOKIES AND PASTRIES FROM THE ITALIAN BAKERIES. WE'VE GOT TO FINISH MOST EVERYTHING BY THIS EVENING BECAUSE THE TRUCK COMES FRIDAY. ON THESE DAYS, WE'RE NOT WORKING AROUND HUGH [SMITHSONIAN PHOTOGRAPHER] ANYMORE, BUT AROUND JULIA'S PLUMBERS AND ELECTRICIANS WHO'VE COME TO DISCONNECT AND TAKE APART ALL THE GAS AND ELECTRIC LINES, WATER LINES, AND PLUMBING IN THIS KITCHEN. BY NOW, THE KITCHEN IS BEGINNING TO LOOK STRIPPED. JULIA'S ASSISTANTS AND SERVICE MEN OF MANY YEARS AND ALL THE MANY FRIENDS WHO COME BY THE HOUSE ARE STARTLED BY THE LOOKS OF A PLACE THEY HAVE LOVED. THE PLUMBER PROMISES TO BRING HIS CHILDREN TO WASHINGTON TO SEE THE EXHIBIT OF THE KITCHEN, AND ALL THE REST SAY THEY ARE GLAD THE MUSEUM IS TAKING THE KITCHEN. BUT EVERYBODY, INCLUDING EACH OF US, IS JUST A LITTLE SAD. OUR WORK HERE IS COMING TO AN END.[10]

MONDAY: Lunch: Cold cuts & tomatoes
               Dinner: fish, salad, veg, toast, fruit

TUESDAY: Lunch: Fruit
               Dinner: Hamburger, tomatoes, celery sprouts, cukes

WEDNESDAY: Tuna or salmon; fruit
               Dinner: Lamb, lettuce, toms, celery

THURSDAY: Lunch: 2 eggs, cott. cheese; veg; tst
               Dinner: chicken, spinach, peppers, beans

FRIDAY: Lunch: Cheese, spinach, toast
               Dinner: Fish, veg, salad, toast

SATURDAY: Lunch: Fruit
               Dinner: Chicken, tomatoes, fruit

SUNDAY: Chicken, toms, carrots, cabbage, broccoli, fruit
               Dinner: steak, lettuce, cukes, celery, toms, sprouts

Was Julia dieting? This weekly diet card, found in the bottom of the junk drawer, caught us by surprise.

The first group of crates and boxes arrived at the museum on November 19. Rayna noted that the boxes that had taken four days to pack were unloaded from the truck in about thirty minutes. Most of the boxes were taken to an empty gallery on the museum's first floor, where they would be unpacked and the objects formally processed into the collections.

A selection of frequently used ceramic mugs from one of Julia's kitchen cabinets: pear and cherry Fruit Du Jour mugs by Shafford, one of several striped mugs, and an asparagus mug by Fitz & Floyd, 1988

JULIA CHILD'S KITCHEN

Painted ceramic egg cups by Eden and mixing bowl made by RRP Co., Roseville, Ohio

"I'M ABSOLUTELY DELIGHTED THAT THE SMITHSONIAN IS TAKING MY KITCHEN."

JULIA CHILD'S KITCHEN

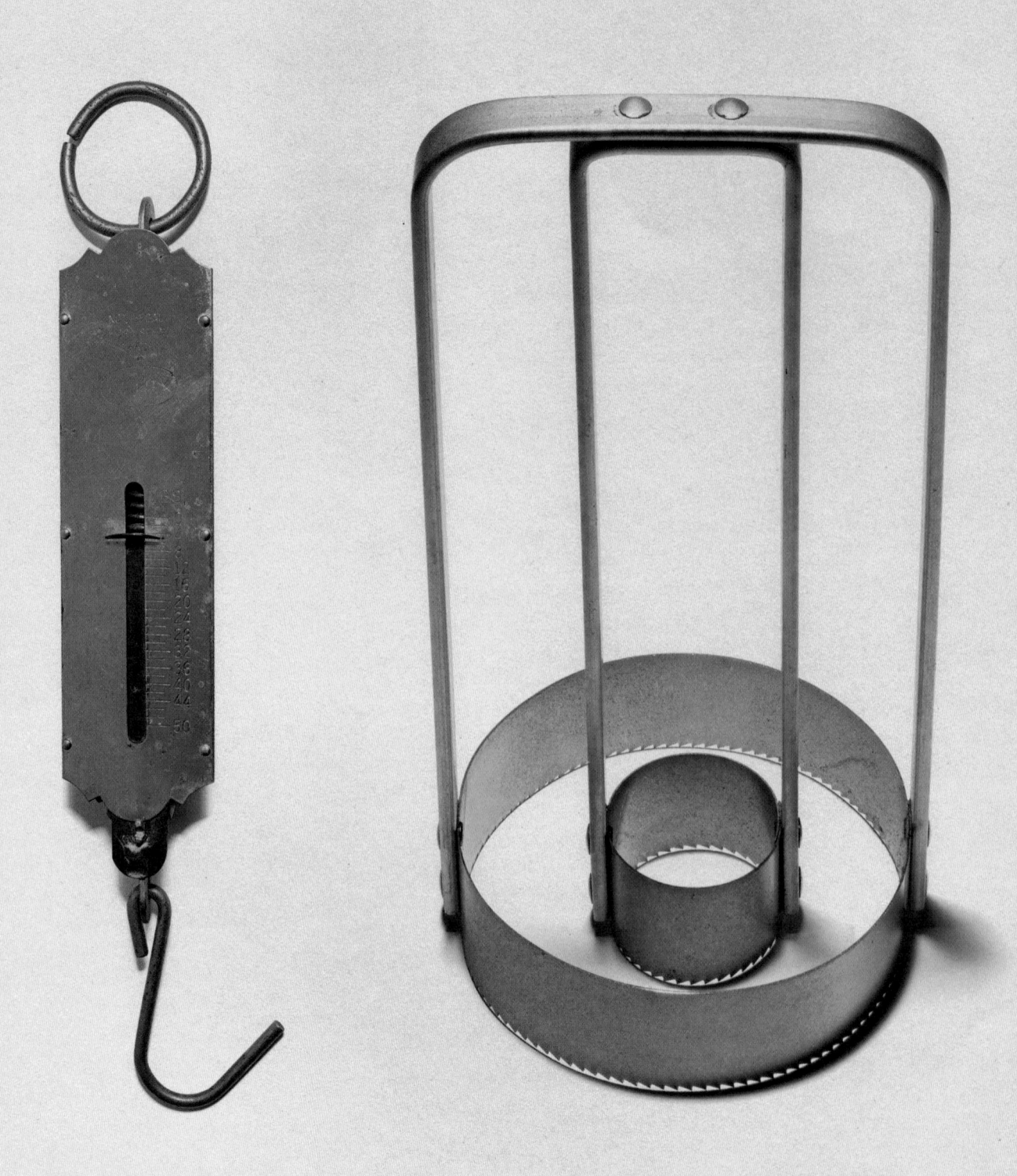

left: Spring scale. *right:* Doughnut cutter / pineapple corer

214   CHAPTER 6

JULIA CHILD'S KITCHEN

left: Three-dimensional fish mold for making fish mousse. *right:* Painting on tin of San Pasqual, the patron saint of cooks and kitchens. The red chiles indicate an association with New Mexico.

"I'M ABSOLUTELY DELIGHTED THAT THE SMITHSONIAN IS TAKING MY KITCHEN." 215

TEAM TWO: THE BIG STUFF...AND THE KITCHEN SINK

Joe Criste, an exhibit specialist in the museum's Historic Restoration Shop, was tapped to lead the second team to remove the cabinetry, door and window moldings, and large appliances from Julia's kitchen. He flew to Boston in advance to scope out what the team would need to get the big stuff safely removed and crated for shipment to the museum. With just a tape measure, pencils, and a yellow pad of paper, he verified measurements of the cabinetry and recorded details like light switches, electrical outlets, and exact locations for the recessed lighting units in the ceiling. He also measured the big appliances to provide the crate builders with the dimensions they would need to build shipping crates. Joe admitted he was surprised to see that some of the kitchen cabinets had no backs; the shelves were nailed to hanging strips attached to the wall. This information was critical for making sure the team would have appropriate material to support the cabinets for shipping.

On December 2 and 3, Joe and his colleagues Peter Albritton, Rob Barrett, and Geoff Ward packed a van with tools and supplies and drove from Washington to Cambridge, arriving on the 4th. There they met up with project manager Nanci Edwards and jumped right into the plan.

With the entire team on hand, they set about removing the cabinetry from the walls and floor. As they worked, they moved items into the wide central hall of the house and then outside where the crate builders were working. Things went fairly smoothly until they discovered that a particular corner cabinet would not fit through the door. After scoping out the size of the kitchen windows, they removed the glass and handed the cabinet outside to two members of the team, who perched on the air conditioner to receive the cabinet from the other two.

Joe also recalled that the Smithsonian team felt badly about leaving holes in the drywall after removing the door and window trim. Early the next morning Rob Barrett took off in the museum's van and drove around Cambridge looking for a construction site. He found one and noticed there were pieces of unused drywall in the site's dumpster. After asking permission of the contractor, Rob filled up the van with clean drywall and returned triumphantly to Irving Street, where the Smithsonian team made repairs to the interior of Julia's kitchen, making it more presentable.[11] Finally, with everything removed, one challenge remained—Julia's airport-grade vinyl floor covering. The team assessed the condition and discussed the likelihood that the glue used to attach the vinyl to the floor in the early 1960s could have contained asbestos. Deciding unanimously to exercise caution and

Removing the cabinetry: Smithsonian historic restoration specialists Geoff Ward (white T-shirt), Rob Barrett (striped shirt), and Peter Albritton (blue shirt) accomplishing the task of removing the cabinets without damaging them

prioritize safety, they found a loose corner piece that was not glued down and cut a small sample to take back to the museum. The idea was either to track down the manufacturer in case the product was still on the market after forty years, or to scan the sample and create a pattern that could be printed out on paper. Ultimately, the latter approach was taken, and the flooring in Julia's kitchen at the Smithsonian is essentially wallpaper mounted on a firm wooden surface. To this day, team members remove their shoes before entering the kitchen to clean and inspect artifacts, or for photography. We call this our "socks-only" policy.

opposite: Julia's cabinets just before they were emptied by the museum team. Also note the stainless-steel pole mounted on the ceiling, a remnant from the days of filming in the kitchen. This pole, for holding TV lights, was packed and taken to the museum and is visible in the kitchen there.

SEALWRAP
CLEAR • TOUGH • SELF-SEALING
SUPERB FOOD SERVICE FILM
BORDEN

The Garland range sits on a dolly in the central hall of Julia's home, ready to be wheeled outside to the crate builders

Once all the crates and boxes were loaded into the moving van, Julia's assistant Stephanie appeared with copies of *In Julia's Kitchen with Master Chefs* for each member of the team, as well as the van driver. While individuals started paging through the volume finding recipes they wanted to try, Stephanie wrangled everyone to stand near the truck holding their books. "We're done! Say 'soufflé!'" and with a click of the camera, the packing of Julia's 1,200 or so parts and pieces of her home kitchen was completed.

With the kitchen packed and loaded into a truck, the team paused with their copies of *In Julia's Kitchen with Master Chefs* before leaving Cambridge. From left, Smithsonian staff Joe Criste, Nanci Edwards, Rob Barrett, and Geoff Ward. The trucking company's driver and workers are at the right.

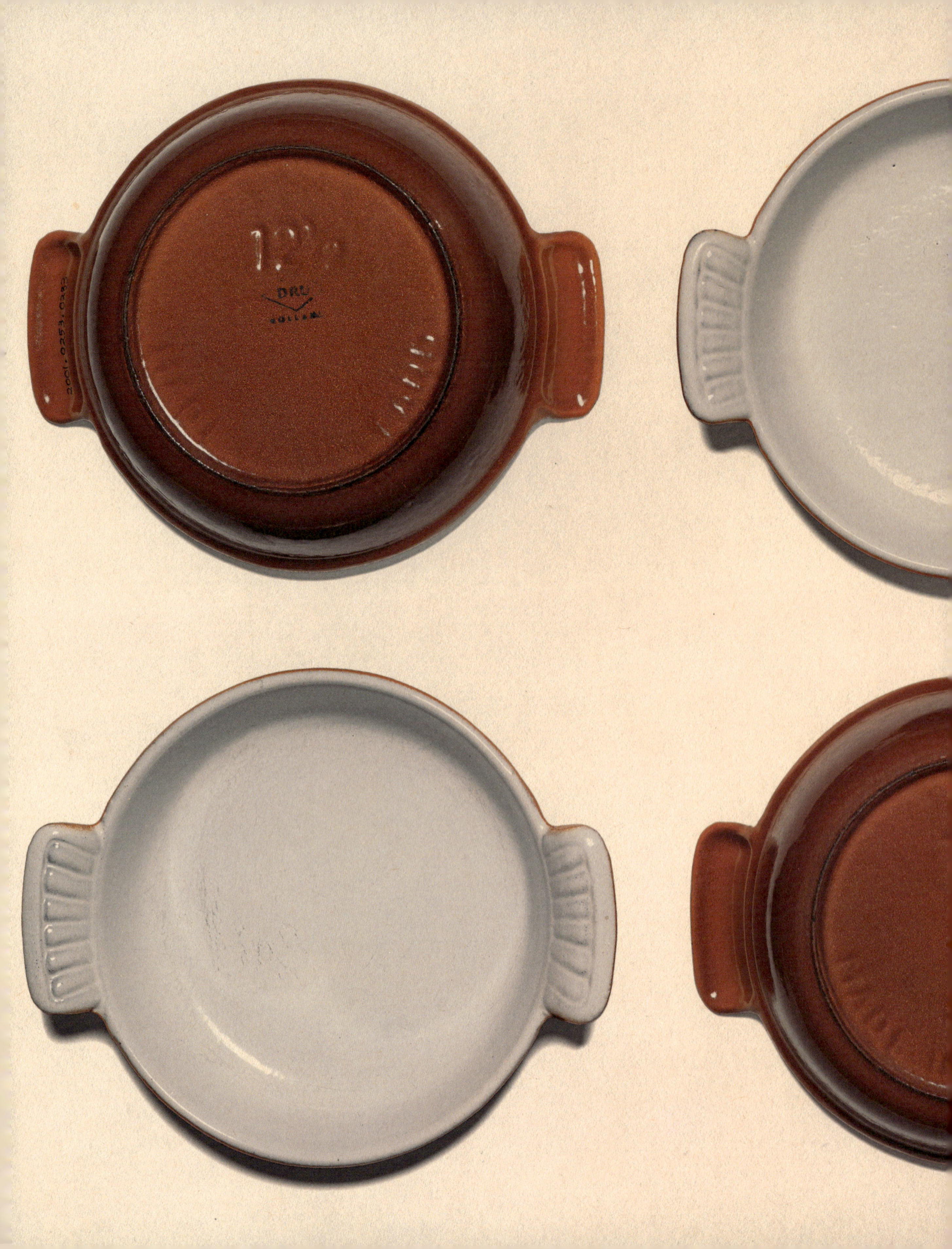
DRU

CHAPTER 7

"If I can influence anyone…"

As any staffer will tell you, one of the most exciting places in a museum is the loading dock on days when new collections arrive. At the National Museum of American History, staff awaiting a shipment will wend their way to the building's lower level, passing pallets of supplies for the museum's café and stores before finally reaching the mechanism that opens the enormous overhead doors and exposes the secure dock. In the fall of 2001, excitement over the arrival of two big shipments totaling some fifty-five boxes and crates containing Julia Child's kitchen was infectious. Collections Manager Steve Velasquez and colleagues from the museum's Objects Processing Facility (OPF), the Historic Restoration shop, and the Food History curatorial team were on the scene with carts, dollies, hand trucks, and flatbeds to help move the material to various places for processing. Ordinarily, all objects are taken directly into the OPF space for unpacking, examination, and processing, but this was no ordinary situation. The material was so extensive, the OPF receiving area could not accommodate it. Instead, the project manager, Nanci Edwards, had arranged for the cabinetry and architectural elements to be taken to the Historic Restoration workshop while the bulk of the collection was wheeled into the massive freight elevator (that can accommodate historic vehicles and other very large objects) and then into an empty gallery on the museum's first floor. This brilliant solution assured the security of the collection and provided a delightful treat for museum visitors: The gallery had an entire wall of windows through which the public could watch the unpacking and processing of Julia's kitchen in real time.

If the loading dock is thrilling for museum staff, watching museum staff at work seems to be equally thrilling for visitors. Curiosity about what goes on behind the scenes is not just a plot device for movies, *Raiders of the Lost Ark* and *Night at the Museum* notwithstanding. Many museums have discovered that welcoming visitors into the day-to-day work of caring for objects and specimens promotes greater understanding of the professional standards and skills behind the public-facing exhibitions. In recent years at the National Museum of American History, for example, visitors have been able to observe the painstaking efforts of conservators working to stabilize the Star-Spangled Banner, the 1814 flag that inspired our national anthem. Over ten years, conservators removed over 1.7 million stitches that were holding the flag to a linen backing, which had been attached in 1914 to allow the flag to be displayed. Conservators found that by 1998 the linen itself was deteriorating and trapping airborne pollutants. Their painstaking work took place in a secure, temperature- and humidity-controlled lab with a wall of windows that allowed millions of visitors to file past, observe the conservators at work, and gain a real sense of the size and fragility of the flag, as well as the care required to preserve it for perpetuity.

The opportunity to unpack and process Julia Child's kitchen in front of the public was too intriguing to ignore, especially in the weeks and months following the 9/11 terrorist attacks, when many people were not inclined to travel or visit public spaces, including museums. Those who did found an 850-square-foot gallery shaped rather like a piece of pie, with windows along what would be the crust. As they gazed in, the scene was one of careful, deliberate, often joyful, and per-

previous spread: A few of Julia's gratin pans
opposite left: A bomb-sniffing dog and extra security officers inspected the shipments of material from Cambridge. Staff who were on hand when the Garland range arrived noticed that the dog was especially interested in what were likely fragrant remnants from more than forty years of Julia's cooking. *opposite right:* Steve Velasquez begins unpacking the Garland range.

petual movement as the curatorial staff opened crates and made some surprising discoveries, such as finding Paul Child's banana stickers still on the underside of the kitchen table. Here was proof of something we had heard about from various family members: that stickers from Paul's breakfast bananas sometimes ended up where they would provoke a laugh when found.

"SUCH A CURIOUS PROCESS..."

Rayna Green, Nanci Edwards, and Steve Velasquez determined the gallery layout, setting up tables for the various steps in the cataloging process: unpacking, measuring, describing, tagging, numbering with a unique catalog number, photographing, and building storage boxes to house the objects. Museum conservator Richard Barden assessed the condition of objects and noted those that would need special cleaning or treatment. Volunteers from the Culinary Historians of Washington (CHOW) and the Washington, DC, chapter of the American Institute of Wine & Food (AIWF) helped in myriad ways. Susan Riecken, for example, collected a reference set of first editions of Julia's books and copies of magazine and newspaper articles about Julia, at one point unwittingly competing against Rayna Green for an item on eBay. Susan was also essential to processing the objects. In "Notes from a Cataloger's Diary," she recorded her thoughts about marking each object with its unique catalog number, a key task for collections management in museums. From the article, an entry dated Monday, February 11, 2002:

left: Curator Rayna Green tracking objects and describing them for the museum's records. *right:* Conservator Richard Barden examining objects in the gallery, including the flashlight, makeup, pad of paper, jar lids, and other contents of Julia's junk drawer in the foreground

above: **Fruit stickers found on the underside of Julia's kitchen table.**

> "The numbering business is something I want to be good at, and it turns out that I am. I love finding the right spot on each object for the number to be painted, and my pleasure in having a steady hand and legible, even beautiful, writing feels downright illicit in this context. It feels wrong to be defacing Julia's whisks and gratin pans this way, never mind the Garland range! Such a curious process, this transformation of utilitarian objects into *objets*!"[1]

This transformation of objects from frequent use to being preserved for perpetuity is witnessed time and again by museum people, and for some, there is always a momentary cloud that marks the transition, the passage of time. Underlying the excitement of working with Julia Child's kitchen is the very real fact that Julia is no longer living in Cambridge and welcoming friends, family, and television viewers into her kitchen. This sense of discomfort has tinged the experience of visiting Julia's kitchen by people who knew her well. Jacques Pépin recalled, "Frankly, for me when I went to the Smithsonian and I saw it through the window, it was freakish to me. Sitting there. Now in a museum looking at it behind glass, it was a bit scary."[2] Yet the value of preserving the material culture of individuals, communities, places, and events is made clear as people from across the country

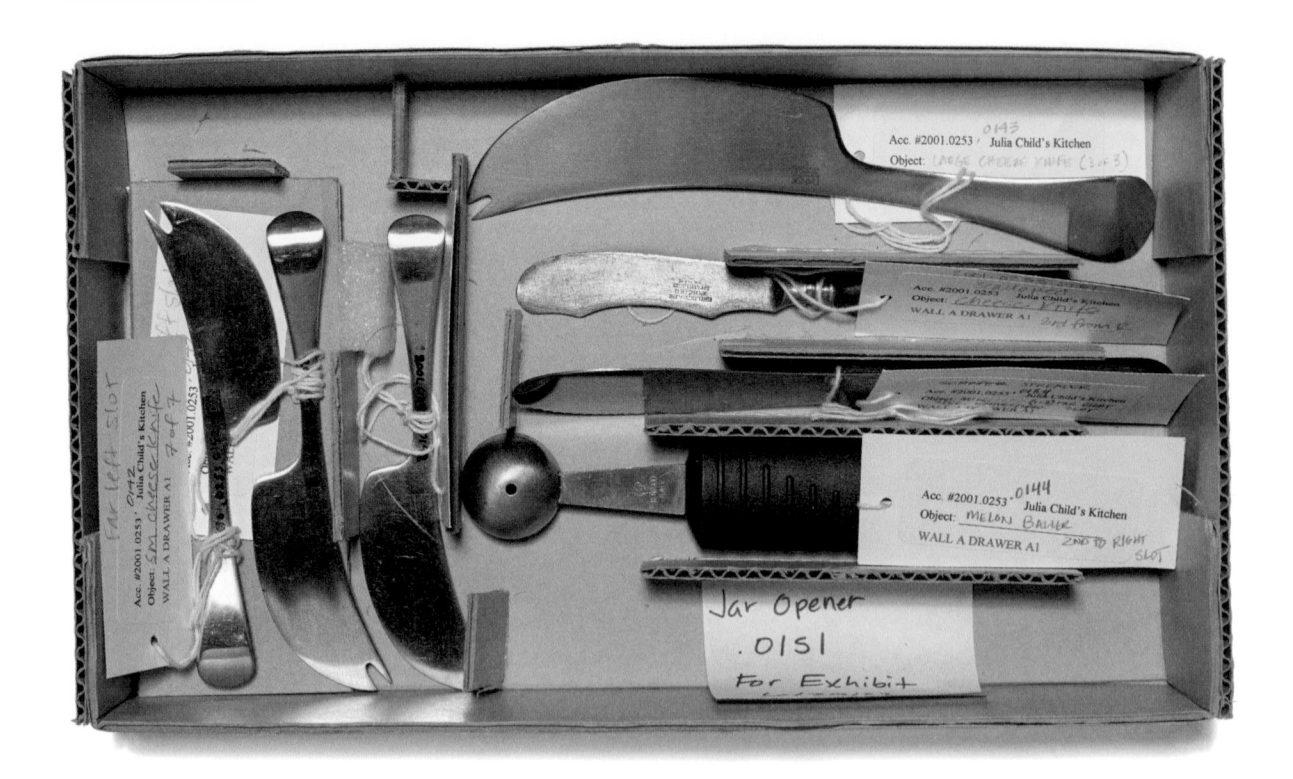

above: An example of kitchen tools tagged, cataloged, and safely housed in the museum. These tools were stored in one of the kitchen drawers and are therefore not on display.
opposite: Julia and the beloved Garland range, 1975

and around the world gain an understanding of history and culture through objects, documents, and stories shared by museums. Musing further about Julia's kitchen at the Smithsonian, Jacques replied, "Certainly [it communicates] a moment in time, a moment in time that was a happy time, when we were together. The beauty of cooking—there is no political implication or gender or religious or any of that type of complication. As I have said [before], 'Everyone is the same in the eye of the stove.'"[3]

"IT'S JULIA CHILD'S KITCHEN! AND THERE'S JULIA CHILD!"

As the unpacking and cataloging continued, the team became more aware of visitors' excitement, largely because we could hear their enthusiasm as they gazed upon us. What had been a doorway into the gallery was fitted out with an acrylic viewport that left several inches of space open at the top. We could hear people approaching and encountering a sign and large photographic cutout of Julia. We heard, "Oh, it's Julia Child's kitchen!" multiple times every day, and sometimes the speaker mim-

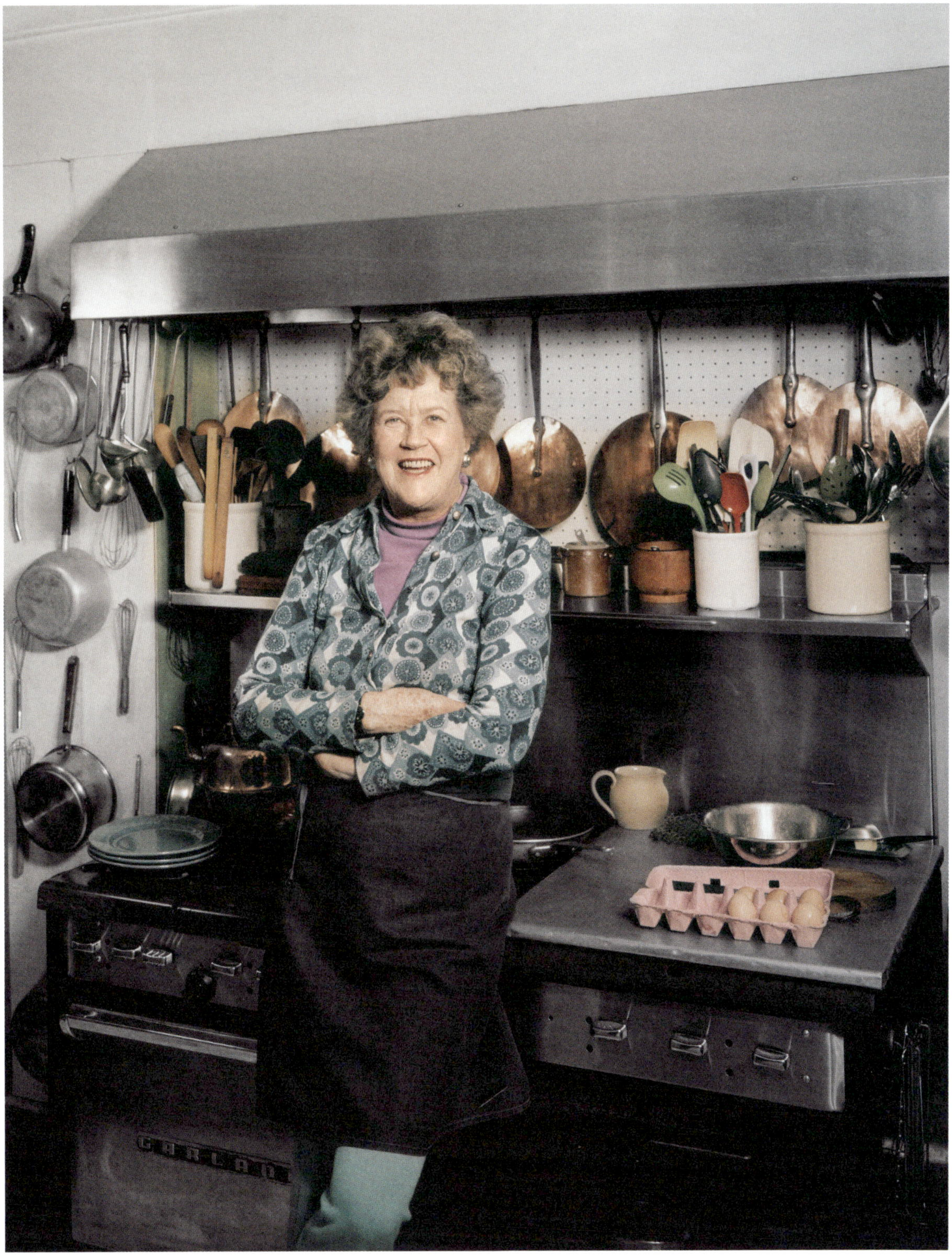

icked Julia's distinctive warble with something like, "It's *Juuulia's* kitchen! Is she making *salll-sa*?" We heard this and wondered, "Did Julia make much salsa?" and quietly noted that the speaker was a dad with two eye-rolling teens in tow. Not long after, Rayna noticed five young men wearing ball caps and baggy trousers peering into the space. "Julia Child is seriously awesome," said one as they moved past the viewport.

As we worked, we harbored the hope of reassembling the kitchen inside the gallery in time for Julia's ninetieth birthday on August 15, 2002. In Smithsonian time, this is magical thinking. To collect and process more than one thousand objects and build an exhibition with them in less than a year and without funds in hand was, well, nuts. But every challenge we had encountered since Rayna's initial call to Julia back in August 2001 had been resolved, it seemed, just in time. This had happened often enough, suggesting to us that "Julia karma" was paving the way.[4]

We floated the idea informally among colleagues to gain a sense of whether we had any support. Many people were excited by the tremendous energy and atmosphere of good will that hung over the pie-shaped gallery, now called, "What's Cooking? Julia Child's Kitchen at the Smithsonian." Others advised us to select some iconic objects to feature, as that was an approach more easily achieved. But as we labored in the gallery, we kept hearing the opinions, hopes, and dreams of our visitors. "I love seeing all the whisks and her pots and pans. But I can't wait to see the whole thing put together!" "I want to see just how Julia arranged her kitchen, the part you can't see on TV." "I wonder when they are going to have the kitchen ready for the public?"

How could we let such enthusiasm drift into the void? Rayna, Nanci, and I decided to take turns stepping outside of the gallery to speak with visitors, answer their questions, and ask a few of our own. This marked the beginning of a relationship with the public that the project team has endeavored to bolster whenever possible. Our informal chats revealed a deep well of admiration for Julia and her ability to make ordinary cooks feel empowered to try new things. Time and again, we heard stories of how people grew up watching *The French Chef* on television, with or without a parent, and feeling inspired to try recipes from *Mastering the Art of French Cooking*. We learned about a group of women in Colorado who made cakes for Julia on her August birthday every year. We heard that Julia made them want to learn more about cooking and about how much they enjoyed stocking up on cookware, just like Julia. Trying not to lead the witness, we asked what in particular they wanted to see in the museum about Julia. More times than not, the response was, "The kitchen. All of it."

Armed with these data, albeit not scientifically collected, we gained permission to investigate how the rebuilt kitchen might be displayed in the gallery as well as any auxiliary exhibition elements, such as photographs, graphics, and interpretive panels. Designer Marcia Powell joined the team to create drawings for a potential exhibition, while the crate opening and objects processing continued.[5] The beehive of activity, strangely reminiscent of what we had learned about Julia's kitchen during recipe testing and meal prep, was an ongoing attraction in the museum. But at one point, on Monday, May 6, Susan Riecken found herself working all alone in the gallery. She wrote, "Hunched over a cataloging data sheet as I measured a cast-iron casserole, a woman and young child peered in. The woman spoke to the child with animation and authority. 'Why look! It's Julia Child's kitchen! And there's Julia Child!'"[6] When we heard this report from the day, we all sighed, "If only."

Paul and Julia in the kitchen, October 25, 1983

"BON APPÉTIT! JULIA CHILD'S KITCHEN AT THE SMITHSONIAN"

In the spring of 2022, the team received the green light to move forward with creating an exhibition featuring Julia's kitchen in the gallery space that had served so well as an objects processing area and space for public engagement.[7] As things came together, "Julia karma" was once again much in evidence: Volunteers continued to support the work, donors made contributions, and in-kind support arrived in many forms. Geoffrey Drummond, Julia's TV producer in the nineties, compiled a video, "Julia Child's Kitchen Wisdom," to play on a loop in the gallery. The ninety minutes of clips from her forty years on television would enliven the space with Julia's distinctive voice and augment the other exhibition elements.

The intent was always to show Julia's kitchen exactly as it had looked when she left it in 2001, but one problem remained. The Smithsonian team did not collect the distinctive wall of copper pots because Julia had already promised to lend it to her friend and fellow AIWF founder Robert Mondavi for his new museum project in Napa, California. Designer Marcia Powell, along with Billy Powell and others in the cabinet shop, created a brilliant solution: They filled in the wall space with an acrylic window into which the outlines of the pots were routed, using a photograph of the wall taken during the packing-up process as a guide (see photo on page 109). This acrylic wall proved both attractive and brilliant as it allowed museum visitors a substantial viewport into which they could gaze at the astonishing array of equipment, tools, and kitchen objects that Julia and Paul had amassed over many years.

Thus it was that on August 18, 2002, Julia Child stepped into her home kitchen inside the National Museum of American History and memorably declared her desire to turn something on and start to cook. Later that day we celebrated the opening of the exhibition, "Bon Appétit! Julia Child's Kitchen at the Smithsonian." Surrounded by family, AIWF members, and longtime friends, including a few of her old colleagues from the OSS, Julia voiced her approval of

In the cabinet shop, Joe Criste and Rob Barrett installed Julia's sink back in her cabinetry for the exhibition.

the installation, with just a hint of emotion. Our strict attention to installing the kitchen's many objects exactly where they had been when Julia left her home in Cambridge less than a year prior was rewarded with her appreciation. That evening, as guests strolled through the museum sampling marvelous dish after marvelous dish created by area chefs to honor Julia on her ninetieth birthday, the team dared to exhale—but not entirely, for the press event and public opening awaited us early the next morning.

"WE WANT HER TO SEE HER HERITAGE."

We gathered back in the museum the following morning for a live TV segment on NBC's *Today* show, followed by a press event. Julia and Rayna Green would be inside the kitchen, responding to questions from an interviewer in New York. As airtime approached, the rest of us stepped back, starved for sleep but saturated with excitement and emotion. Julia and Rayna were seated at the table inside the kitchen and wired for sound when I heard a voice asking, "Where's Paula?" As I peered inside the kitchen, Julia pointed to one of the knives on the magnetic strip to the left of the sink and asked me to straighten it; its handle had dipped slightly, but noticeably. Without hesitation, I took off my shoes (to protect the paper floor) and tiptoed around the microphone wires. With a gloved hand I adjusted the offending knife and retreated just moments before television viewers witnessed Julia Child inside her kitchen for the last time.

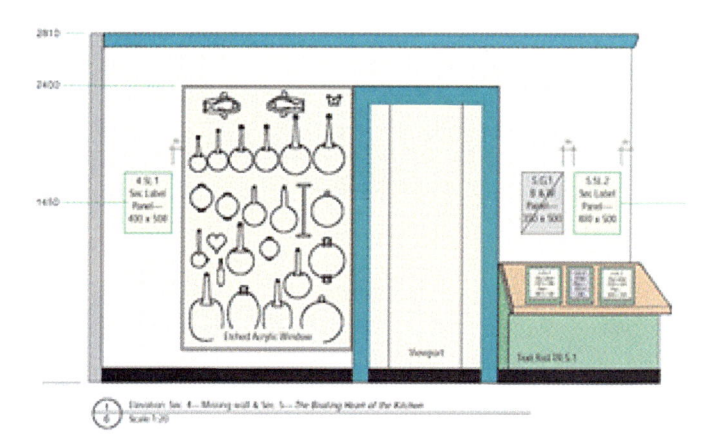

above: Intern Christine Yokoyama installing Julia's hooks on her pegboard for hanging the pans in their proper places. *left:* Marcia Powell's design for the acrylic wall with the outlines of the copper pot wall routed into the surface.

The press event went without a hitch as Julia charmed everyone with her humility and humor. She expressed awe at the team's thorough approach, echoing remarks she had shared with the *Boston Globe* earlier in the week: The Smithsonian team "took tremendous notes when they came. They wrote down everything, even the toothpicks."[8] When asked about her secret for living such a long life, she replied, "Red meat and gin," with a gleam in her eye.[9] The gathering wrapped up shortly before 10:00 A.M., when the building would be opening to the public, and yet, at ninety years old, Julia went off for more interviews and a full social schedule in Washington. Was she aware that there were people, at least two wearing chef's coats, queued up to enter the building right at opening?

When we emerged, after checking the gallery one last time, there was a line of people forming outside of the gallery. As we greeted these enthusiastic fans of Julia, we noticed a young couple in their chef whites holding their infant. Without a prompt, they explained, "We're chefs on the Eastern Shore of Maryland, and we want our daughter to see her heritage." This was one of many testimonies we heard from first-day visitors about Julia's inspiring role in their own lives.

As the days and months went by, we observed visitors in the gallery and noticed an unusual sense of uplift. People seemed relaxed and comfortable. They lingered in the space. They watched huge chunks of the ninety-minute video, upending the conventional wisdom of exhibition developers who, based on research, estimate that visitors spend less than a minute watching videos while standing inside a gallery. With no room for a bench in the tiny space, visitors often sat on the floor together like kids gathered around the TV for Saturday morning cartoons. They spoke to each other, and even to people they didn't know. They compared notes about attachments for their stand mixers. They exclaimed over objects that were just like theirs, from the copper polenta pot to the cast-iron skillets to cookbooks on the shelves and the Rubik's cube next to the telephone. They talked about cooking and their favorite recipes. They wondered aloud about particular tools, and what that handsaw was doing hanging on the wall in the kitchen (it's a butcher's saw for cutting up meat and bone). And they talked about Julia and memorable TV moments: how she dropped a chicken, a fish, a turkey—none of which happened, by the way—but people remember that she just kept going, which is, really, the teachable point of the story.[10]

Meanwhile, we gave tours to various groups and happily received feedback. One group of fourth graders sent follow-up notes, including a report, "Our Trip to

Julia Child's Kitchen," from Sarah S. in November 2003. Her final sentence surely would have generated a nod from Julia: "You should go to her exhibit and watch her shows and learn her cooking."[11] Julia would have delighted in the museum staff members who occasionally dropped into the gallery for a respite; it was clear there were many fans of Julia and cooking among us. Before opening hours we sometimes encountered security officers and building maintenance staff, often men, who were checking out the video for tips on cooking various dishes.

left: Julia's polenta pot *below*: Julia's bone saw that hangs above the butcher block table in the kitchen

First breakfast on the terrace at La Pitchoune, September 1, 1979

CELEBRATE AND GRIEVE

When Julia Child died on August 12, 2004, just three days shy of her ninety-second birthday, word swept through the museum, as it must have in culinary schools, food media offices, restaurants, markets, shops, and the homes of millions of fans across the country. We'd known this day would come, and when it did, we sought each other out and then froze in place, sitting together silently for who knows how long. By the time we made our way to the "Bon Appétit!" exhibition, there were flowers lovingly placed by an anonymous admirer of Julia near the gallery entrance. We soon learned that the admirer was a Smithsonian staff conservator who had made frequent pilgrimages to the kitchen since its opening. Over the course of the day, many people brought flowers—and a few even brought wrapped butter—to not only celebrate Julia's life but also grieve at the place they now associated most with their favorite cooking teacher and culinary muse: Julia's kitchen at the Smithsonian.

REUNITING THE COPPER AND ITS KITCHEN

Interest in Julia Child doesn't seem to wane. Years after her death in 2004, we noted a steady stream of interest in visiting the kitchen. Even for people who don't know exactly who she is, the kitchen provides a layered portrait of her culinary work and educational impact. And the kitchen as a kitchen is mesmerizing to people. It seems like a homey space, one where visitors imagine sitting down for a cup of tea with a friend. It also seems old-timey, except when one really looks closely at the professional knives, no-nonsense cutting tools, and the array of pots,pans, and specialty cookware. We have observed visitors guiding others to the wall panels and the video, "Julia Child's Kitchen Wisdom," that still plays in a new and updated gallery. The video often provides the link of recognition some visitors need to place Julia in the context of television cooking shows that are more recent and familiar. At the same time, every so often a new book, film, or television series reignites a big spark of interest in Julia Child and her life.

    This was certainly the case with the 2009 release of the film *Julie & Julia*.[12] Based on Julie Powell's 2005 book that chronicled her attempt to cook all 524 recipes in *Mastering the Art of French Cooking*, Volume One, within a calendar year, the film inspired a whole new generation of Julia fans. Actors Meryl Streep (as Julia) and Amy Adams (as Julie) portrayed the title characters in a way that resonated with audiences and expanded public interest in Julia's kitchen at the

Smithsonian. Shortly after the film was released, I witnessed a young girl running into the gallery shouting, "Mom! Look! It's Meryl Streep's kitchen!" Mom gently set the record straight, but the unbridled enthusiasm for the kitchen itself did not need adjustment of any sort.

Julie & Julia coincided with the unfortunate demise of Robert and Margrit Biever Mondavi's museum and cultural center, Copia: The American Center for Wine, Food & the Arts in Napa.[13] Julia had lent her wall of copper pots to the center in 2001, and with Copia's closing, the artifacts were reunited with the rest of the kitchen through a donation from Julia's family and The Julia Child Foundation for Gastronomy and the Culinary Arts, a not-for-profit foundation she had established before her death. The loss of a cultural organization is never a cause for celebration, but the confluence of the *Julie & Julia* film and the arrival of the spectacular wall of copper and cast-iron at the museum would have been any PR maven's dream. We called it another case of "Julia karma."

The exhibition team decided not to install the pegboard wall where it would have been within the kitchen's footprint. Rather, the acrylic viewport that echoed the wall was determined too important for visitor access to lose. Thus, the repatriated wall of copper cookware was installed against a gallery wall, but lined up to its kitchen location so visitors can see how it functioned historically. At a special event to reveal the new installation of the wall, *Julie & Julia*'s director, Nora Ephron, spoke about her own history with Julia's cookbooks and her admiration for Julia's television acumen and comedic timing. Like many guests at the museum that evening, Ephron lingered in the gallery, gazing into the kitchen, and pointing out the objects and elements that resonated with her own considerable life in food.

CLASS IN THE KITCHEN

By 2010, "Bon Appétit!" was showing signs of age. The exhibition was expected to be on view for about two years, the period typically allotted for projects in that tiny gallery. But Julia's kitchen was approved for continuation due to its resonance with the public; it had become a destination in the museum and among visitors to Washington, DC. Staff at the museum's information desks grew accustomed to directing people to the exhibition. Three French chefs breathlessly asked, "Où est Julia?" as they hurried to pay their respects while in Washington for business. Locals made pilgrimages to the kitchen on a regular basis and added it to itineraries for visitors from out of town. Even the sightseeing trolleys that conveyed visitors around DC

The first installation of Julia's kitchen at the Smithsonian in 2002

added the kitchen to its sites of interest. "And here is the National Museum of American History, home of the Star-Spangled Banner, the ruby slippers [from the movie *The Wizard of Oz*], and Julia Child's kitchen!" With so much attention, it wasn't surprising that the gallery needed a refresh, a facelift. And, frankly, the team was champing at the bit to create a larger exhibition that would put Julia Child and her kitchen in the greater context of twentieth-century food history. Julia's influence could be appreciated as part of an expanded view of the changing social, cultural, technological, and political landscape of food. Our desire to explore those complex layers of food and food history found an opportunity when the museum had to partially close in 2011 for long-awaited upgrades to its public spaces.[14]

When a much larger gallery was identified on the first floor in the museum's east wing, the project was given approval by the museum's management team to create an exhibition that would include Julia's kitchen. Officially, the gallery would be ours through 2017.[15] As part of planning for the new exhibition, Steve Velasquez and I worked with Mary Coughlin, an objects conservator and assistant professor in the Museum Studies graduate program at George Washington University, to supervise a seminar that would assess the condition of several groups of objects in

Nora Ephron, Susy Davidson, and Phila Cousins celebrate the arrival of Julia's copper pots at the museum and the successful launch of Ephron's film *Julie & Julia* in 2009.

Julia Child's kitchen. In the Spring 2011 semester, we worked with a class of five GWU Museum Studies students to evaluate the condition of objects and make recommendations to incorporate preventive conservation measures into the new exhibition. This project preceded the intricate task of packing up the kitchen to move to a new space.

Because the course met during museum hours, the students worked in full view of the public. Before entering the kitchen, the students, like staff, donned socks to protect the paper-covered floor, and gloves to prevent any transfer of dirt or oils between hands and objects. Once inside, they practiced appropriate care of the kitchen table and countertops by covering them with sheets of soft, flexible polyethylene foam before using them gently as work surfaces. During the class sessions the students recorded the condition of some four hundred objects. For some, they added custom-cut pieces of a stable, polyester film to isolate objects at points of contact. This was especially important in the case of plastic spatulas and other tools contained in ceramic crocks above the Garland range. Indeed, plastics in the kitchen, found in some tools, the dish rack and dishwashing gloves, Julia's personal telephone book binder, and several books on the bookcase, generated the most concern, as the inherent deterioration revealed by weeping and off-gassing of acidic vapor negatively impacted surrounding objects.[16]

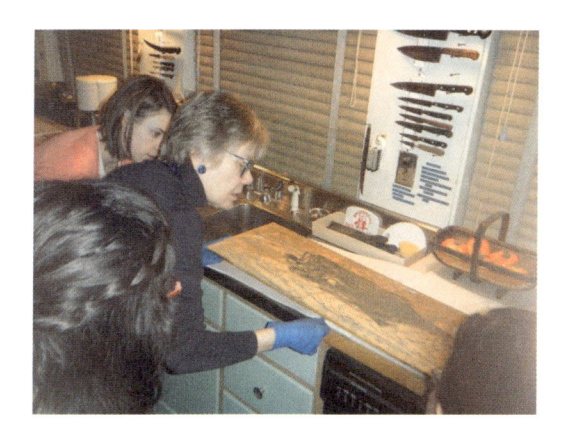

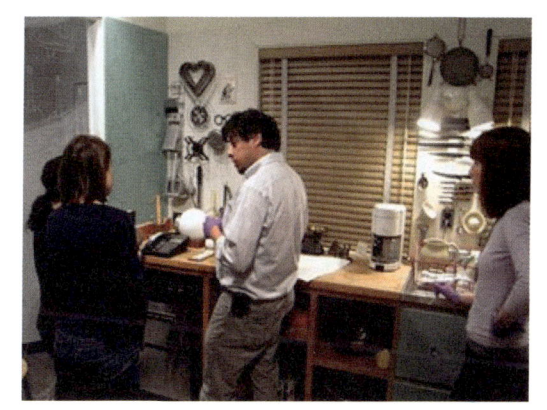

The students, teachers, and curators discussed the particular challenges of caring for a complex object—a kitchen—that was on continuous and long-term view. The museum's desire to display the kitchen just as it was when Julia left it in 2001 had to be weighed against our responsibility to preserve the objects on view for the long term. Over the years the curatorial and conservation staff continued to assess the condition of the objects in the kitchen and have cleaned and applied basic, noninvasive treatment for some, while removing a few, such as a couple of plastic spatulas, from the exhibition to isolate them in storage.

Although the students were initially self-conscious about working in front of the public, they eventually focused entirely on the tasks at hand. During class, at least one curator stood outside the kitchen door to explain what was happening and to answer questions. As always, visitors told stories of their cooking experiences and their admiration for Julia. But for those fourteen weeks in the spring of 2011, they also asked questions about museum work and object conservation. Several young

left: Curator Helena Wright examining the condition of one of the fish prints in Julia's kitchen with George Washington University students.
right: Steve Velasquez explains how to protect the countertop when examining objects. George Washington University students and their course instructor, the object conservator Mary Coughlin, conducted basic assessments of objects that had been on view for almost a decade.

people asked about the graduate program, thinking it would be cool to work in a museum.[17] In addition to completing survey checklists and writing papers, the students also wrote blog posts about their work assessing discrete groupings of objects.[18] On reflection, this project extended the educational role of Julia's kitchen in yet another direction, one she would have likely supported with great enthusiasm.

"FOOD: TRANSFORMING THE AMERICAN TABLE"

All in all, Julia's kitchen was out of the public eye for less than a year, during which time the team, led by Steve Velasquez, packed everything up and moved it to a secure staging area. Plans for the exhibition, "FOOD: Transforming the American Table," were shaping up and included a new gallery for Julia's kitchen. This exhibition space, which was 3,700 square feet compared with 850 in the original location, provided an opportunity for debating the best location for the kitchen, as it would now share space with a host of different stories, objects, imagery, and other components. Led by designer Clare Brown, the team debated whether to place the kitchen in the back of the gallery, effectively making visitors seeking the kitchen walk past (and hopefully interact with) the other food history stories on the way to reaching their goal. In the end, however, the team decided to build the kitchen right at the gallery's threshold, to draw people to the exhibition and to reward the devoted pilgrims who seek out Julia's kitchen with nothing short of fervor. This placement would also allow visitors to walk almost entirely around the kitchen, providing more ways to see the details and to create more space for reflection and interaction. Significantly, the new location would also permit the museum to correct a conservation issue that had vexed the team for years: The kitchen would get its own ceiling, to protect it from atmospheric dust and convey a more realistic sense of the room as a room. What's more, after nearly ten years, the scratches and daily hand and nose prints left by enthusiasts on the original acrylic viewports had become increasingly difficult to clean. The new installation would feature new, sturdy, custom-built viewports.

In terms of the interpretive framework, we realized that the original 1950–2000 timeframe for the exhibition narrative was compatible with the kitchen itself, reflecting as it does that period of tremendous change in what and how we eat. The objects within—from the late forties in Paris to 2001, when Julia donated the kitchen—represent home cooking, culinary education, and an era of expanding

Entrance to the exhibition "FOOD: Transforming the American Table"

professionalism among American cooks. Her influential story and enduring educational message would set up the rest of the exhibition, where other stories and touchstone objects reflecting changes in food, and its production, distribution, preparation, and consumption, would be revealed and explored.[19]

Along a wall near the entrance to the exhibition stretches a major section called "New and Improved!" The stories there explore how new technologies and innovative processes accelerated the establishment of the industrial food system in the postwar period. While these changes helped provide many Americans with an abundant and affordable food supply, they also led to serious consequences that are ongoing: the effects of highly processed foods on the health of people and communities, the impacts of industrialized food production on wages and the safety of workers, the economic costs of centralized production on smaller producers and regions, and the significant and cumulative environmental impacts of large-scale food production. These issues are addressed in a series of case studies that feature the rapid growth of the lettuce industry; the expansion of the commercial production of baked goods and the rise of snack foods; the ongoing lack of access to food for many Americans, even during periods of national prosperity; the link between supermarkets and suburban expansion; the introduction of new tools and materials for kitchen cookware to help home cooks; and the explosion of fast-food, supersized, and drive-through dining.

Narratives that ran counter to the excitement of the "New and Improved!" food scene in the United States are grouped within a section that stretches along the opposite wall of the gallery. Under the heading "Resetting the Table," the stories reveal how migrants from Asia, Africa, the Middle East, and Central and South America have redefined "American" cuisine. The ingredients, flavors, dishes, culinary techniques, social practices, and food spaces reflect the tremendous cultural diversity of the country since the passage of the Immigration and Nationality Act in 1965.[20] This part of the exhibition also showcases material from the sixties and seventies counterculture movements that rejected mainstream, industrial food production in favor of more communal models of producing food, eating, and living. The rise of vegetarian restaurants, artisanal food production, organic and fresh emphases on restaurant menus, farmer's markets, school gardens, and other examples of a more regional and local approach to food are also explored through objects and graphics.

"FOOD: Transforming the American Table" also looks at the rise of wine and winemaking since the repeal of Prohibition in 1933, along with the origins of the modern craft beer industry. These industries share some key components: the desire to create beverages with deep historical and cultural roots in the United States that can compete in the marketplace but maintain and even transcend standards of quality, while drawing from a sense of place and community. These ideas are very much in line with the shifts in food production away from industrialized and centralized to a more craft and artisanal model that are also represented in the exhibition.

"FOOD" opened to the public in November 2012, and due to its relevance and popularity, the project was extended. In 2019, the gallery was updated and refreshed, with Julia's kitchen remaining as the welcoming presence at the entrance.

opposite through page 250: Views from "FOOD: Transforming the American Table" at the National Museum of American History

BREWING
A REVOLUTION
BUFFALO
BILL'S
OPEN
We Brew
DRAFT BEERS

OLD VINES AND
NEW BLOOD
BUFFALO
BILL'S
OPEN
We Brew

Technologies Old and New

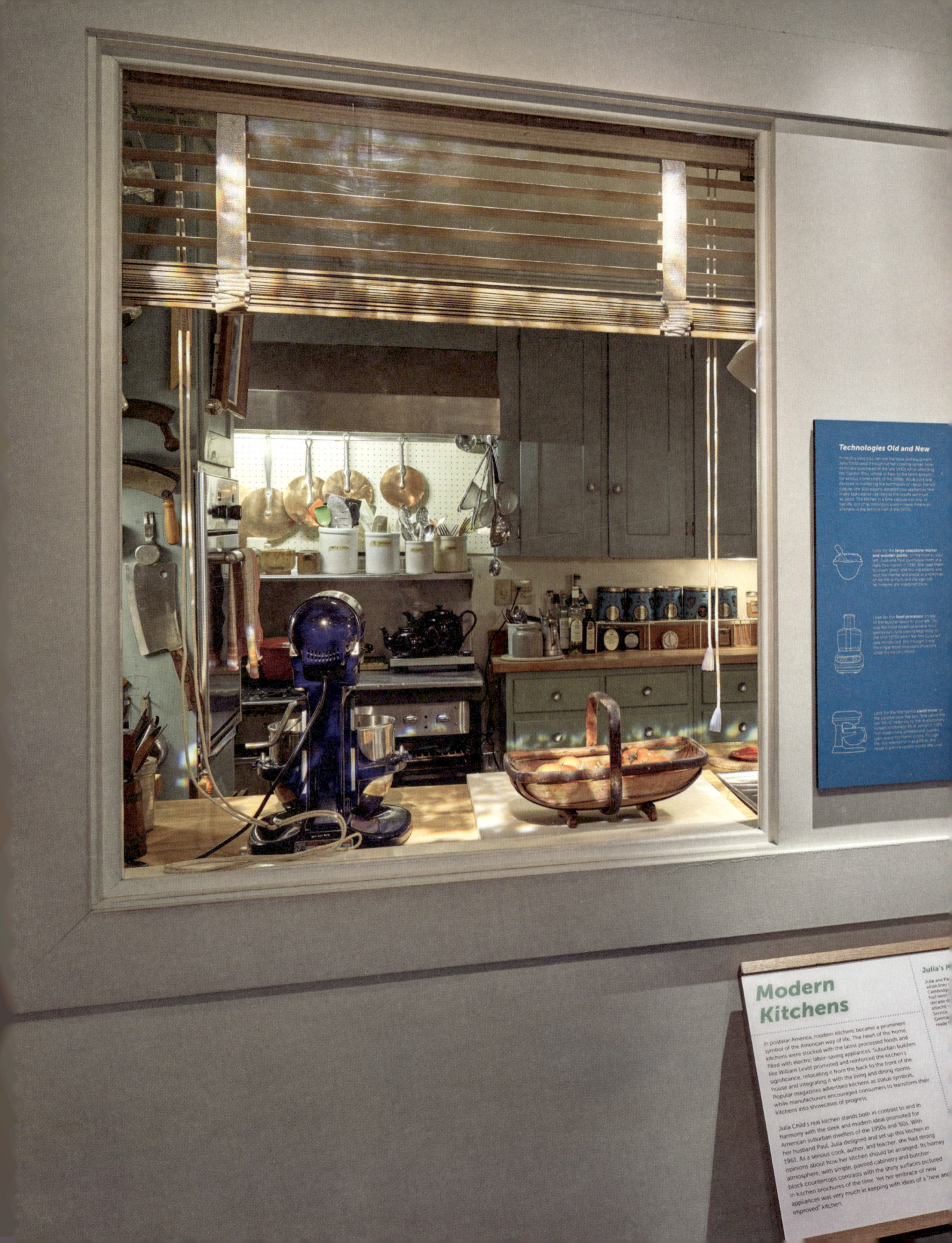

Modern Kitchens

In postwar America, modern kitchens became a prominent symbol of the American way of life. The heart of the home, kitchens were stocked with the latest processed foods and filled with electric labor-saving appliances. Suburban builders like William Levitt promoted and reinforced the kitchen's significance, relocating it from the back to the front of the house and integrating it with the living and dining rooms. Popular magazines advertised kitchens as status symbols, while manufacturers encouraged consumers to transform their kitchens into showcases of progress.

Julia Child's real kitchen stands both in contrast to and in harmony with the sleek and modern ideal promoted for American suburban dwellers of the 1950s and '60s. With her husband Paul, Julia designed and set up this kitchen in 1961. As a serious cook, author, and teacher, she had strong opinions about how her kitchen should be arranged. Its homey atmosphere, with simple, painted cabinetry and butcher block countertops contrasts with the shiny surfaces pictured in kitchen brochures of the time. Yet her embrace of new appliances was very much in keeping with ideas of a "new and improved" kitchen.

The Real Thing
A Place for Everything
Built for a Tall Cook
Work Zones
New Kitchen Built to Fit Your Wife

Wine
for the Table

Fifty States of Wine

FOOD ON THE GO

jack will speak to you

SHORTCUTS FOR HOME COOKS

SUPERMARKET INNOVATIONS

"WHERE'S THE FOOD?"

Visitor surveys of the "FOOD" exhibition provided valuable feedback and, not surprisingly, Julia's kitchen received enthusiastic comments and high scores among survey takers. Visitors who walked through the gallery with family and friends enjoyed the experience of seeing familiar objects and stories, from TV dinners and microwave meals, to snacking and drive-through dining, to the *Moosewood Cookbook* and Alice Waters's bouillabaisse cauldron from Chez Panisse, her acclaimed restaurant in Berkeley, California, that in 1971 committed to serving dishes created with local and organic ingredients, to food-related political movements and the rise of Mexican foods and flavors throughout the United States. Still, we heard from some visitors that they were disappointed not to have food or live cooking demonstrations associated with the exhibition. Some respondents asked, "Where's the food?"

By this time, the team was already brainstorming ways to take food history toward a more active and interactive space. With colleagues in the public programming department, we experimented with different themes, topics, and program models, resulting in a series of after-hours panel discussions and tastings in the museum's Victory Garden.[21] Through a robust schedule of talks, tours, objects-out-of-storage, and book-signings, the team built an enthusiastic and loyal audience for food history.

As we continued to evaluate our programs and their reach, we also wondered: Could we take Julia's educational message about the importance of learning about food and cooking into a purpose-built space? Might we organize live cooking demonstrations or even cooking classes in a kitchen theater of sorts? Could we carve out a separate gallery to collaborate with our Smithsonian colleagues from other museums on exhibitions featuring their research and collections reflecting diverse aspects of food history and culture?[22]

These ideas crystallized around the major renovation project underway in the museum's west end, where the space formerly occupied by the "Bon Appétit" exhibition was slated for public programming. Before long, a demonstration kitchen and public plaza were sketched into the plans, essentially extending and expanding the food history project. We knew in our bones that Julia would have fully supported the commitment to cooking inside the museum and putting culinary history literally onstage. The idea also involved using cooking and food as an accessible way of engaging museum visitors in a broader exploration of important themes and topics in American history. Could we combine our historical research and collecting with cooking?

Chef Curtis Aikens presented the first cooking program on the museum's kitchen stage.

"COOKING UP HISTORY"

In a word, the answer was "yes!" The first floor of the museum's renovated west end opened in July 2015 with the first cooking demonstrations drawing a standing-room-only crowd. Curtis Aikens, one of Food Network's first chefs, created three summertime dishes that reflected his Georgia upbringing, while speaking with Smithsonian host Jessica Carbone about the ingredients, cooking techniques, family recipes, and his personal journey in food. Curtis owned the stage and, in fact, jumped off to mingle with the crowd. With such a strong beginning we were convinced that the kitchen stage was a viable way to extend Julia's message about food, cooking, and social interaction with the public. And it was also a place to discuss larger issues sur-

"Cooking Up History" host Ashley Rose Young with cookbook author and editor Toni Tipton-Martin during a cooking demonstration at the museum on February 21, 2020

rounding food and culture: Chef Curtis spoke about the essential place of kitchen gardens and the value of generational knowledge that was part of his childhood in Georgia. He also spoke about how he, like other chefs concerned with community health, was altering some of the old family recipes, replacing some ingredients with options that promote long-term health. These messages of culinary knowledge, access, health, and community brought the program to a place that intersected with issues that were and still are very much in the news and on the minds of people across the country.

For the next six months, the team tweaked the programmatic model, delivering unique programs with guest chefs every Friday for twenty-five weeks. As a history museum, we endeavored to link each program with objects and exhibitions that visitors could explore on their own. Committed to welcoming a diversity of voices and cultural traditions to the museum, we believed that food and cooking provided an accessible and relatable way to begin. Since 2015, many of the featured guest chefs and community cooks credited Julia with inspiring their interest in cooking and giving them the courage to make it a career. "Cooking Up History," presented monthly, became a signature museum program that even continued over Zoom during the most challenging years of the global pandemic in 2020 and 2021.[23] Smithsonian kitchen manager Kathy Phung and the historian/host Ashley Rose Young have created an excellent program model that is easily adapted for programming objectives and special circumstances. In the spirit of Julia, the demonstration kitchen and back-of-house prep kitchen come alive with the sounds of culinary work, conversation, tasting, and cleanup, just like Julia's home kitchen did for so many years.

THE JULIA CHILD AWARD

Since 2015, The Julia Child Foundation for Gastronomy and the Culinary Arts has presented its annual award to an individual or group that has made a significant difference in the way Americans eat, drink, and cook. Because the National Museum of American History is the home of Julia's kitchen, the award is presented at an annual museum gala. The awardee is selected each year by an independent jury made up of professionals in the fields of food, media, restaurants, and culinary education. Neither the museum nor the foundation is represented on the jury.

Each year the museum's food history team is informed of the awardee's identity and sets to work with the recipient to create a program that reflects their culinary journey. The process of getting to know the recipients and to engage them in dialogue about their sources of inspiration, the important touchstones on their career trajectory, and how they are working to help encourage the next generations, is one of the highlights of our work. In addition to co-creating a memorable gala

Chefs Mary Sue Milliken and Susan Feniger meeting with Julia in their Los Angeles restaurant, 1982

program with the Julia Child Foundation, we at the museum try to collect objects and documents for the permanent collections that will be available for use in exhibitions, publications, programs, and other educational materials. When possible, we have organized temporary exhibitions of these materials. After nine years, we understand how remarkable these objects are, taken together, as they represent diverse journeys that relate to excellence and to Julia Child's legacy.

The other essential aspect of the Julia Child Award is hearing from the recipients about their relationships to Julia. Jacques Pépin, Rick Bayless, Mary Sue Milliken, Susan Feniger, Toni Tipton-Martin, Danny Meyer, and Grace Young all knew or at least met Julia personally and have shared their memories with gala audiences and public programs. José Andrés, Danielle Nierenberg, and Sean Sherman may not have met Julia, but all have a connection with her and admire her tremendous ability to reach and inspire people. They credit her with changing ideas and attitudes about food; supporting chefs, restaurants, and restaurant workers; and bringing joy to millions.

above: Celebrating Toni Tipton-Martin receiving the Julia Child Award in 2021 are (left to right) master mixologist and educator Tiffanie Barriere, who presented the award; Dr. Anthea M. Hartig, Elizabeth MacMillan Director of the National Museum of American History; Toni Tipton-Martin; and Eric W. Spivey, Chairman of the Board of Trustees of The Julia Child Foundation for Gastronomy and the Culinary Arts.

JULIA CHILD'S KITCHEN

this page, top to bottom: Jacques Pépin receiving the first Julia Child Award in 2015, presented by Daniel Boulud; Mary Sue Milliken and Susan Feniger receiving the award in 2018; Chef José Andrés receiving the award in 2019 for his innovative restaurants and culinary work as well as his humanitarian organization, World Central Kitchen; and Grace Young speaking as she received the award in 2022 for her work as a cookbook author, culinary historian, and Chinatown activist

"IF I CAN INFLUENCE ANYONE..." 255

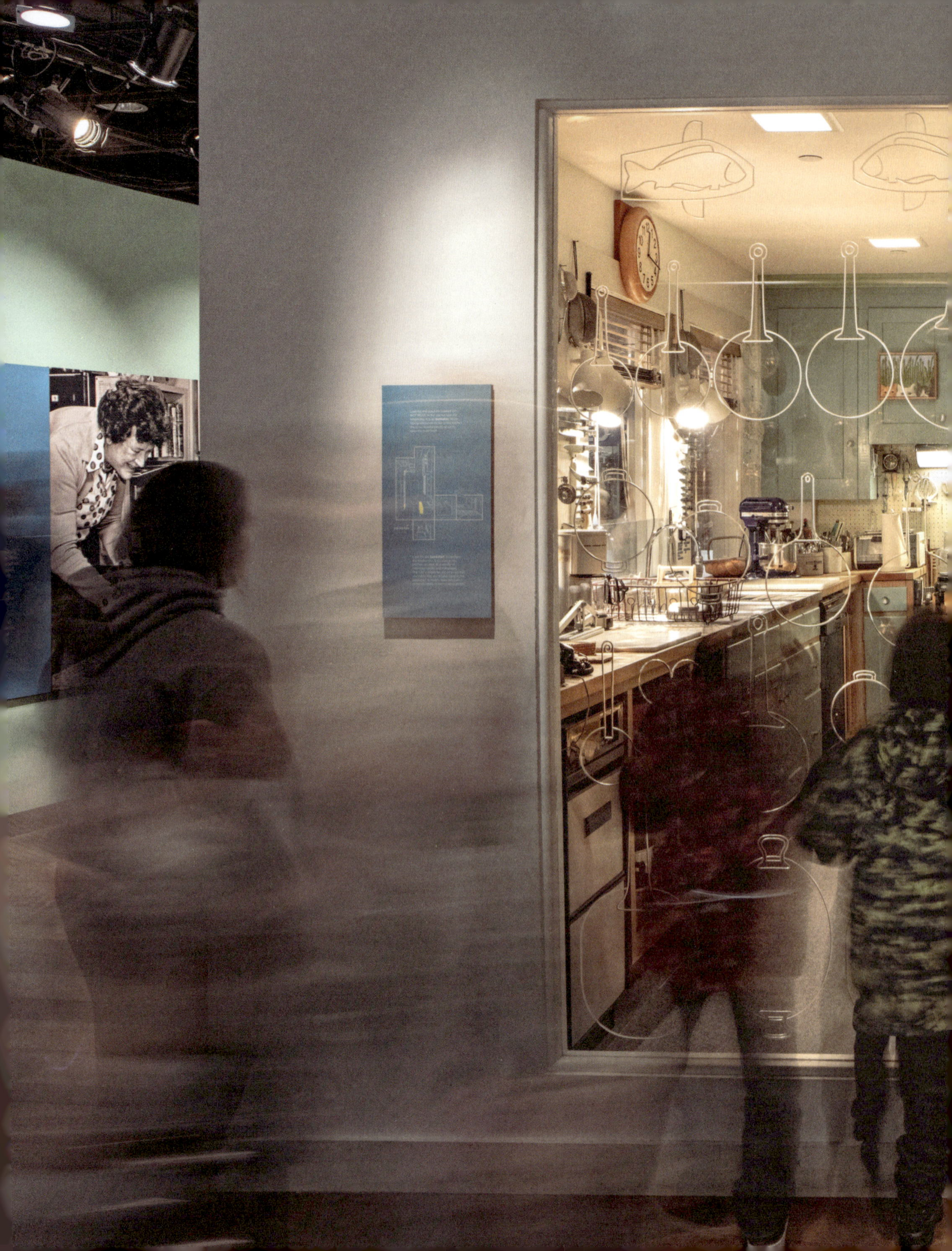

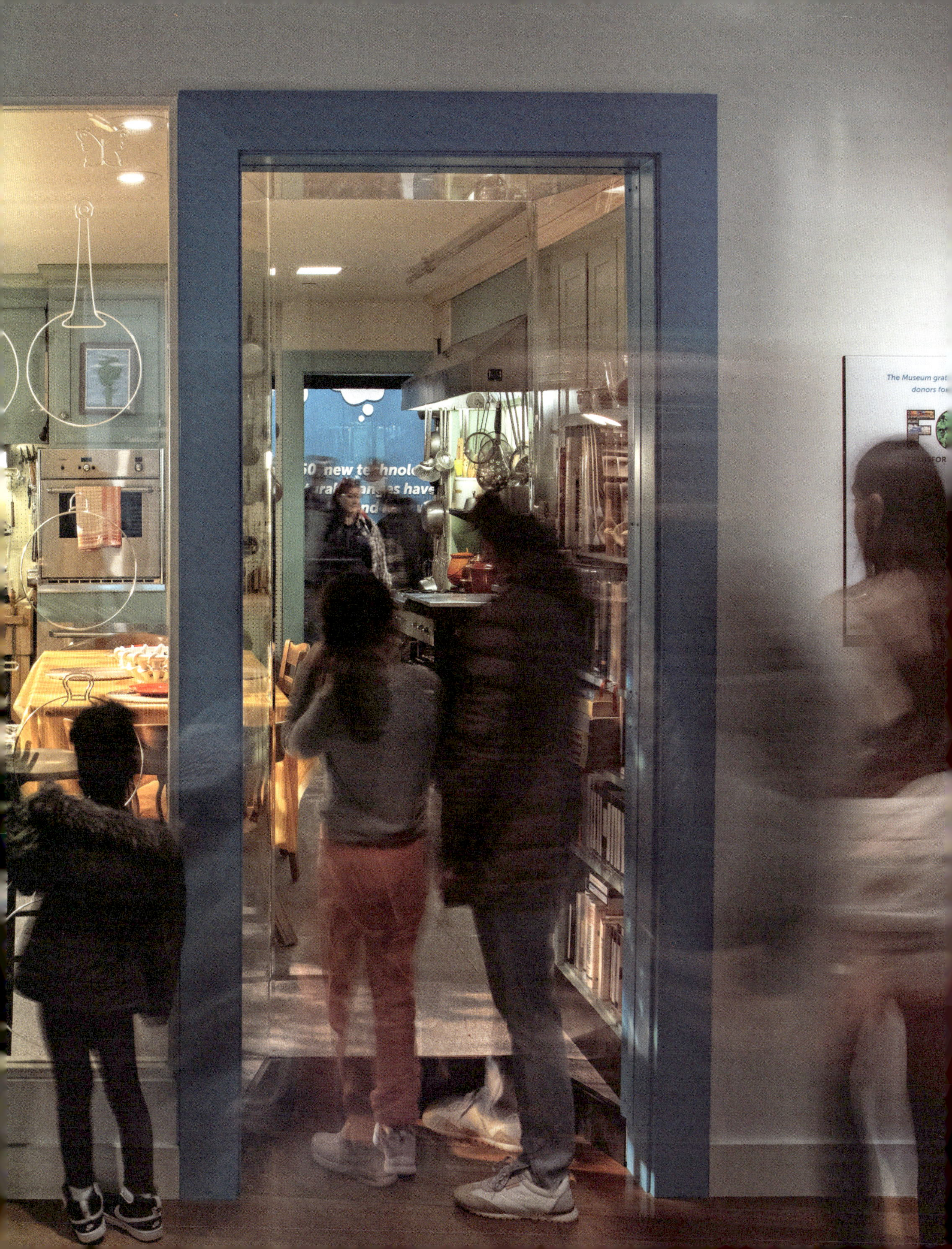

JULIA CHILD'S KITCHEN

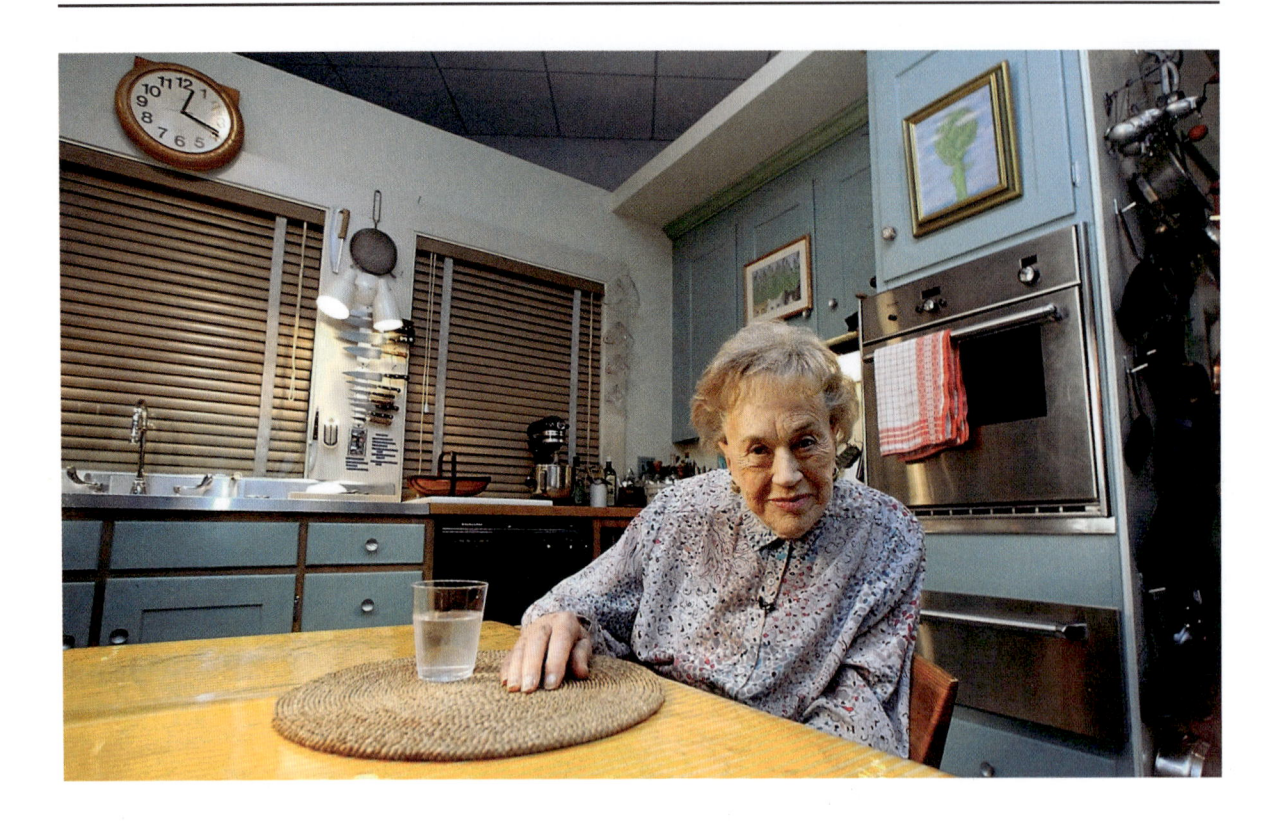

Julia Child's kitchen has always been more than just a room with a giant stove and pegboard-covered walls. For forty years on Irving Street in Cambridge, Massachusetts, it was a place of dedicated experimentation and innovation, countless hours of research and writing, inspired teaching and learning, lively discussions and conversations, and abundant friendship, fun, love, and marvelous, memorable meals. Since its move to the National Museum of American History in 2001 and its public unveiling the following year, the kitchen has drawn the attention of people from across the country and around the world who find something of themselves within its walls as well as a sense of uplift and joy.

Caring for Julia's kitchen is a labor of love that I have shared over more than two decades with many colleagues at the National Museum of American History. We remove fingerprints from the viewports, dust the surfaces and floor, monitor the condition of cookware and fixtures, and answer myriad questions from the public. And sometimes we have been known to spend a few minutes hanging out with visitors in front of the video featuring clips from Julia's cooking shows that plays adjacent to the kitchen. We laugh right along with everyone else when Julia tells us how we, too, could theoretically make omelets for three hundred people in twenty minutes.

After so many years, the public interest in Julia's kitchen at the Smithsonian has not diminished. People still seek it out among all the stellar offerings of the National Museum of American History. I have encountered visitors entering the building or stepping into an elevator who ask me where they can see Julia's kitchen. It's not as though I walk around with "Ask me about Julia Child!" emblazoned on my forehead, so I can't explain why this happens on a regular basis. But it delights me to the point where I have offered to drop whatever I was doing to spend ten minutes with these newfound fans of Julia in the gallery. I have heard many stories about cooking adventures that often end with the sentiment "Well, it was worth a try and I had fun," which Julia would surely endorse. More than once, as I've stood by the kitchen speaking with visitors, I have had to assist a couple of enthusiastic pilgrims who thought they could walk through the industrial-strength acrylic viewports. But luckily, to my knowledge no one has been injured in their quest for a better view inside Julia's kitchen.

I have heard many visitors to the exhibition comment on how comfortable and inviting the kitchen looks and how different it is from the kitchen designs that are currently prominent features in home renovation projects on television or gorgeously portrayed in glossy magazines. As Julia herself said in 1981, "People always expect me to have a decorator's kitchen, but I wanted a kitchen for cooking."[1]

previous spread: A swirl of museum visitors around Julia's kitchen, November 24, 2023. *opposite:* Julia Child in her kitchen at the museum on August 19, 2002. This would be the last time she sat among her culinary tools in her favorite room.

Naturally, kitchens and kitchen design, like ideas about what makes a meal and mealtime, are very different than they were in the early sixties when Julia and Paul Child were setting up their Cambridge kitchen. Julia's layered, lived-in, colorful, and cooked-in kitchen contrasts in every way with the sleek, neutral-toned, vaulted spaces anchored by giant islands typical of

This needlepoint sign with Julia's typical sign-off hangs in the kitchen above a doorway.

contemporary designer kitchens. Julia's penchant for having tools and cookware visible is at odds with modern notions of clutter-free counters; labels on the walls, à la Paul Child, are out of the question. Evidence of cooking is also absent.[2] This contrast is on the minds of many visitors, who recognize that Julia's is not what they imagine a "gourmet" kitchen to be. In the next breath, however, they will often say something about how Julia was so real, so down-to-earth, and such a good cook, she didn't need the fancy accoutrements of the stark designer kitchens of the 2000s. Indeed, for Julia, today's kitchen design trends would be about as attractive as those plastic World's Fair "kitchens of the future" she ignored in 1961.[3]

What about cooking? What do visitors have to say about their own habits of meal preparation? In informal conversation, people will admit they are often too busy or tired to properly cook a meal as they imagine Julia would have done. And forget about eating together as a family when there are so many activities away from home that demand attention. Yet after another moment or two, these same visitors will reveal their favorite recipes for when they do put on an apron and grab a skillet. The more they talk, the more detailed their stories about cooking become. Julia would be pleased—even irregular bouts in the kitchen are better than abandoning cooking at home completely.

This book has foregrounded the words and stories of people who spent significant time with Julia, and sometimes Paul as well, in their home kitchen. It's only fitting, therefore, that Julia should have the last word. As we sat with her in the kitchen in 2001, aware that we would soon have a role in her legacy, she mused that she "was very proud, indeed" that the Smithsonian wanted her kitchen, and added, "If I can influence anyone to go into the culinary profession as a career, I'm very happy and if I can influence anyone to keep into the kitchen and make it a real family room and part of your life, I will have succeeded beyond hope."[4] Two decades later, we can tell that Julia's message about learning to cook and to care about food still resonates with the American public. Julia Child's educational and inspirational legacy is alive and well in her home kitchen in Washington, DC.

When Dorie Greenspan told me that Julia always looked you in the eye and made you feel as though you were the only person in the room, I remembered this photograph from the opening of the exhibition "Bon Appétit! Julia Child's Kitchen at the Smithsonian" in August 2002. I waited in line to speak with Julia, and when I sat down the photographer was waiting for us to face the camera for a picture. But Julia's eyes were on mine, and I wasn't about to break that connection. Those few moments with her have stayed with me as I've tried to do justice to her story and legacy in this volume. Thank you, Julia!

Julia Child and Paula Johnson, August 18, 2002

In 2000, Julia received the Légion D'Honneur, France's highest honor, for her pivotal role in introducing Americans to French cuisine and cookery. The medal is on display near her kitchen in the exhibition "FOOD: Transforming the American Table."

APPENDIX A

About The Julia Child Foundation for Gastronomy and the Culinary Arts

The Julia Child Foundation for Gastronomy and the Culinary Arts was created by Julia in 1995 and began operating in 2004. Its mission is to honor and further Julia's legacy, which centers on the importance of understanding where food comes from, what makes for good food, and the value of cooking. Headquartered in Santa Barbara, California, the Foundation is a nonprofit that makes grants to support culinary history research, scholarships for culinary training, food writing, and food media, as well as professional development and food literacy programs. Over the last decade, the Foundation has made more than $3 million in grants to other nonprofits. In 2015, the Foundation created the Julia Child Award, presented in association with the Smithsonian's National Museum of American History. The annual award honors an individual who has made a profound and significant difference in the way America cooks, eats, and drinks, and is accompanied by a $50,000 grant from the Foundation to a food-related nonprofit selected by the recipient. Previous recipients include Jacques Pépin, Rick Bayless, Danny Meyer, Mary Sue Milliken, Susan Feniger, José Andrés, Danielle Nierenberg, Toni Tipton-Martin, Grace Young, and Sean Sherman. For more information, visit www.juliachildfoundation.org and www.juliachildaward.com.

Sean Sherman (Oglala Lakota) received the Julia Child Award in 2023.

Zoe Fess and Elena Terry (Ho Chunk) spoke about traditional systems of knowledge and demonstrated cooking with Indigenous ingredients at the National Museum of American History in November 2022.

APPENDIX B

About the Smithsonian Institution, the National Museum of American History, and the Smithsonian Food History Project

The Smithsonian Institution is the world's largest museum, education, and research complex, with twenty-one museums and the National Zoo, working to preserve and increase understanding of science, history, art, and culture. Founded in 1846 with funds from the Englishman James Smithson (1765–1829), the Institution was established "for the increase and diffusion of knowledge," a mission that continues to this day. Across its museums, more than 157 million objects help visitors—in person, in publications, through programming, and online—explore who we are, where we've been, and where we're headed. For more information, visit https://si.edu.

The National Museum of American History is one of the Smithsonian's most-visited museums and is the only museum in the country dedicated to preserving and exploring the full history of the United States. It serves as the custodian of the nation's historical collections, which number 1.8 million objects and more than three shelf-miles of archival material. The museum is home to treasured objects that reflect our complex past: the desk used by Thomas Jefferson to draft the Declaration of Independence; the Star-Spangled Banner—the 1814 flag that inspired our national anthem; the 1830s steam locomotive *John Bull*—the oldest locomotive in existence still capable of operation; a section of the Greensboro lunch counter—the site of protests during the civil rights movement in the 1960s that led to the desegregation of public spaces; a short-handled hoe used by labor leader Cesar Chavez, who fought for better conditions for agricultural workers; artifacts representing presidential campaigns and the roles of the presidents and first ladies; the ruby slippers worn by Judy Garland in the 1939 film *The Wizard of Oz*; the Yellow Cloud electric guitar used by the musical artist Prince; and Julia Child's home kitchen from Cambridge, Massachusetts, to name just a few.

Opened in January 1964 as the National Museum of History and Technology, the museum was renamed the National Museum of American History in 1980 to reflect its scope of interests and responsibilities more accurately. Under the leadership of Dr. Anthea Hartig, the Elizabeth MacMillan Director and the first woman to head the National Museum of American History, the museum is welcoming and serving diverse audiences from across the nation and around the world. Through incomparable collections, rigorous research, and dynamic public outreach, the National Museum of American History seeks to empower people to create a more just and compassionate future by examining, preserving, and sharing the complexity of our past. The doors of the museum are always open online, and the virtual museum continues to expand its offerings, including online exhibitions and PK–12 educational materials and programs. The public can follow the museum on social media and for more information go to https://americanhistory.si.edu.

ABOUT THE SMITHSONIAN FOOD HISTORY PROJECT, NATIONAL MUSEUM OF AMERICAN HISTORY

The Smithsonian Food History project was launched in 1996 when Warren and Barbara Winiarski of Napa Valley, California, provided generous support for a research and collecting initiative on the history of winemaking in America. From that beginning, the project has grown into a multiyear effort to include researching and collecting objects and archives relating to food history as well. The museum's interdisciplinary team of curators, historians, collections specialists, archivists, and educators continues to conduct research around the country and further build the institution's archival and artifact collections. The project's collections, publications, exhibitions, and programs address topics across a wide spectrum of food and drink, including culinary history, food-related technologies and innovations, food traditions from diverse regions and communities across the United States, food security and justice, and food and climate change. Through objects, documents, photographs, and digital audio and video files, the project uses food history to enrich our understanding of American history.

The project invites individuals and communities from near and far to gather on-site and online for conversations and interactive experiences. By exploring American food history, museum audiences will have a great understanding of the role they play in shaping how we grow, distribute, prepare, conserve, and share food and drink in the United States.

Please visit https://americanhistory.si.edu/explore/topics/food.

Resources

JULIA'S COOKBOOKS AND TELEVISION SERIES

BOOKS BY JULIA CHILD

Mastering the Art of French Cooking (with Simone Beck and Louisette Bertholle). New York: Alfred A. Knopf, 1961.

The French Chef Cookbook. New York: Alfred A. Knopf, 1968.

Mastering the Art of French Cooking, Vol. II (with Simone Beck). New York: Alfred A. Knopf, 1970.

From Julia Child's Kitchen. New York: Alfred A. Knopf, 1975.

Julia Child & Company (in collaboration with E. S. Yntema). New York: Alfred A. Knopf, 1979.

Julia Child & More Company (in collaboration with E. S. Yntema). New York: Alfred A. Knopf, 1979.

The Way to Cook. New York: Alfred A. Knopf, 1989.

Julia Child's Menu Cookbook. New York: Wings (Random House), 1991.

Cooking with Master Chefs. New York: Alfred A. Knopf, 1993.

In Julia's Kitchen with Master Chefs (with Nancy Verde Barr). New York: Alfred A. Knopf, 1995.

Baking with Julia (written by Dorie Greenspan). New York: William Morrow, 1996.

Julia and Jacques Cooking at Home (with Jacques Pépin). New York: Alfred A. Knopf, 1999.

Julia's Kitchen Wisdom. New York: Alfred A. Knopf, 2000.

My Life in France (with Alex Prud'homme). New York: Alfred A. Knopf, 2006.

People Who Love to Eat Are Always the Best People. New York: Alfred A. Knopf, 2020.

TELEVISION SERIES AND SPECIALS

The French Chef. WGBH (Boston), PBS, 1962 (pilot) 1963–73 (series).

Julia Child & Company. WGBH (Boston), PBS, 1978–79.

Julia Child & More Company. WGBH (Boston), PBS, 1979–80.

Good Morning America. ABC, 1980–95.

Dinner at Julia's. WGBH (Boston), PBS, 1983–84.

Julia Child & Jacques Pépin: Cooking in Concert. PBS, 1993.

Cooking with Master Chefs. PBS, 1993–1994.

In Julia's Kitchen with Master Chefs. PBS, 1994–96.

Julia Child & Jacques Pepin: More Cooking in Concert. PBS, 1995.

Baking with Julia. PBS, 1996–98.

Julia & Jacques Cooking at Home. PBS, 1999–2000.

Acknowledgments

JULIA CHILD tested recipes, cooked with family and friends, and taped three television series in her home kitchen. I've surely said those words hundreds of times during talks and tours at the National Museum of American History. But I always wondered... what was it *really* like to cook with Julia, sit down to a meal, edit a cookbook, test recipes, or cook for TV in that kitchen? To begin finding out, I sat down with people who had experienced the buzz and the joy of life with Julia in her favorite room. Their stories, told in their own words, make this book sing, and I am most grateful for their contributions.

I want to thank JACQUES PÉPIN, whose foreword sets up the book beautifully, and whose long relationship with Julia remains one of the great culinary matches of our time. My heartfelt thanks extend to PHILA COUSINS and ALEX PRUD'HOMME, Julia's close family members, who spoke of Julia and the kitchen with gusto and love. Others who shared their memories are SUSY DAVIDSON, GEOFFREY DRUMMOND, DORIE GREENSPAN, STEPHANIE HERSH, CHRISTOPHER KIMBALL, MARIAN MORASH, RUSSELL MORASH, SARA MOULTON, PATRICIA PRATT, NANCY SILVERTON, and SHERROD STURROCK.

This book is a visual feast thanks to the photographers who captured the essence of Julia and her kitchen, starting with the late PAUL CHILD, whose documentation of their life together in France and at 103 Irving Street remains a treasure trove. The photographs by CHRISTOPHER HIRSHEIMER, MICHEAL MCLAUGHLIN, ALBIE WALTON, ULRIKE WELSCH, RICK FRIEDMAN, ARNOLD NEWMAN, and TIM SLOAN add warmth and texture to the narrative. Special thanks to staff at the SCHLESINGER LIBRARY and HARVARD RADCLIFFE INSTITUTE, staff in the SMITH COLLEGE ARCHIVES, MAUREEN HARLOW and the PBS MEDIA LIBRARY, and VANESSA WALTON KEEFE for help with images in their archives.

JACLYN NASH'S photographs of the objects and museum spaces provide an intimate view into Julia and her kitchen. Jackie is marvelous to work with—our object photo sessions will remain a delightful memory. I also want to recognize HUGH TALMAN and RICHARD STRAUSS, both Smithsonian photographers, whose wonderful images predate Jackie's work on the project and also appear in this volume.

I wish to thank DR. ANTHEA M. HARTIG, whose understanding of Julia Child and her impact on American history was apparent from her first day on the job in 2019 as the first woman director of the National Museum of American History. She immediately embraced membership on Team Julia, and her support of food history helped nourish the project through the dark days of the pandemic.

THE JULIA CHILD FOUNDATION FOR GASTRONOMY AND THE CULINARY ARTS has been a marvelous partner to the museum's Food History Project for more than a decade. This book would not have been possible without the encouragement of ERIC W. SPIVEY, TODD SCHULKIN, LAUREN SALKELD, and TANYA STEEL.

My colleagues from Smithsonian Enterprises—JILL CORCORAN, PAIGE TOWLER, and AVERY NAUGHTON—proved to be a dream team, and their expertise at critical junctures will not be forgotten. Likewise, the team from ABRAMS—LAURA DOZIER, LISA SILVERMAN, and DEB WOOD—were a joy to work with, and I'm grateful that their wisdom and talents for making beautiful books were brought to this one.

I appreciate the assistance from DC-area chefs and teachers RIS LACOSTE, GWYNN NOVAK, and ROBERT WEIDMAIER for helping sort out details for certain culinary tools. And I am tremendously grateful to colleagues who commented on drafts, jumped on phone calls, and bolstered my spirits, including RAYNA GREEN, NANCI EDWARDS, and STEVE VELASQUEZ. Steve, as the first collections manager and now as curator in the Division of Home and Community Life, confirmed data on hundreds of objects with assistance from curatorial interns REEZA BALDONADO, MEGAN MCKELVEY, and NIKO RODRIGUEZ. Object conservators DAWN WALLACE, MEREDITH SWEENEY, and TAMSIN MCDONAGH provided advice and focused care.

JOE CRISTE from the museum's historic restoration shop clarified details about removing the kitchen from the Cambridge house in 2001 and continues to share his knowledge of the kitchen's cabinetry gained from installing, deinstalling, and reinstalling the kitchen in the museum. In addition to Joe, PETER ALBRITTON, ROB BARRETT, and GEOFF WARD of the original team and now STEVE WALCZAK, MARY MILLER, JONATHAN MORRIS, LEO KERR, SHAWNIE MCRANEY, SEAN SWEENEY, DON BOYCE, and LAURA MCCLURE have picked up the mantle and are using their amazing skills to keep the kitchen in good shape.

I want to extend special thanks to Smithsonian librarian KATRINA BROWN and editor LESLIE POSTER. Other members of the museum's Team Julia provided moral support and enthusiasm along the way: KARI FANTASIA, VALESKA HILBIG, SARAH LOUX, ELISE LUTHI, DANA MARINE, THERESA MCCULLA, KATHY PHUNG, KATHY SKLAR, EMMALINE SMITH, AND ASHLEY ROSE YOUNG. KATHY FRANZ, TANYA GARNER, KATHARINE KLEIN, MELINDA MACHADO, and CHRISTINE RUSSO also offered assistance and encouragement.

A heartfelt thanks to the visitors who have lingered at Julia's kitchen and spoken with me, as well as everyone who has supported the museum's food history project. In that respect, there is no one deserving greater acknowledgment than WARREN and BARBARA WINIARSKI, whose generous and prescient gift to fund our research into American wine history led to the establishment of the Smithsonian Food History Project. Their support over many years has made possible a tremendous range of our research, collecting, and public programming.

Friends and family who have sustained me over the course of this project include JESSICA CARBONE, DIANE DENHAM, SUSAN FARNSWORTH and SKYE, DEBORA KODISH, BETH LEONINI, LINDA LIVERS, MELISSA MCLOUD, KATHERINE OTT, LESLIE PROSTERMAN, BECKY SCHNEIDER, ANNE WITTY, LOUISE WOERNER, and DON KOLLMORGEN. My family, especially JINI, ERIN, and AVA, have cheered me along. And CARL should receive a medal for holding things together on the home front, and for preparing tasty meals for a curator writing about cooking and kitchens but unable to shift from laptop to cooktop in time for dinner.

Notes

A note about the papers of Julia and Paul Child, which include letters, news clippings, receipts, and Paul's photographs that appear in this work: Donated by Julia, the collection is archived as The Julia Child Papers at the Arthur and Elizabeth Schlesinger Library on the History of Women in America, Radcliffe Institute for Advanced Study, Harvard University, Cambridge, Massachusetts (to be referred to as Julia Child Papers here). The collection is open to researchers by appointment. A finding aid is available online at https://hollisarchives.lib.harvard.edu/repositories/8/resources/9746.

In addition, there are many sources generated by the Smithsonian's National Museum of American History (NMAH), including a taped interview with Julia in her kitchen. A transcript of this interview is filed with the Julia Child collection in the NMAH Division of Home and Community Life.

INTRODUCTION

1. See Julia Child and Alex Prud'homme, *My Life in France* (New York: Alfred A. Knopf, 2006); Noel Riley Fitch, *Appetite for Life: The Biography of Julia Child* (New York: Anchor Doubleday, 1997); Helen Lefkowitz Horowitz, *Warming Up Julia Child* (New York: Pegasus Books, 2022); Alex Prud'homme, *The French Chef in America* (New York: Alfred A. Knopf, 2016); Joan Reardon, ed., *As Always, Julia: The Letters of Julia Child & Avis DeVoto* (Boston and New York: Houghton Mifflin Harcourt, 2010); Laura Shapiro, *Julia Child, A Life* (New York: Viking Penguin, 2007); Bob Spitz, *Dearie: The Remarkable Life of Julia Child* (New York: Alfred A. Knopf, 2012). Cookbooks by Julia Child and her television series are listed in Resources. (page 267)
2. There is a rich body of scholarship on museums and material culture, including a volume of essays that was instrumental in sparking my interest in the field: Ian M. G. Quimby, ed. *Material Culture and the Study of American Life* (New York: W. W. Norton & Company, 1978). Since then, of course, the field has expanded in many ways and across many disciplines, with journals and graduate programs focused on objects, communities, power, and the shifting roles of museums. Among more recent volumes are Steven Lubar and Kathleen M. Kendrick, *Legacies: Collecting America's History at the Smithsonian* (Washington, DC, and London: Smithsonian Institution Press, 2001) and Steven Lubar, *Inside the Lost Museum: Curating the Past and Present* (Cambridge, Mass., and London: Harvard University Press, 2017).
3. For background on museums, material culture, and the digital age, see Susana Smith Bautista, *Museums in the Digital Age: Changing Meanings of Place, Community, and Culture* (Lanham, Md.: Altamira Press, 2014).
4. Child and Prud'homme, *My Life*, 3.
5. Quoted in Gail Cameron Wescott, "Mastering the Art of Living," *Smith Alumnae Quarterly* (Winter 2002–2003), 44.
6. Alice Julier, "Julia at Smith," *Gastronomica* (Summer 2005): 47.
7. Wescott, "Mastering," 42–44.
8. Julier, "Julia," 48.
9. Polly Frost, "Julia Child Interview, August 1989," in *Julia Child: The Last Interview and Other Conversations* (Brooklyn, NY, and London: Melville House Publishing, 2019), 58.
10. "Government girls" of World War II, see Mary Beth Franklin, "The War Girls," *Washington Post*, January 28, 1997.
11. Jennet Conant, *A Covert Affair* (New York: Simon & Schuster Paperbacks, 2011), 15.
12. Quote "the war was the change in my life" in Fitch, *Appetite*, 82. For more on the World War II experience, see Conant, *A Covert Affair*, 2011.
13. The meal in Rouen is best described by Julia herself. See Child and Prud'homme, *My Life*, 18.
14. Smithsonian Institution (hereafter "SI") interview with Julia Child, September 11, 2001.
15. Child and Prud'homme, *My Life*, 57–59.
16. Ibid., 110.
17. Child and Prud'homme, *My Life*, 132–34, 156–62, 172–74, 193–95; Reardon, *As Always*, e.g., 124–26.
18. Typing was definitely one of Julia's skills. On her application for employment after the war, she noted that her former position as a clerk for the U.S. Information Center in 1942 had involved researching names, titles, and agencies of government officials and typing the information on small cards. She noted, "Typed over 10,000 little white cards in two months." Julia Child Papers, MC660, Box 140, File 9.

19. Bernard DeVoto's low opinion of American cutlery was a long-standing irritation, starting with the article, "The Paring Knife at the Crossroads," published in *Harper's Magazine* in April 1939. He wrote, "The same conditions hold for kitchen cutlery. It is practically all made of stainless steel now, which means that it is practically all no good. At approximately twice the price you paid ten years ago you can get a good butcher knife, but you can't get a good paring knife at any price." Julia's letter to DeVoto and Avis's response are published in Reardon's *As Always, Julia*, 7–10.
20. Reardon, *As Always*, 258–59.
21. Judith Jones, *The Tenth Muse: My Life in Food* (New York: Alfred A. Knopf, 2007), 60–61.
22. Child and Prud'homme, *My Life*, 226.

CHAPTER 1: "THE KITCHEN NEEDED COMPLETE RETHINKING."

1. A history of Julia's house can be found at https://historycambridge.org/james/James%203.html.
2. Julia Child, "Julia Child," in *Architectural Digest Celebrity Homes*, Paige Rense, ed. (Los Angeles: The Knapp Press, 1977), 219.
3. Ibid.
4. The National Museum of American History has responded to many requests for the names or formulas of the shades of blue and green selected by Paul Child for the kitchen at 103 Irving Street in Cambridge. We do not know the exact formulas but have determined that the colors in the kitchen are close to Benjamin Moore's Covington Blue and Sherwood Green (or possibly Stem Green). In 2012, a Mr. Gilbert from New Hampshire visited the kitchen at the museum and spoke with me about having worked for a contractor named Ralph Osmond to refinish the countertops in the 1980s. Gilbert followed up in an email and reported that he had spoken with Dave Brown, the painter who was also working in the kitchen at the time, about the colors. Brown recalled that he "used Benjamin Moore Stain Impervo oil base paint and made up the color on the spot using cobalt blue with some yellow tint and a few drops of raw sienna. If he were to do it again, he would probably use an eggshell finish." Brown and Gilbert had eaten their lunch from McDonald's in the kitchen and had put the folded wrappers behind the stove as a prank. Email to author, January 30, 2013.
5. Nancy Carlisle and Melinda Talbot Nasardinov, *America's Kitchens* (Boston: Historic New England, 2008), 147–49.
6. Nancy Craig, "The Best Kitchens Are Planned by Exasperated Women," *House Beautiful,* May 1956, 180–87.
7. Alexandra Lange, "The Woman Who Invented the Kitchen," *Slate*, October 25, 2012.
8. Alex Prud'homme, *The French Chef in America* (New York: Alfred A. Knopf, 2016), 34.
9. Julia Child, "The Kitchen Julia Built," *New York Times Magazine*, May 16, 1976, 82.
10. Julia Child and Paige Rense, ed. "Julia Child." In *Architectural Digest Celebrity Homes* (Los Angeles: The Knapp Press, 1977), 219.
11. Julia Child, "The Kitchen Julia Built," *New York Times Magazine*, May 16, 1976, 80.
12. Child and Rense, *Architectural Digest*, 1977, 219.
13. *The World's Fair House: American Contemporary Styling at Its Best: A Home Decorator's Guide to Modern Material and Souvenir Book of the Formica Exhibition, New York World's Fair 1964–1965* (Cincinnati: Formica Corp., c. 1964).
14. Quote: "This is the way it should be" from SI interview with Julia Child, September 11, 2001.
15. Correspondence from Paul Child to Charles Child, March 6, 1962, Julia Child Papers, MC 644, Box 07, Folder 77.
16. Correspondence from Paul Child to Charles Child, November 1, 1962, Julia Child Papers, MC 644, Box 07, Folder 77.
17. Child, "The Kitchen Julia Built," *New York Times Magazine*, 80.
18. Bill Stumpf and Nicholas Polites, "Julia's Kitchen: A Design Anatomy," *Design Quarterly* 104 (Minneapolis, Minn.: Walker Art Center, 1977), 16.
19. Alex Prud'homme and Katie Pratt, *France Is a Feast* (London: Thames & Hudson Ltd., 2017).
20. SI interview with JC, 2001.
21. For a brief history and illustrations of Moustiers ceramics, see *Moustiers Ceramics: Gifts from the Eugene V. and Clare E. Thaw Collection, Works from the Permanent Collection* (New York: Cooper Hewitt, Smithsonian Design Museum, August 2017–January 21, 2019).
22. Simone Beck and Julia Child, *Mastering the Art of French Cooking*, Vol. Two (New York: Alfred A. Knopf, 1970), 535.
23. Noel Riley Fitch, *Appetite for Life: The Biography of Julia Child* (New York: Anchor Doubleday, 1997), 218.
24. SI interview with JC, 2001.
25. Fitch, *Appetite*, 223.
26. SI interview with JC, 2001; Wikipedia entry for Bjorn Egge: https://en.wikipedia.org/wiki/Bj%C3%B8rn_Egge.

27. Craig Claiborne, "Cookbook Review: Glorious Recipes," *New York Times*, October 18, 1961, 47.

CHAPTER 2: "THIS IS MY TEST KITCHEN AS WELL AS EVERYTHING ELSE."

1. Chapter title quote from Smithsonian Institution interview with Julia Child, September 11, 2001; Mary Elizabeth Falter, "The Hospitable Kitchen of a Distinguished Cook," *House & Garden*, February 1964, 132.
2. *House & Garden*, July 1962, 113.
3. "Washington Cook Book," *House & Garden*, July 1962, 113–18.
4. Correspondence from Paul Child to Charles Child, March 6, 1962, Julia Child Papers, MC644, Box 07, Folder 77.
5. Ibid.
6. Julia Child and Alex Prud'homme, *My Life in France* (New York: Alfred A. Knopf, 2006), 236–37.
7. Robert Rice, "Onward and Upward with the Arts: Diary of a Viewer," *New Yorker*, August 30, 1947, 44–52.
8. See William I. Kaufman, ed., *Cooking with the Experts: Over 400 Simple, Easy-to-Follow, Taste-Tempting Recipes Selected by Television's Best Cooks* (New York: Random House, 1955).
9. Kathleen Collins, *Watching What We Eat: The Evolution of Television Cooking Shows* (New York and London: Continuum, 2009), 27–29 and 49–59; Dana Polan, "James Beard's Early TV Work: A Report on Research," *Gastronomica* 10, no. 3 (August 1, 2010): 23–33. https://doi.org/10.1525/gfc.2010.10.3.23; Dana Polan, *Julia Child's The French Chef* (Durham, NC, and London: Duke University Press, 2011); Ashley Rose Young, "Lena Richard: America's Unknown Celebrity Chef," Smithsonian Institution. *Sidedoor* (podcast), June 2020. https://www.si.edu/sidedoor/ep-8-americas-unknown-celebrity-chef.
10. According to APTS (America's Public Television Stations), a nonprofit membership organization, "Public television stations have been serving America since the early 1950s, when the Federal Communications Commission reserved a portion of the broadcast spectrum for noncommercial educational purposes. KUHT-TV Houston was the first public television station to go on the air, in 1952, and Alabama Public Television launched the first statewide public broadcasting network in 1955. President Eisenhower proposed the first federal support for public television in the National Defense Education Act of 1958, to explore the power of television in improving instruction and student outcomes in elementary and secondary schools, and the Public Television Finance Act of 1962 provided federal funds to dramatically expand the number of public television stations in the United States . . . In 2023, there are 170 licensees operating more than 350 public television stations across the country." https://apts.org/about/public-tv.
11. SI interview with Russell Morash, March 21, 2023.
12. SI interview with Marian Morash, March 21, 2023.
13. SI interview with RM, 2023.
14. Correspondence from Paul Child to Charles Child, January 19, 1963, Julia Child Papers, MC644, Box 07, Folder 78.
15. Correspondence from Paul Child to Charles Child, January 26, February 9, and May 18, 1963, Julia Child Papers, MC644, Box 97, Folder 78.
16. *Mastering the Art of French Cooking* sold more than 100,000 copies during its first year (https://npg.si.edu/blog/julia-child%E2%80%99s-100th-birthday) and 600,000 copies by March 1969 (https://www.thedailymeal.com/cook/25-best-selling-cookbooks-all-time-slideshow/).
17. For the story of La Pitchoune, see Child and Prud'homme, *My Life*, 245–48. In June 1992, with Paul's health in serious decline, Julia handed the keys to La Pitchoune to Simca's sister-in-law, 300–302.
18. Child and Prud'homme, *My Life*, 253.
19. Ibid., 252.
20. Julia Child Papers, Correspondence, 1925–1992. Subseries B. Cookery, 1951–1992. Beard, James, 1966–1972. MC644, Folder 129–130.
21. Julia Child Papers, Beard, James, 1966–1972. MC644, Folder 129–130.
22. SI interview with JC, 2001. Also see Simone Beck and Julia Child, *Mastering the Art of French Cooking*, Vol. Two (New York: Alfred A. Knopf, 1970), ix–x.
23. Beck and Child, *Mastering*, Vol. Two, 70.
24. Julia's Georgetown house: https://boundarystones.weta.org/2017/04/26/julia-childs-washington-roots; Child and Prud'homme, *My Life*, 205. Bart Barnes, "CIA Official Sherman Kent, 82, Dies," *Washington Post*, March 14, 1986.
25. SI interview with JC, 2001.
26. Alex Prud'homme, *The French Chef in America*, 142-143.
27. Gail Perrin, "How Julia Child Learned to Cook," *Boston Globe*, November 5, 1975, 36.

28. Judith Jones, "Julia: The Ever-Curious Cook," *Gastronomica* 5:3 (Summer 2005), 26–27.
29. Paul's health challenges and their impacts on Julia and their marriage are best described by Alex Prud'homme, *The French Chef in America*, 142–45.
30. David Nussbaum, "In Julia Child's Kitchen, October 5, 1998," *Gastronomica* 5:3 (Summer 2005), 29.
31. Ruth Lockwood was the associate producer on WGBH's *The French Chef* and continued to work with Julia and others, including Joyce Chen on twenty-six episodes of *Joyce Chen Cooks* in 1966–67. She remained a lifelong friend and associate of Julia Child. Marian Morash was the chef on *The Victory Garden* television program (which was also produced by her husband, Russell Morash) and is the author of *The Victory Garden Cookbook* (1982). She cofounded and served as executive chef of the Straight Wharf Restaurant in Nantucket, a professional kitchen run entirely by women. Pat Pratt was a lifelong friend of Julia's and was often on the scene to provide culinary and administrative assistance. Rosemary Manell worked with Julia behind the scenes as a sous chef, food stylist, friend, and artist. Sara Moulton followed in Julia's footsteps by writing cookbooks and appearing on food television. Writer and culinary associate Susy Davidson became the first coordinator and the executive director of the Julia Child Foundation, a position she held until 2011. Elizabeth Bishop's legacy in food and wine is carried out at Boston University's Elizabeth Bishop Wine Resource Center. And Nancy Verde Barr's role as one of Julia's trusted associates in the kitchen and for public appearances is told in her memoir, *Backstage with Julia: My Years with Julia Child* (Hoboken, NJ: John Wiley & Sons, 2007). All of these women deserve recognition for their work and strong relationships with Julia over many decades. My sincere apologies to anyone I may have overlooked, as Julia's associates were numerous, loyal, and critically important to her work and success.
32. Sara Moulton cofounded the New York Women's Culinary Alliance, served as executive chef of *Gourmet* magazine, and was food editor for ABC's *Good Morning America*. She is the author of five cookbooks and has hosted her own cooking shows, including *Sara's Weeknight Meals*.
33. Smithsonian Institution interview with Sara Moulton, March 8, 2023.
34. Julia Child and E. S. Yntema, *Julia Child & More Company* (New York: Alfred A. Knopf, 1979), 21.
35. Noel Riley Fitch, *Appetite for Life: The Biography of Julia Child* (New York: Anchor Doubleday, 1997), 399; Child and Yntema, vi–vii.
36. SI interview with SM, 2023.
37. Ibid.
38. Ibid.
39. Ibid.
40. Robert Cooke, "The Soup of Life," *Boston Globe*, September 25, 1973; Sarah Zielinksi, "Julia Child and the Primordial Soup," *Smithsonian Magazine*, September 22, 2010. https://www.smithsonianmag.com/science-nature/julia-child-and-the-primordial-soup-35465592/
41. Irvin Molotsky, "S. Dillon Ripley Dies at 87; Led the Smithsonian Institution During Its Greatest Growth," *New York Times*, March 13, 2001.
42. SI interview with SM, 2023.
43. Smithsonian Institution interview with Dorie Greenspan, May 10, 2023.

CHAPTER 3: "THIS IS CERTAINLY THE SOUL OF OUR HOUSE.

1. SI interview with Stephanie Hersh, September 9, 2021.
2. Alex Prud'homme was one of the young members of the family who regularly visited Paul and Julia, his great uncle and aunt. He observed, "There were times when Julia grew wistful about not having a child and grandchild, as her siblings did, and commiserated with Simca about their lack of progeny. Yet, Julia acknowledged that had she conceived she would have devoted her energy to her children and would not have had the career that she did." Alex Prud'homme, *The French Chef in America*. New York: Alfred A, Knopf, 2016, 146.
3. Philadelphia Cousins, "Fond Memories of Julia Child's Kitchen," National Museum of American History. *O Say Can You See?* (blog), August 14, 2012. https://americanhistory.si.edu/blog/2012/08/fond-memories-of-julia-childs-kitchen.html.
4. SI interview with Alex Prud'homme, February 3, 2023.
5. SI interview with Julia Child, September 11, 2001.
6. SI interviews with Russell Morash and Marian Morash, 2023.
7. SI interview with Jacques Pépin, 2023.
8. Julia Child, "The Kitchen Julia Built," *New York Times Magazine*, May 16, 1976, 76–80.
9. "This is certainly the soul of our house." SI interview with JC, 2001.

10. Child, "The Kitchen Julia Built," 76–80.
11. SI interview with AP, 2023.
12. Erin Blasco, "Chris Kimball Remembers Eating and Cooking with Julia Child." NMAH. *O Say Can You See?* (blog), November 7, 2012. https://americanhistory.si.edu/blog/2012/11/chris-kimball-remembers-eating-and-cooking-with-julia-child-1.html.
13. Frank J. Prial, "When Dining with Julia and Paul Child, There's No Mystique Surrounding Wine," *New York Times*, February 1, 1975. Reprinted in *Kansas City Star*, February 16, 1975 [accessed via Julia Child Papers, MC 644, Box 98, Scrapbook].
14. See George M. Taber, *Judgment of Paris: California vs. France and the Historic 1976 Paris Tasting That Revolutionized Wine* (New York: Scribner, 2005). The story of the Paris tasting and bottles of the two winning vintages are on display in the "FOOD" exhibition at the National Museum of American History. Also see Matt Kramer, "Wine Talk with Julia Child," *Wine Spectator*, March 1–15, 1986, 25–27. 1.
15. The wine tracker was offered to the Smithsonian as part of the original donation in 2001. There are a handful of objects, including the wine tracker, that were not located in the kitchen proper but were deemed integral to the overall collection.
16. Jacques Pépin's paintings grace the pages of his cookbooks, such as two of my favorites, *Chez Jacques: Traditions and Rituals of a Cook* (New York: Stewart, Tabori & Chang, 2007) and *Jacques Pépin: Heart & Soul in the Kitchen* (Boston and New York: Houghton Mifflin Harcourt, 2015). His menu paintings are well known among colleagues and friends, and his *Menus: A Book for Your Meals and Memories* (New York: Harvest, 2018) provides painted templates for readers to record their menus and details of meals they wish to remember.
17. Noel Riley Fitch, *Appetite for Life: The Biography of Julia Child* (New York: Anchor Doubleday, 1997), 372.

CHAPTER 4: "EVERYBODY SHOULD LISTEN TO THE COOKS."

1. Simone Beck and Julia Child, *Mastering the Art of French Cooking*, Vol. Two (New York: Alfred A. Knopf, 1970), 517–55.
2. SI interview with Julia Child, September 11, 2001.
3. Julia Child, "Create a Kitchen to End All Kitchens," *Boston Sunday Herald Advertiser*, May 16, 1976, A17.
4. Ibid.
5. Ibid.
6. See, for example, David Kamp, *The United States of Arugula: The Sun Dried, Cold Pressed, Dark Roasted, Extra Virgin Story of the American Food Revolution* (New York: Broadway Books, 2006); Warren J. Belasco, *Appetite for Change: How the Counterculture Took on the Food Industry, 1966–1988* (New York: Pantheon Books, 1989). The expanded interest in food and cooking from global cultures is reflected in popular books for the period, perhaps none so clearly as the *Time-Life Foods of the World* set of twenty-seven cookbooks (1968).
7. Among the influential works that explore the impacts of the post-World War II industrial food system in the United States are Warren Belasco, *Appetite for Change: How the Counterculture Took on the Food Industry 1966–1988* (New York: Pantheon Books, 1989); Tracie McMillan, *The American Way of Eating: Undercover at Walmart, Applebee's, Farm Fields and the Dinner Table* (New York: Scribner, 2012); Michael Moss, *Salt, Sugar, Fat: How the Food Giants Hooked Us* (New York: Random House, 2013); Marion Nestle, *Food Politics: How the Food Industry Influences Nutrition and Health* (Berkeley: University of California Press, 2003); Michael Pollan, *The Omnivore's Dilemma* (New York: Penguin Press, 2006).
8. G. S. Bourdain, "Julia Child Is Stirring Up More Treats," *New York Times*, December 24, 1978, Section D, 27. Speaking about the launch of her new series, "Julia Child & Company," she stated, "with this series, I'm getting away from what I call 'the French straitjacket.' I do some good American dishes, like a really fine old-fashioned potato salad, corned beef hash, how to corn your own beef and even homemade English muffins."
9. SI interview with Alex Prud'homme, February 3, 2023.
10. Ibid.
11. Ibid. Julia kept her microwave in the pastry pantry and not in the kitchen proper. It was not collected by the Smithsonian.
12. Irving Nachumsohn (changed to Naxon) was awarded U.S. patent number 2,187,888 for an electric "cooking apparatus" in 1940. Commercial production of the "Naxon Beanery" began in the 1950s. In 1970, Naxon sold his business to the Rival Manufacturing Company in Kansas City, which rebranded the slow cooker as the Crock-

Pot. The National Museum of American History collected the archives of Irving Naxon in 2023. The collection is housed in the museum's Archives Center.
13. Receipts for Crock-Pots purchased by Julia Child are from the Julia Child Papers, MC 660, Box 12, File 2.
14. Julia Child and E. S. Yntema, *Julia Child & Company* (New York: Alfred A. Knopf, 1979), 76. She also provided a recipe for "Crock-Pot or Slow Cooker Beans" in her 2000 book with David Nussbaum, *Julia Child's Kitchen Wisdom: Essential Techniques and Recipes from a Lifetime of Cooking* (New York: Alfred A. Knopf, 2000), 38. Julia's slow cooker was stored in one of the pantries adjacent to the kitchen and was not collected by the Smithsonian.
15. Rita Leinwand, "Interview with Julia Child," *Bon Appétit*, September 1978, 89.
16. Child, "Create a Kitchen," 13.
17. SI interview with JC, 2001.
18. Ibid.
19. Ibid.
20. Ibid.
21. Correspondence from Mrs. Jo N. Wilson to Julia Child, September 5, 1972, Julia Child Papers, MC644, Box 18.
22. Fred Bridge was the founder of Bridge Kitchenware in New York City, a leading supplier of cookware for professional and home cooks. He sold cookware for sixty-three years and was widely recognized for his depth of knowledge about kitchen tools and equipment. In his obituary on May 7, 1996, in the *New York Times*, the *Times'* former food editor, Craig Claiborne, is quoted: "He was the greatest in his field. He had a profound influence on everyone who was serious about cooking." His book with coauthor Jean E. Tibbetts, *The Well-Tooled Kitchen* (New York: William Morrow, 1991), is still an important reference and a joy to peruse.
23. Correspondence from Julia Child to Mrs. George Orescou, February 21, 1978, Julia Child Papers, MC644, Box 18.
24. "Ask Santa for a Food Processor," *McCall's*, December 1977, Julia Child Papers, MC 644, Box 18, File 231.
25. Julia Child, *From Julia Child's Kitchen* (New York: Alfred A. Knopf, 1975), ix and 153.
26. SI interview with JC, 2001.
27. The sieve was not collected by the Smithsonian as it was located outside of the kitchen proper.
28. Child, "Create a Kitchen," 13.
29. Regal Ware ad, 1972. Food History Reference Files, National Museum of American History.
30. Julia tossed the rolling pin as she demonstrated rolling pin techniques on Episode 20, "Croissants," on *The French Chef* television series 3. The program aired March 24, 1965.
31. SI interview with JC, 2001.
32. Quote: "Good rolling pins are awfully important," from SI interview with JC, 2001.
33. SI interview with JC, 2001.
34. Sandy Allen, "Helpful Cooking Hints Offered by Julia Child," *Stamford Advocate*, October 3, 1975.
35. Lynn Dean, "Audience Samples Variety of Omelettes as Julia Child Cooks While Talking," *Stamford Advocate*, October 28, 1975. Julia Child Papers, MC644, Box 98, Scrapbook.
36. Child, *From Julia Child's Kitchen*, 215.
37. SI interview with JC, 2001.
38. Dave Cathey, "John Bennett, Oklahoma's Chef Emeritus, Passes Away," *Oklahoman*, July 22, 2019.
39. John Bennett, as told to Dave Cathey, "Oklahoma Chef John Bennett Recalls Meeting, Working with Julia Child," *Oklahoman*, August 15, 2012.
40. Correspondence from Paul Child to Charles Child, May 29, 1962. Julia Child Papers, MC 644, Box 07, Folder 77.
41. SI Interview with JC, 2001.
42. Simone Beck, Louisette Bertholle, and Julia Child, *Mastering the Art of French Cooking*, vol. 1 (New York: Alfred A. Knopf, 1961), 8.
43. SI Interview with JC, 2001.
44. Ibid.
45. Correspondence with Pat Pratt, 2016. See also Paula J. Johnson, "A Tale of Two Fish Prints," National Museum of American History. *O Say Can You See?* (blog), August 11, 2016. https://americanhistory.si.edu/blog/tale-two-fish-prints-julia-childs-kitchen.
46. Ibid.
47. "Nids de pommes de terre" or potato nests (baskets) are formed using two small sieves or a proper bird's nest fryer, which has a long handle and double-nested wire basket. Grated potato is pressed into the first basket and the other is nested on top. The baskets are dipped into hot oil and fried for about three minutes. The insert basket is removed and the potato nest is turned onto a surface. Julia used them to hold souffléed potatoes or French fries, as well as clams, smelts, creamed chicken, or sweetbreads. See Child, *From Julia Child's Kitchen*, 415.

48. Conversation and correspondence with Sherrod Sturrock, March 25, 2020.

CHAPTER 5: "WELCOME TO MY HOUSE AND TO MY KITCHEN."

1. Bryan Miller, " 'New York Master Chefs' on PBS," *New York Times,* January 17, 1985. https://www.nytimes.com/1985/01/17/arts/new-york-master-chefs-on-pbs.html.
2. Smithsonian Institution interview with Geoffrey Drummond, 2023.
3. SI Interview with GD, 2023; "sheepdog" quote from Julia Child, "The Kitchen Julia Built," *New York Times Magazine,* May 16, 1976, 76.
4. SI interview with GD, 2023.
5. See Julia Child, *Cooking with Master Chefs* (New York: Alfred A. Knopf, 1993). Significant representation of women chefs reflects the gains in culinary school admissions since the 1940s, when only 2 percent of students at the Cooking Institute of America were women. By 1980, 21.3 percent of CIA students were women, and in 2016 the percentage of women was over 50 percent, the first time women's admissions surpassed those of men. Source: Culinary Arts & Chef Training | Data USA.
6. A beautifully illustrated book from the series *In Julia's Kitchen with Master Chefs* was published by Alfred A. Knopf in 1995 and contains the recipes, notes on ingredients and techniques, and photographs taken during the taping in Julia's home kitchen.
7. Episode of *In Julia's Kitchen with Master Chefs* featuring Leah Chase, available on YouTube here: https://youtu.be/9vjnBHCn7Bg?si=5PLEcLY8KZuATvu . Leah Chase's recipes and cooking tips from the show are published in Julia Child, *In Julia's Kitchen with Master Chefs* (New York: Alfred A. Knopf, 1995), 190–98.
8. Madhur Jaffrey's books include *Vegetarian India: A Journey Through the Best of Indian Home Cooking* (New York: Alfred A. Knopf, 2015), *Madhur Jaffrey's World Vegetarian* (New York: Clarkson Potter Reprint, 2002), *A Taste of India* (New York: Atheneum Books, 1986), *At Home with Madhur Jaffrey: Simple, Delectable Dishes from India, Pakistan, Bangladesh, and Sri Lanka* (New York: Alfred A. Knopf, 2010), and others. Zarela Martinez's books include *Food from My Heart: Cuisines of Mexico Remembered and Reimagined* (Hoboken, NJ: John Wiley & Sons, 1995), *The Food and Life of Oaxaca, Mexico: Traditional Recipes from Mexico's Heart* (New York: Macmillan, 1997), and *Zarela's Veracruz: Mexico's Simplest Cuisine* (Boston and New York: Houghton Mifflin Harcourt, 2004).
9. SI Interview with GD, 2023.
10. Ibid.
11. SI interview with Nancy Silverton, 2023.
12. Alex Prud'homme, *The French Chef in America: Julia Child's Second Act* (New York: Alfred A. Knopf, 2016), 267.
13. See Laura Shapiro, *Julia Child: A Life* (New York: Viking Penguin, 2007), 135–44; and Edith Efron, "Dinner with Julia Child," *TV Guide,* December 5–11, 1970, 46.
14. SI interview with GD, 2023.
15. Ibid.
16. SI interview with GD, 2023; Christopher Hirsheimer, "Watching Julia," *Saveur* no. 27 (1998), 45.
17. SI interview with GD, 2023.
18. Smithsonian Institution interview with Dorie Greenspan, 2023. Greenspan and her husband, Michael, gave Julia the cutout cat to add to her menagerie of feline figures.
19. Staff listing for the February 1–March 9, 1998, taping of *Julia and Jacques Cooking at Home* accessed in the Julia Child Papers. SI interview with GD, 2023.
20. SI interview with Stephanie Hersh, 2021.
21. Ibid.
22. Julia Child, *The Way to Cook* (New York: Alfred A. Knopf, 1989), 24–25. The recipes are enhanced by beautiful color photographs of steps in the process and the finished dish. Julia's trusted associate Rosemary Manell (who also created the cats and asparagus painting that hangs in Julia's home kitchen) was the food stylist for the volume.
23. SI Interview with SH, 2021.
24. Smithsonian Institution interview with Nancy Silverton, 2023.
25. Ibid.
26. Ibid.
27. Ibid. For the recipe, see Dorie Greenspan, *Baking with Julia* (New York: William Morrow, 1996), 386–88.
28. SI interview with DG, 2023.
29. Ibid.
30. "A Three-Tiered Wedding Cake with Martha Stewart," Parts 1 and 2, can be viewed in reruns on public television. The recipe and detailed instructions are included in Greenspan, *Baking with Julia,* 293–306.

31. Greenspan, *Baking with Julia*, 1996. The book won the Julia Child Cookbook Award from the International Association of Culinary Professionals and was the James Beard Foundation Cookbook Award recipient.
32. Jacques Pépin, in Child, Pépin, and Nussbaum, *Julia and Jacques Cooking at Home* (New York: Alfred A. Knopf, 1999), ix.
33. Ibid., viii.
34. SI interview with JP, 2023.
35. Jacques Pépin in *Julia and Jacques Cooking at Home*, viii.
36. Julia Child in *Julia and Jacques Cooking at Home*, vi.
37. SI Interview with GD, 2023.
38. SI interview with Jacques Pépin, 2023.
39. Julia Child and Jacques Pépin, *Julia and Jacques Cooking at Home*, vi–ix.

CHAPTER 6: "I'M ABSOLUTELY DELIGHTED THAT THE SMITHSONIAN IS TAKING MY KITCHEN."

1. John Leland, "At Home with Julia Child; Change of Scene, If Not Cuisine." New York Times, July 26, 2001.
2. SI interview with Julia Child, September 11, 2001.
3. Julia Child and E. S. Yntema, "Dinner for the Boss," in *Julia Child & Company* (New York: Alfred A. Knopf, 1979), 117–18. Julia's corn cutter was manufactured by The Secret Farmhouse, Little River, CA 95456.
4. Jackie Sayet, "Chef Allen Once Took Julia Child Stone Crabbing, and Guess Who Pulled the Traps?" Miaminewtimes.com, August 5, 2009.
5. SI interview with Geoffrey Drummond, 2023.
6. Rayna Green Collections Committee memorandum, 2001.
7. The house was sold, and the proceeds partially funded the building of a 60,000-square-foot Campus Center, which opened in 2002 and was named the Julia McWilliams Child '34 Campus Center.
8. Rayna Green, "Project Diary," National Museum of American History. *What's Cooking? Julia Child's Kitchen at the Smithsonian* (website), 2001. https://americanhistory.si.edu/kitchen/diary05_03.htm.
9. Indeed, the Schlesinger Library on the History of Women in America, located at the Harvard Radcliffe Institute in Cambridge, Massachusetts, includes extensive collections of Julia Child's papers and other archival material.
10. Rayna Green, "Project Diary," *What's Cooking?*
11. SI interview with Joe Criste and Nanci Edwards, February 7, 2023.

CHAPTER 7: "IF I CAN INFLUENCE ANYONE . . ."

1. Susan Riecken, "Notes from a Cataloger's Diary," *Gastronomica* 5:3 (Summer 2005), 125–27. Riecken's article is also the source of the quote, "Such a curious process, this transformation of utilitarian objects into *objets*!"
2. SI interview with Jacques Pépin, 2023.
3. Ibid.
4. The project benefited from the generosity of fans of Julia and friends of the museum along the way. The project gratefully received funds or in-kind donations to cover the costs of shipping, exhibition materials, website development, the opening event, and the like. Some of these donations arrived just in time, which created a sense of miracles happening due to the overwhelming affection people had for Julia.
5. Many people on the museum's staff, along with volunteers, labored to bring the collection into the museum, process it, and create the first exhibition. I have tried to acknowledge everyone in the Acknowledgments but want to note here that to a person, the team was motivated to complete the myriad tasks in recognition and celebration of Julia's generous donation.
6. Reicken, "Notes," *Gastronomica*, 127.
7. Interim director Marc Pachter and associate directors Dennis Dickinson and Maggie Webster were especially helpful.
8. Sheryl Julian, "Still Partying at 90," *Boston Globe*, Aug. 14, 2002, E 93.
9. "Red meat and gin" was one of her often-used answers to questions about her longevity, as reported by Tim Fish, "Julia Child Celebrates 90th Birthday at Copia," *Wine Spectator*, August 6, 2002. https://www.winespectator.com/articles/julia-child-celebrates-90th-birthday-at-copia-21361.
10. Julia had long passed into oral tradition, where stories that may not be factually correct are told time and again because they embody and communicate an essential and powerful message.
11. Note from a visit by students at St. Peter's Interparish School, in Washington, DC, in November 2003, in project reference files.
12. Julie Powell, *Julie & Julia: My Year of Cooking Dangerously* (New York: Little, Brown, 2005);

Julie & Julia (film), written and directed by Nora Ephron, Sony Pictures (August 7, 2009).

13. Robert and Margrit Biever Mondavi's original vision for Copia as a center for exhibitions, educational courses, films, musical performances, events, and restaurant spaces was never realized. On reflection a few years after its closing in 2009, Margrit Biever Mondavi pointed out that the timing was bad, opening as it did shortly after the terrorist attacks on September 11, 2001. She also wrote, "It was too ambitious, too big of a dream, and maybe ahead of its time. It came and it went so fast." Margrit Biever Mondavi with Janet Fletcher, *Margrit Mondavi's Sketchbook: Reflections on Wine, Food, Art, Family, Romance, and Life* (Oakville, Calif.: Robert Mondavi Winery, 2012). Since 2016, the Copia building has been renovated and serves as a branch campus of the private college, the Culinary Institute of America (CIA).
14. The upgrades were part of PSRP-III, the third phase of museum renovations which focused on the museum's West Wing.
15. The 2017 deadline came and went as the exhibition's popularity kept has kept it on view. A 2019 refresh has ensured its life well beyond the original deadline.
16. Mary Coughlin, "Bon Appétit? Plastics in Julia Child's Kitchen," *Objects Specialty Group Postprints*, vol. 20 (2013), 1–15.
17. Paula J. Johnson, "Prep Work in Julia Child's Kitchen," National Museum of American History. *O Say Can You See?* (blog), May 16, 2011.
18. "Caring for Julia Child's Kitchen," NMAH YouTube Channel, January 2012: Caring for Julia Child's Kitchen https://www.youtube.com/watch?v=4MSzg-txl58; Amanda Browe, "Tracking the Condition of Objects in Julia Child's Kitchen," NMAH. *O Say Can You See?* (blog), May 27, 2011; Christine Klepper, "What's on Julia Child's Bookshelf?" NMAH. *O Say Can You See?* (blog), June 3, 2011: https://americanhistory.si.edu/blog/2011/06/whats-on-julia-childs-bookshelf.html; Anneliese Bustillo, "Everyday Discoveries in Julia Child's Kitchen," NMAH. *O Say Can You See?* (blog), June 10, 2011; Lauren Anderson, "What Do Julia Child's Spatulas Say About Preservation?" NMAH. *O Say Can You See?* (blog), June 17, 2011: https://americanhistory.si.edu/blog/2011/06/what-do-julia-childs-spatulas-say-about-preservation.html; Caitlin Dichter, "Cats with Asparagus and 'Forkery' in Julia Child's Kitchen," NMAH. *O Say Can You See?* (blog), June 24, 2011: https://americanhistory.si.edu/blog/2011/06/cats-with-asparagus-and-forkery-in-julia-childs-kitchen.html.
19. For a discussion of the exhibition development, see Paula J. Johnson, "Growing Food History on a National Stage: A Case Study from the Smithsonian's National Museum of American History," in *Food and Museums*, Nina Levent and Irina D. Mihalache, eds. (London: Bloomsbury Academic, 2016), 113–29.
20. The Immigration and Nationality Act of 1965, also known as the Hart-Cellar Act, was passed by the 89th Congress and signed into law by President Lyndon B. Johnson on October 3, 1965. It essentially opened the door to more people from outside Western Europe to apply for citizenship.
21. The team's "Food in the Garden" series in collaboration with horticulture colleagues in the office of Smithsonian Gardens proved to be an effective pilot for bringing people to the museum garden after-hours, with food and drink and an informal panel discussion. Such programs are entry points to history for many.
22. An internal and unpublished feasibility study helped shape the scope of the project, which resulted in a demonstration kitchen but not a changing exhibition gallery or retail space devoted to food history.
23. For program descriptions and recipes, see: https://americanhistory.si.edu/explore/topics/food/cooking-up-history.

AFTERWORD

1. Curtis Hartman and Steven Raichlen, "Julia Child: The Boston Magazine Interview," *Boston Magazine*, April 1981, 78. Julia Child Papers, MC644, Box 983.
2. A trend among wealthy homeowners calls for two kitchens—the main kitchen for show and the back kitchen where someone else prepares food, as if the activity of cooking must be hidden from guests. See Ronda Kaysen, "A Kitchen for the Kitchen," *New York Times,* September 16, 2022.
3. For a discussion of modern kitchen designs and the role of media, see Sophie Donelson, *Uncommon Kitchens* (New York: Abrams, 2023) and "Forget the Perfect White Kitchen. You Have Better Options," Interview with Sophie Donelson by Evan Kleiman, KCRW, *Good Food* (podcast), August 11, 2023: https://www.kcrw.com/culture/shows/good-food/kitchen-design-food-identity-marinades-mangos/perfect-white-kitchen-sophie-donelson-design.
4. SI interview with Julia Child, September 11, 2001.

Photograph Credits

Page 1, Hugh Talman, NMAH
Pages 2–7, photographs by Paul Child, © Schlesinger Library, Radcliffe Institute, President and Fellows of Harvard College
Page 14, Richard W. Strauss, NMAH
Page 17, Christopher Hirsheimer
Page 21, Richard W. Strauss, NMAH
Page 24, Smith College Yearbook, 1934, Smith College Archives, Smith College Special Collections, InMagic_Record_2074
Page 25, family photo courtesy of Phila Cousins
Page 27, Hugh Talman, NMAH
Page 28 (left), Paul Child, © Schlesinger Library, Radcliffe Institute, President and Fellows of Harvard College
Page 28 (right), Paul Child, Julia Child Image, photograph & related rights™/© 2024 The Julia Child Foundation for Gastronomy and the Culinary Arts
Page 29, Hugh Talman, NMAH; 30, NMAH
Pages 32–33, Paul Child, © Schlesinger Library, Radcliffe Institute, President and Fellows of Harvard College
Page 34, Hugh Talman, NMAH; 35–39, NMAH Food History Files
Page 40, Paul Child, © Schlesinger Library, Radcliffe Institute, President and Fellows of Harvard College
Page 41, Smithsonian Institution Libraries
Page 42 (left), Paul Child, © Schlesinger Library, Radcliffe Institute, President and Fellows of Harvard College
Page 44, NMAH Food History Files
Page 45, illustration by Paul Child/© 2024 The Julia Child Foundation for Gastronomy and the Culinary Arts
Pages 47–49, 55, Paul Child, © Schlesinger Library, Radcliffe Institute, President and Fellows of Harvard College
Page 61, NMAH Food History Files
Page 71, Arnold Newman/Arnold Newman Collection via Getty Images
Page 76, Ulrike Welsch/Boston Globe via Getty Images
Page 77, Paul Child, Julia Child Image, photograph & related rights™/© 2024 The Julia Child Foundation for Gastronomy and the Culinary Arts; 79, Jim Scherer
Page 80, courtesy of Susy Davidson
Pages 82, 84–86, Paul Child, © Schlesinger Library, Radcliffe Institute, President and Fellows of Harvard College
Page 88 (left), Hugh Talman, NMAH
Page 88 (right), William Truslow, courtesy of Phila Cousins
Page 91, courtesy of Alex Prud'homme
Page 94 (top and bottom left), courtesy of Susy Davidson
Page 94 (right), Anthony P. Gawrys, courtesy of Anthony P. Gawrys
Pages 98–99, Hugh Talman, NMAH
Page 100 (left), NMAH
Page 100 (right), Richard W. Strauss, NMAH
Page 101 (left), Hugh Talman, Smithsonian Institution Archives
Page 102, Courtesy of Susy Davidson
Page 104, Jacques Pepin via NMAH Archives Center
Page 109, Hugh Talman, NMAH
Page 111, © Dan Wynn Archive and Farmani Group, Co LTD
Page 113, NMAH Food History Files
Page 115, Hugh Talman, NMAH
Page 119, Richard W. Strauss, NMAH
Page 120, Schlesinger Library, Radcliffe Institute, President and Fellows of Harvard College
Page 124, Paul Child, © Schlesinger Library, Radcliffe Institute, President and Fellows of Harvard College
Page 127, Schlesinger Library, Radcliffe Institute, President and Fellows of Harvard College
Page 137, NMAH Food History Files
Pages 142–143, Hugh Talman, NMAH
Page 151, Micheal McLaughlin
Page 152 (right), Paul Child, © Schlesinger Library, Radcliffe Institute, President and Fellows of Harvard College
Page 160, Paul Child, Julia Child Image, photograph & related rights™/© 2024 The Julia Child Foundation for Gastronomy and the Culinary Arts
Pages 162–165, Hugh Talman, NMAH
Pages 170–171, Micheal McLaughlin
Page 172, Courtesy of Geoffrey N. Drummond
Pages 173–174 (left), Micheal McLaughlin
Page 174 (right), Courtesy of Geoffrey N. Drummond
Pages 177–179, Christopher Hirsheimer

Page 183, PBS Media Archive
Page 186 (top and bottom left), Christopher Hirsheimer
Page 189, Christopher Hirsheimer
Page 193 (left), Rayna Green, NMAH
Page 193 (right), Paula Johnson, NMAH
Page 198, Julia and Paul Child, Hans Namuth, 1977, National Portrait Gallery, Smithsonian Institution, gift of the Estate of Hans Namuth, © 1991 Hans Namuth Estate, courtesy Center for Creative Photography, University of Arizona
Page 204, Hugh Talman, NMAH
Page 201, still from video for NMAH by Dean Gaskill
Page 217, Nanci Edwards, NMAH
Page 219, Hugh Talman
Page 220, Nanci Edwards, NMAH
Page 221, Stephanie Hersh, NMAH
Page 224, Smithsonian Institution Archives
Page 226, NMAH

Page 227, Richard W. Strauss, NMAH
Page 229, Albie Walton
Page 231, Rick Friedman/Corbis via Getty Images
Pages 232–233 (right), Paula Johnson, NMAH
Page 233 (left), Marcia Powell, NMAH
Page 236, Paul Child, Julia Child Image, photograph & related rights™/© 2024 The Julia Child Foundation for Gastronomy and the Culinary Arts
Page 239, Richard W. Strauss, NMAH
Page 240, Hugh Talman, NMAH
Page 241, Paula Johnson, NMAH
Page 253, Mitzi Trumbo, Courtesy of Mary Sue Milliken
Page 258, Tim Sloan/Staff via Getty Images
Page 261, Richard W. Strauss, NMAH
Page 280, photograph by Jaclyn Nash
All other Smithsonian collections photography, Jaclyn Nash, NMAH

A trug meant for fresh produce sits on a countertop near one of Julia's kitchen windows. The papier mâché tomatoes have been added by the museum to suggest the trug's purpose.

Index

Note: Page numbers in *italics* include one or more images.

A

Adams, Amy, 237
Adams, Jody, 173
Aikens, Curtis, 251, *251*, 252
Akoto, Charlotte, 183
A La Carte Communications, 170, 176, 188
Albritton, Peter, 216, *217*
Alford, Jeffrey, 184
Alfred A. Knopf, 31
Alssid, Rebecca, 171, 187
American Institute of Wine & Food (AIWF), 102, 105, 175, 184, 192, 226
America's Test Kitchen (television program), 100
Andrés, José, 254, *255*, 263
aprons, *168–169*, 170, 206
Architectural Digest, 22, 41
artful animals in kitchen
    cats, *158–161*
    fish, 158, *158, 162–165*
As Always, Julia, 30
Aunt Ju-Ju, 87–88

B

baking sheets, *96*
Baking with Julia (book), 144, 184, 276n31
Baking with Julia (television program), 83, 174, 175, *181–184*, 275n30
Baldonado, Reeza, *196*
banana stickers, 226, *227*
Barbeau, Monique, 173
Barden, Richard, 226, *226*
Barr, Nancy Verde, 78, 273n31
Barrett, Rob, 216, *217, 221, 232*
Barriere, Tiffanie, *254*
Bastianich, Lidia, 170
basting brushes, *167*

Bayless, Rick, 173, 254, 263
Beard, James, 64, 70, 113, 134, 149
Beck, Simone "Simca," *28–30*, 70, *71*, 81
Bennett, John, 149
Bergin, Mary, 183
Berkowitz, George, 152
Bernzomatic Corporation, *153*
Bertholle, Louisette, 28–30
Bierman, Alexis, *203, 204*, 205
Bishop, Liz, 78, 80, 105, 273n31
blenders, *135*
Blom, David, 183
blowtorch, *153*
"Bon Appétit! Julia Child's Kitchen"
    dismantling and packing Julia's kitchen for, *193–196*, 199, *201–206*, 209–210, 212, *216–218*
    opening of, *232–233*, 261, *261*
    popularity of, 238–239
    public observation of unpacking, processing, and reassembling of Julia's kitchen for, 228, 230
    unpacking, processing, and reassembling material from Julia's kitchen for, *224–227*, 228, *232*, 277n5
    visitors to kitchen, 23, 234–235, 237
    wall of pots installation, 238
    wall of pots substitute, 232, *233*
books and bookshelf, 44, *44, 115–117*, 167, 274n6
Boston Globe, 22, 234
Boulud, Daniel, 173, *173, 255*
Braker, Flo, 183
Brassart, Élizabeth, 28, *29*
Bridge, Fred, 274n20
Bridge Kitchenware, 126, *127*, 134, 274n20
Brody, Lora, 183

Brown, Clare, 241
buffalo iron, *148–149*
Bugnard, Max, *28, 29*, 148

C

Calvel, Raymond, 72
Cambridge home, 34–35, *86, 166–167*, 177, *177*, 205, 277n7. *See also* kitchen (Cambridge)
Carbone, Jessica, 251
cats (art), *158–161*
ceramic egg cups, *213*
ceramic mugs, *212*
champagne bottle stopper, French, *195*
Chase, Leah, *173*–174
Chen, Joyce, 113, 137, 273n31
Cheryl (assistant of Julia), 206
"Cheshire pin," 144, *145*
Chez Panisse, 250
"the chicken sisters," 152
Child, Julia
    American regional specialties and, 114, 274n8
    as Aunt Ju-Ju, 87–88
    awards and honors, 174, *174*, 262
    being childless, 273n2
    birthday, 170
    birth family, 24
    bluefish caught by, *162–164*
    Bugnard and, *28, 29*, 148
    characteristics, 16, 100, 171, 177
    Chinese food and, 26
    as culinary education supporter, *28–30*, 102, 105, 150, 171, 175, 187, 192, 261
    death, 181, 237
    diet card of, *211*
    enabling home cooks to master French cooking, 113–114
    gay men and, 175

INDEX   281

Child, Julia (*cont.*)
    move to Santa Barbara, 192, 205
    ninetieth birthday, 20–21, 230, 233
    at opening of "Bon Appétit! Julia Child's Kitchen at the Smithsonian," 232–233
    Pépin and, 15–17, 171
    physical appearance of, 28
    Planned Parenthood and, 167
    public's love for, 23, 230–231, 232, 234, 259, 277n4
    "Red meat and gin," 234, 277n9
    Today show segment, 233–234
    typing skills, 270n18
    women's places in professional kitchens and, 175
    during World War II, 25–26, *27*
    youth, 24–25
Child, Julia: photographs, *1–7, 21, 47, 79, 80, 82, 88, 94, 101, 124, 171, 172, 173, 174, 183, 201, 258*
    in basement kitchen, *177*
    with Beck, *71*
    with Bugnard, *28*
    in China, *25*
    with "fright knife," *152*
    with Garland range, *229*
    with Jacques and Drummond, *189*
    with Johnson at "Bon Appétit! Julia Child's Kitchen at the Smithsonian" exhibit, *261*
    with Jones, *77*
    at La Pitchoune, *236*
    with Milliken and Feniger, *253*
    in Paris kitchen, *28, 40, 49*
    with Paul, *76, 111, 200, 231*
    with Paul and Prud'homme, *91*
    with Pépin, *17, 178, 186*
    at Smith College, *24*
Child, Julia: publications, 267
    As Always, Julia, 30
    Baking with Julia, 184, 276n31
    Cooking with Master Chefs, 172
    first editions for Smithsonian, 226

Julia and Jacques Cooking at Home, 17, *17*, 78
Julia Child & Company, 121
From Julia Child's Kitchen, 135, 148
From Julia's Kitchen, 46
In Julia's Kitchen with Master Chefs, 221
Mastering the Art of French Cooking (Vol 1), 22, 29–30, *34*, 56, 63, 70, 108, 135, 149, 230, 237
Mastering the Art of French Cooking (Vol 2), 70, 77, 108, 135, 230
My Life in France, 30
The Way to Cook, 180, 276n22
Child, Julia: television programs and specials, 267
    Baking with Julia, 83, 144, 174, 175, 181–184, 275n30
    clips shown at Smithsonian exhibit, 232
    Cooking with Master Chefs (television program), *172–173*, 181
    Emmy award, 174, *174*
    The French Chef, 22, 63, 64, 65, 67, 93, 105, 144, 152, *152*, 206, 230, 273n31, 275n30
    Julia and Jacques Cooking at Home, 17, *17*, 78, 174, *178*, 179, 187–188
    Julia Child & Company, 79, 105
    Julia Child & More Company, 78–80, 105
    In Julia's Kitchen with Master Chefs, 170, 173–174, 175, 176, 183
Child, Paul, *91, 94, 102, 111, 200, 231*
    banana stickers and, 226, *227*
    on bluefish caught by Julia, 163–164
    career of, 25, 26, 31, 34
    on Culinary Institute students, 150

    death, 78, 172
    fish print by, 165
    The French Chef and, 65–69
    health, 77, 172
    on kitchen bookshelf, 44
    kitchen renovation and, 21, 36, 38, 41, *42*, 110
    label maker and, 56, *57*
    L'École des Trois Gourmandes, *28–30*
    Mastering the Art of French Cooking (Vol 2), *76*, 77
    meeting and marriage, 25, 26
    photographer, 48
    as photographer, *76, 77, 124*
    reading to Julia, 60
    tea and, *26*
    wine and, 101, *101*, 102–103
China, Julia in, *25*, 26
Claiborne, Craig, 56, 274n20
Clark, Patrick, 172
clay coin banks, *14*
convenience food, 56, 113, *113*
cooking shows, 64, 152, 175, 176. *See also* specific programs
"Cooking Up History" (Smithsonian Institution National Museum of American History), 251–252, *264*, 278n22
Cooking with Master Chefs (book), 172
Cooking with Master Chefs (television program), *172–173*, 181
Copia: The American Center for Wine, Food & the Arts, 192, 232, 238, 277n13
copper kettle, 52, *53*
corn cutter/scraper, 197, *197*
Coryn, Sidonie, 77
Coughlin, Mary, 239–240, *241*
countertops, 46, *47*
Cousins, Phila, 80, 87–88, 184, 195, *240*
Crew, Spencer, *101*
Criste, Joe, 216, *221*, 232
Crock-Pots, *120–121*, 274n12, 275n14
Cuisinart, 81, 134

Culinary Arts Certificate program (Boston University), 171, 175, 187
Culinary Historians of Washington (CHOW), 226
Culinary Institute of America, 149, 175
Cunningham, Marion, 183–184
cutlery, 30–31, *207,* 271n19

D

Davidson, Susy, 78, *80,* 81, *240,* 273n31
Del Grande, Robert, 172
Desaulniers, Marcel, 184
DeVoto, Avis, 30–31, 88
DeVoto, Bernard, 30–31, 271n19
Dickinson, Dennis, 277n7
Dickson, Robert, 149
Dickson Bros., 121, 126
dinner parties, 78–81, 88, 92, *104*
dinnerware, *87,* 89–90
Dionot, François, *21*
dirty dishes, 96, *96*
Dodge, Jim, 173
Donna, Roberto, 173
doughnut cutter, *214*
Drummond, Geoffrey, 184, 199, *201*
    basic facts about, 170–171
    first meeting with Julia, 171–172
    with Julia and Jacques, *189*
    Julia and Jacques Cooking at Home and, 179
    "Julia Child's Kitchen Wisdom" and, 232, 237
    on Julia's kitchen, 175
    In Julia's Kitchen with Master Chefs and, *174,* 176
    A La Carte Communications, 170, 176, 188
    New York's Master Chefs and, 170
Duguid, Naomi, 184
Duhamel, Albert, 63

E

E. Dehillerin cookware specialty store, 42

Edwards, Nanci, 193, *193,* 205, 206, 216, *221,* 225, 226, 230
egg cups, *213*
Egge, Bjørn, 52
Egge, Eline, 52
electric frying pan, *139*
Elizabeth Bishop Wine Resource Center, 105
Encyclopedia Britannica, 44
Eng, Jeff, *21*
Ephron, Nora, 238, *240*

F

Farberware, 134
Farbinger, Marcus, 184
Fearing, Dean, 173
Fess, Zoe, *264*
Feniger, Susan, 172, *253, 254, 255,* 263
Field, Carol, 173
Fischbacher, Jean, 70
fish (art), 158, *158, 162–165*
fish mold, *215*
Fleckner, John, 193
Food History Project (Smithsonian Institution National Museum of American History), 266
food industry, postwar, 56, 113, *113,* 242–244, 274n6
"Food in the Garden" series (Smithsonian Institution National Museum of American History), 278n21
food mills, 51, *51*
food processors, 134–135, *136*
food television, 64, 152, 175, 176. *See also* specific programs
Forestier, Danielle, 184
Forgione, Larry, 170
France
    La Pitchoune, 70, 166, *236*
    Paris kitchen, *28, 40, 49*
The French Chef (television program), 22, 64, 206
    Bishop and, 105
    "fright knife/memorial cleaver and," 152, *152*

    impact of, 230
    I've Been Reading and, 63
    Marian Morash and, 273n31
    Russ Morash and, 93
    pilot for, 63
    preparing for, 65–69
    rolling pin toss, 144, 275n30
    television technology and, 65
"fright knife," 152, *152*
From Julia Child's Kitchen, 135, 148
From Julia's Kitchen, 46
fruit bowl, 51, *51*

G

gadgets, *154–157*
Gand, Gale, 184
garbage disposal, 56, *57*
Garland range, *53, 55,* 74, *75,* 220, 224, 229
Gawrys, Anthony, 94, *94*
General Electric Interval Timer, *66*
Georgetown kitchen, 74
Germon, George, 173
Gilbreth, Lillian, 38
Ginsu knives, 126
Giroux, Michelle, *21*
Graff, Richard, 102, 105
Granton knives, 126
gratin pans, *109, 141, 222–223*
Gray, Todd, *21*
Green, Rayna, *100, 193,* 201, 204, 226
    acquisition of first editions of Julia's publication by, 226
    acquisition of Julia's kitchen and, 194, 196, 202–203, 205, 212
    diary of, 206, 209–210
    exhibit layout and, 226
    Julia's move to Santa Barbara and, 192
    relationship with public and, 230
    Today show segment, 233
Greenspan, Dorie, 83, 144, 182–183, 184, *186,* 261, 276n18
Greenspan, Michael, 276n18

Gross, Christopher, 173
Groveman, Lauren, 184

H

Hamersley, Gordon, 173, 176
Hart-Cellar (Immigration and Nationality) Act (1965), 244, 278n20
Hartig, Anthea M., *254*, 265–266
Hazan, Marcella, 113
Hearon, Reed, 173
Heller, Susan, 176
Henckel knives, 126
Hersh, Stephanie, *179*–181, 183, 184, 194, 201, 206, 221
Hirsheimer, Christopher, 188
horsehair sieves, 136
House Beautiful, 38
House & Garden, 22, *60*–62
Hyde, Temi, *79*

I

I Love to Eat (television program), 64
Immigration and Nationality Act (1965), 244, 278n20
In Julia's Kitchen with Master Chefs (book), *221*
In Julia's Kitchen with Master Chefs (television program), *170, 173–174,* 175, 176, 183
International Association of Culinary Professionals, 175
In the Kelvinator Kitchen (television program), 64
I've Been Reading (television program), 63

J

Jaeggi & Sons, 126
Jaffrey, Madhur, 173, 174
James, William, 34
Johnson, Lyndon B., 278n20
Johnson, Paula, *100,* 193, *193, 201,* 206, 230, 233, *261*
Jones, Judith, 31, 70, 72, 77, *77*
Joyce Chen Cooks (television program), 273n31
Julia and Jacques Cooking at Home (television program), 17, *17,* 78, 174, *178,* 179, 187–188
Julia Child Award, *253–255,* 263
Julia Child & Company (book), 121
Julia Child & Company (television program), 79, 105
Julia Child Foundation for Gastronomy and the Culinary Arts, 81, 253–*254,* 263, 273n31
Julia Child & More Company (television program), *78–80,* 105
"Julia Child's Kitchen Wisdom" (Drummond), 232, 237
"Julia karma," 230, 232, 238
Julie & Julia, 237–238

K

Kasper, Lynne Rossetto, 173
Katzman, Natan, 170
Kelly, Mary Lou, 95
Kennedy, Robert Woods, 36
Kent, Sherman, 74, 148–149
kettle, 52, *53*
Killeen, Johanne, 173, 184
Kimball, Christopher, 100, *100*
Kitchell, Alma, 64
kitchen (Cambridge), *48, 49*
  Baking with Julia taped in, 175
  ca. 1962, *32–33*
  cabinets, *216–219*
  described by Pépin, 16
  dismantling and packing material from Julia's kitchen by Smithsonian staff, *193–196,* 199, *201–206,* 209–210, 212, *216–218*
  efficiency of, 38, 41–42
  flooring, 39
  importance of, to career, 23
  Julia and Jacques Cooking at Home taped in, *178,* 179, 188
  Julia at opening of "Bon Appétit! Julia Child's Kitchen at the Smithsonian," 232–233, 261, *261*
  In Julia's Kitchen with Master Chefs taped in, 175, 176
  junk drawer, *226*
  layout, *35*
  organization of, 83
  as part of Smithsonian's FOOD: Transforming the American Table exhibit, 239–250, *256–257,* 277nn14–15
  popularity of "Bon Appétit! Julia Child's Kitchen at the Smithsonian," 238–*239*
  public observation of unpacking, processing, and reassembling of Julia's kitchen in Smithsonian, 228, 230
  renovating, 21, *32–33,* 35–36, 38, 41, 110, 171–172, 271n4
  in Smithsonian's National Museum of American History, 16–17, 20, *21,* 23, *239*
  telephone, 184, *185*
  transformation of, for television, *177–179*
  unpacking, processing and reassembling material from Julia's kitchen by Smithsonian staff, *224–227,* 228, *232,* 277n5
  visitors to Smithsonian exhibit and, 234–235, 237, *256–257*
  walls, 271n4
kitchen (Cambridge basement), 177, *177,* 179
kitchen (Georgetown), 74, *75*
kitchen (La Pitchoune), *71*
kitchen (Paris), *28, 40, 49*
KitchenAid, 136
kitchens, American
  contemporary trends, 259–260, 278n2
  postwar modern, *36–38,* 41
knives, 41, *100, 124–133*
Kominiak, Craig, 184
Kramer, Stanley, 170

L

label maker, 56, *57,* 83
Lacoste, Ris, *21*
Lagasse, Emeril, 152, 172
La Pitchoune ("The Little Thing"), 70, *71,* 166, *236*
L'École des Trois Gourmandes (The School of Three Hearty Eaters), *28*–30
Le Cordon Bleu, 28, *28,* 29
Leeds, Jamie, *21*
Le Pavillon restaurant, 72
Les Dames d'Escoffier, 175, 202
Lewis, Edna, 113
Liederman, David, 92
"Life in the Universe" exhibit (Smithsonian Institution National Air and Space Museum), 82
Livingston, Mary, 82
Lockwood, Ruth, 78, 273n31
Lomonaco, Michael, 173
Love, Norman, 184
Lucas, Dione, 64

M

Mackie, Leslie, 184
Malgieri, Nick, 184
mallet, 148, *148*
manche a gigot, 197, *197*
Manell, Rosemary, 78, *80,* 184, *203,* 273n31, 276n22
Margolis, Carolyn, 192
Martinez, Zarela, 173, 174, *174*
Mastering the Art of French Cooking (Vol 1), 22, 29–30, *34,* 56, 63, 70, 108, 135, 149, 230, 237
Mastering the Art of French Cooking (Vol 2), 70, 77, 108, 135, 230
McCall's magazine, 134
McCully, Helen, 16, 70, 72
McManus, Esther, 184
McWilliams, John, 94, *94*
McWilliams, Julia. *See* Child, Julia
measuring cups, *166*
meat tenderizers, *190*–*191*
Medrich, Alice, 184
"memorial cleaver," 152, *152*
Meyer, Danny, 254, 263

microwave, 118–*119*
Militello, Mark, 173
Milk Street (television program), 100
Miller, Louise, *178*
Miller, Stanley, 82
Milliken, Mary Sue, 172, *253,* 254, *255,* 263
mixers, 136, *136*
mixing bowl, *213*
Mondavi, Margrit Biever, 238, 277n13
Mondavi, Robert, 192, 232, 238, 277n13
Morash, Marian, 66, 78, *79,* 80, 81, 93, 273n31
Morash, Russell, 66, 93, *102,* 206
mortar and pestle, 50, *50,* 136
Moulinex "Moulinette" electric choppers, 134
Moulton, Sara, 78, *79,* 80–81, 83, 273nn31–32
mugs, *212*
My Life in France (Child and Prud'homme), 30

N

Nachumsohn, Irving, 274n12
Naxon, Irving, 120, 274n12
New York magazine, 46
New York's Master Chefs (television program), 170
New York Times, 56, 101, 274n20
New York Times Magazine, 22
Nierenberg, Danielle, 254, 263
Noreclo, 134
"Notes from a Cataloger's Diary" (Riecken), 226–227
Nussbaum, David, 78, 187, 188

O

Ogonowski, David, 184
Ojakangas, Beatrice, 184
Ortiz, Joe, 184
Ott, Cindy, *204,* 205

P

Pachter, Marc, 277n7

Palladin, Jean-Louis, 172
Palmer, Charles, 172
Parade magazine, 81
pastry sticks, *146*
patron saint of cooks, painting on tin, *215*
Penny (assistant of Julia), 206
Pépin, Gloria, 94, *94, 102*
Pépin, Jacques, 15–*17,* 186
  Cooking with Master Chefs, 172
  dinner party, *104,* 105
  Drummond and Julia and, 171
  first meeting with Julia, *94,* 95, *102*
  with Julia and Drummond, *189*
  Julia and Jacques Cooking at Home, 17, *17,* 78, 174, *178, 179,* 187–188
  Julia Child Award and, 254, *255,* 263
  Julia's Cambridge kitchen described by, 16
  Le Pavillon restaurant and, 72
  on seeing Julia's kitchen in Smithsonian, 227, 228
Phung, Kathy, 252
pineapple corer, *214*
Planned Parenthood, 167, 175
Popular Science, 37
Portale, Alfred, 173
potato baskets/nests, 167, 275n47
potato masher/ricer, 52, *52*
potholder, *208*
pots and pans, *48,* 53, *58*–*59,* 83–85, *106*–*108, 109, 122*–*123, 138, 140*–*143, 150,* 235
  number and range of, in Julia's Cambridge kitchen, 139
  in Paris kitchen, *40*
  as part of design aesthetic, 41–*42, 54, 55*
  recommendations for purchasing, 137
  sent to Smithsonian, 238, *240*
  wall of, installed at "Bon Appétit! Julia Child's Kitchen," 238, 240

wall of, acrylic at "Bon Appétit! Julia Child's Kitchen," 232, *233*
Powell, Billy, 232
Powell, Marcia, 231, 232
Pratt, Berit, 78
Pratt, Herbert, 88, 162–164
Pratt, Pat, 78, 88, *162–164*, 273n31
Prial, Frank, 101
primordial soup, 82
Prud'homme, Alex
    on childhood visits to Julia's Cambridge home, 91–92
    on Julia and microwave, 118
    on kitchen table, 97, 98
    My Life in France, 30
public television, 63, 64–65, 272n10. *See also* specific programs

Q

quarry tiles, 73, *73*

R

Radcliffe College, 205, 209, 277n9
ranges
    electric, in Cambridge kitchen, 67
    Garland, *53, 55*, 74, *75*, *220, 224, 229*
Reardon, Joan, 30
recipes
    Pain Français, 72–73
    stove for testing, 74
    of Washington hostesses' tested for *House & Garden*, 60–62
Regal Ware, 137, *137*
Renggli, Seppi, 170
"Resetting the Table" stories (Smithsonian Institution National Museum of American History), 244, 278n20
Reynolds, Sherrod, 166–167
Richard, Lena, 64
Richard, Michel, 172, 184
Riecken, Susan, 226–227, 231
Ripley, S. Dillon, 82
Rival Crock-Pots, *120–121*, 274n12, 275n14

Robot-Coupe vertical cutter-mixers, 134
rolling pins, 144–*145*, 275n30
Royce, Josiah, 34

S

Sabatier knives, 126
salad spinners, 152, *153*
salamanders (tool), *153*
San Pasqual painting on tin, *215*
Santa Barbara, 192, 205
scale, *214*
Schlesinger Library (Radcliffe College), 121, 209, 277n9
Sherman, Sean, 254, 263, *263*
sieves, *112*, 135, 136, 275n25
Silverton, Nancy, 172, 175, 181–182, 183, *183*
slow cookers, *120–121*, 275n14
Smith College, 24–25, 175, 205, 277n7
Smithsonian Institution, basic facts about, 265
Smithsonian Institution National Air and Space Museum, "Life in the Universe" exhibit, 82
Smithsonian Institution National Museum of American History, 20, 21, 23
    basic facts about, 265–266
    "Cooking Up History," 251–252, *264*, 278n22
    dismantling and packing Julia's kitchen by staff, *193–196*, 199, *201–206*, 209–210, 212, *216–218*
    first editions of Julia's publications, 226
    Food History Project, 266
    "Food in the Garden" series, 278n21
    Julia at opening of "Bon Appétit! Julia Child's Kitchen at the Smithsonian," 232–233, 261, *261*
    Julia Child Award and, 253–255

    "Julia Child's Kitchen Wisdom," 232, 237, *239*
    Julia's kitchen as part of FOOD: Transforming the American Table exhibit, *239–250, 256–257*, 277nn14–15
    Julia's ninetieth birthday, 20–21, 230, 233
    popularity of "Bon Appétit! Julia Child's Kitchen at the Smithsonian," 238–239
    public observation of stabilization of Star-Spangled Banner, 225
    public observation of unpacking, processing, and reassembling of Julia's kitchen, 228, 230
    "Resetting the Table" stories, 244, 278n20
    unpacking, processing, and reassembling material from Julia's kitchen by staff, *224–227*, 228, *232*, 277n5
    visitors to kitchen exhibit, 23, 234–235, 237
    wall of pots, acrylic, 232, *233*
    wall of pots installation, 238, 240
Sneed, Jimmy, 173
"socks-only" policy, 218
Soltner, André, 170
Sontheimer, Carl, 81
Spivey, Eric, *254*
Splichal, Joachim, 173
spring scale, *214*
Sri Lanka, 26
Stachowski, Jamie, *21*
Stewart, Martha, *183*, 184
stone-crab cracker, 198, *198*
stoves
    electric, in Cambridge kitchen, 67
    Garland range, *53, 55*, 74, *75, 220, 224, 229*

Straight Wharf Restaurant, 273n31
Streep, Meryl, 237
Sturrock, Alan, 166
Sullivan, Steve, 184
Sunbeam, 134
Sur Le Table, 126, *127*
Susser, Allen, 198
Szurdak, Jean-Claude, 105

T
table and chairs, *48,* 97–99
Talman, Hugh, 205
tamis, 135, 275n25
tastevin, *101*
tea, *26*
technologies, using new, 118
    blenders, *135*
    food processors, 134–*135,* 136
    microwave ovens, 118–*119*
    mixers, 136, *136*
    slow cookers, *120*–121, 275n14
telephone, 184, *185*
Terry, Elena, *264*
thermometers, *167*
"this NASA machine," 118–*119*
Thorpe Rolling Pin, 144, *145*
Time-Life Foods of the World, 274n6
Tipton-Martin, Toni, *252,* 254, *254,* 263
Today show, 233–234
tools, 110–*112, 112, 151, 228, 235.* See also *specific tools*
    amount of, 110
    importance of cooking with right, 108
    Mastering the Art of French Cooking (Vol 2) and, 108
    as part of design aesthetic, *41, 42, 43*
    quality of, 123
    storing, 110, *147*
Torres, Jacques, 173
To the Queen's Taste (television program), 64
Tower, Jeremiah, 172
Trotter, Charlie, 173
Tutove, Rouleau Magique, 144, *145*

V
Valentine's Day greeting (1964), *45*
Velasquez, Steve, *203, 204,* 205, 206, 224, *224,* 225, 226, 239–240, 241, *241*
The Victory Garden (television program), 273n31
The Victory Garden Cookbook, 273n31
Vongerichten, Jean-Georges, 173

W
Ward, Geoff, 216, *217,* 221
Waring, 134
Waters, Alice, 113, 172, 250
The Way to Cook, 180, 276n22
Wear-Ever, 137
Webster, Maggie, 277n7
West Bend, 137
WGBH, 63. See also *The French Chef* (television program)
whisks, 150, *150*
White, Jasper, 173
wines, *101–103,* 274n15
Wine Spectator, 102
wine-tasting cup, *101*
wire whisks, 150, *150*
women. See also *specific individuals*
    as chefs, 78, 175, 275n47
    convenience foods and, 56, 113
    in cooking shows, 64
    kitchen design and, 37–38
    slow cookers and working, 120
Wright, Helena, *241*
Wüsthof knives, 126

Y
Yan, Martin, *95*
Yeh, Cedric, *204,* 205, 206
Yokoyama, Christine, 233
Young, Ashley Rose, *252, 252*
Young, Grace, 254, *255,* 263

Z
Zinberg, Dorothy, 88

Editor: Laura Dozier
Designer: Deb Wood
Design Managers: Heesang Lee and Liam Flanagan
Managing Editor: Lisa Silverman
Production Managers: Anet Sirna-Bruder, Denise LaCongo, and Hayley Earnest

For Smithsonian Enterprises:
Licensing Coordinator: Avery Naughton
Editorial Lead: Paige Towler
Senior Director, Licensed Publishing: Jill Corcoran
Vice President of New Business and Licensing: Brigid Ferraro
President: Carol LeBlanc

Library of Congress Control Number: 2024933699

ISBN: 978-1-4197-7008-1
eISBN: 979-8-88707-115-2

Copyright © 2024, Smithsonian Institution; copyright © 2024, The Julia Child Foundation for Gastronomy and the Culinary Arts

The Smithsonian name and logo are registered trademarks of the Smithsonian.

Photograph credits can be found on pages 279–280.

Cover © 2024 Abrams

Smithsonian

THE JULIA CHILD FOUNDATION
for Gastronomy and the Culinary Arts

Published in 2024 by Abrams, an imprint of ABRAMS. All rights reserved. No portion of this book may be reproduced, stored in a retrieval system, or transmitted in any form or by any means, mechanical, electronic, photocopying, recording, or otherwise, without written permission from the publisher.

Printed and bound in China
10 9 8 7 6 5 4 3 2 1

Abrams books are available at special discounts when purchased in quantity for premiums and promotions as well as fundraising or educational use. Special editions can also be created to specification. For details, contact specialsales@abramsbooks.com or the address below.

Abrams® is a registered trademark of Harry N. Abrams, Inc.

ABRAMS The Art of Books
195 Broadway, New York, NY 10007
abramsbooks.com

page 1: JC branding iron that hung on pegboard among copper and cast-iron cookware
page 8: One of Julia's measuring cups, marked "J" to ensure its return after being used at cooking demonstrations away from home
page 11: Heart-shaped trivet from Julia's kitchen
page 12: Kitchen towel that was folded over the handle of the wall oven